PART III

ADVOCATE FOR ASSETS BEYOND THE CLASSROOM

CHAPTER 9

Creating Asset-Rich Educational Systems

APPENDIXES

Powerful *Teaching*

Developmental Assets in **Curriculum** and **Instruction**

EDITED BY JUDY TACCOGNA, ED.D.

FOREWORD BY JOHN JAY BONSTINGL

Search INSTITUTE | Practical research benefiting children and youth

A Search Institute Publication

Powerful Teaching
Developmental Assets in Curriculum and Instruction
Edited by Judy Taccogna, Ed.D.

Search Institute
615 First Avenue NE, Suite 125
Minneapolis, MN 55413
612-376-8955; 800-888-7828
www.search-institute.org

Credits
Editors: Kathryn (Kay) L. Hong, Ruth Taswell
Book design and composition: Diane Gleba Hall
Production: Mary Ellen Buscher

DONALD W. REYNOLDS
FOUNDATION

Library of Congress Cataloging-in-Publication Data
Powerful teaching : developmental assets in curriculum and instruction / edited by Judy Taccogna ; foreword, John Jay Bonstingl.
    p. cm.

   ISBN 1-57482-751-0 (pbk.)

   1. Effective teaching—United States. 2. Lesson planning—United States. 3. Teacher-student relationships—United States. I. Taccogna, Judy, 1942–

LB1025.3.P69 2003
371.102—dc21

                                    2003000293

About Search Institute
Search Institute is an independent, nonprofit, nonsectarian organization whose mission is to advance the well-being of children and youth by generating knowledge and promoting its application. The institute collaborates with others to promote long-term organizational and cultural change that supports its mission. For a free information packet, call 800-888-7828.

Search Institute's Healthy Communities ▪ Healthy Youth initiative seeks to unite individuals, organizations, and their leaders to join together in nurturing competent, caring, and responsible children and adolescents. Lutheran Brotherhood, now Thrivent Financial for Lutherans, is the founding national sponsor for Healthy Communities ▪ Healthy Youth. Thrivent Financial for Lutherans Foundation has provided Search Institute with generous support for 2003.

Funding for the development of *Powerful Teaching: Developmental Assets in Curriculum and Instruction* was provided in part by the Donald W. Reynolds Foundation, a national philanthropic organization founded in 1954 by the late media entrepreneur for whom it is named. Reynolds was the founder and principal owner of the Donrey Media Group. Headquartered in Las Vegas, Nevada, it is one of the largest private foundations in the United States.

Thrivent Financial for Lutherans™
A Century of Serving the Lutheran Community™

Contents

List of Handouts

Foreword

Long after your students have forgotten the 14 causes of the War of 1812, the Pythagorean Theorem, and the sonnets of Shakespeare, they will remember a much more important lesson: how you made them feel about themselves and their possibilities in this life.

We became teachers not for the money or glory or personal gain. We became teachers because we want to help young people to learn and grow. We became teachers because we love learning and want to share that love of learning with the young. Above all, we became teachers because we are passionate about guiding young people in the most important learning of all: how to craft a worthwhile life.

We live and teach in a challenging time of ever-increasing emphasis on high academic standards and high-stakes assessments, test-preparation courses, and rote memorization for the sake of high scores on standardized exams. At the same time, we see many young people coming to school hungry and tired. Many of our students (of all ethnic groups and income levels) come to us from homes where there is little or no supervision and adult accountability. In the worst-case scenarios, our kids come to us from domestic situations where they face daily challenges that are truly difficult for many of us to fathom.

We are dedicated to creating the best possible environment in our schools so that every child can and does succeed, and no child is left behind. We want our schools to be true schools of quality. And we want our classrooms to be places where every young person learns how to be true to her or his own best possible self.

In this crucial work of teaching, we can make use of a wonderful set of tools in the form of Search Institute's 40 developmental assets. I have long admired the work of Search Institute, and in my 17 years as a classroom teacher, I benefited enormously from using the institute's materials. They helped me and my students build a kind, supportive, asset-rich environment that makes teaching and learning a joy for us all.

With this new resource, you will find concrete applications of the assets in the classroom that align with good educational practice. Framed by the insight and expertise of Judy Taccogna, education director at Search Institute, the many contributions here from teachers all over the country provide enthusiastic, relevant lessons to guide young people—and educators.

I am sure you will find this new book to be an invaluable treasure chest of great ideas for your own classroom and school. Best wishes for every success!

JOHN JAY BONSTINGL
Author, *Schools of Quality*
Director, The Center for Schools of Quality
Columbia, Maryland
Bostingl@aol.com

Acknowledgments

Asset building in school—or anywhere, for that matter—begins and continues through relationships. Your first impression of a resource about infusing assets into curriculum and instruction may be that such a topic demands dissecting the nature of teaching a content area in order to demonstrate technically how to embed the asset approach. If so, you will be surprised a short way into our contributors' examples.

The warmth and care these 23 asset-building educators show for encouraging the development of assets in their students permeates through what and how they teach. By far my greatest acknowledgments are extended to these individuals who engaged with us over the past year or so in bringing their powerful teaching ideas to life for you. They demonstrate passion for good teaching as well as for connecting with young people and nurturing them above and beyond the curriculum—the embodiment of infusing assets in curriculum and instruction.

I want to acknowledge the steady voice of Peter C. Scales, researcher and member of the Education Core Team at Search Institute, in his overall support for and expertise in infusing assets into schools and school communities. His regular and insightful input into the education work and his creation of the research questions needing answers has guided me for several years and helped crystallize the direction for this resource. His encouragement of teachers to participate in the project was also important.

I appreciate the expertise and perspective of the reviewers of the manuscript as well as the considerable time they invested in making constructive suggestions. Their insights led to significant improvements. I thank Judy Puncochar, education specialist in the Human Relations Program, University of Minnesota, Minneapolis, whose early feedback on diversity issues increased our sensitivity to particular concerns.

I also express my gratitude to the following reviewers of the near-final manuscript: John Jay Bonstingl, director, The Center for Schools of Quality, Columbia, Maryland; Betty Flad, executive administrator for School Support, Beaverton School District, Beaverton, Oregon; Ann Clark, supervisor, Safe and Drug-Free Schools and Communities, Houston Independent School District, Houston, Texas; Peter C. Scales, senior fellow, Search Institute, Manchester, Missouri; Jeanne Harmon, English as a Second Language teacher, Highland Park Middle School, Beaverton, Oregon; Clay Roberts, president, Roberts and Associates and Search Institute senior training consultant, Bainbridge Island, Washington; Marilyn Peplau, Search Institute trainer, New Richmond, Wisconsin; Chris Templin, Search Institute trainer, Colorado Springs, Colorado; Mary Ackerman, director of National Initiatives Division, and Randi Sundet Griner, partner services manager, both from Search Institute, Minneapolis.

Two editors played significant roles in this project, supporting it enthusiastically throughout its creation. Kay Hong, senior editor at Search Institute, provided early and constant support as the resource was conceptualized, contributors were engaged, and early manuscripts became a reality. Having been the editor of earlier institute publications and a video about building assets in schools, she brought a unifying vision to this deeper project and advocated convincingly for it as a sound next step for the asset-building work in education. More recently, Ruth Taswell, associate editor, assumed the daunting role of seeing the manuscript to completion. She did a remarkable job of envisioning the flow of the book and bringing unity to its voice. Her persistent questions were insightful and on target, and pushed me to clarify and shape more precisely. Working with both Kay and Ruth has been a highlight of my time at Search Institute. Their sensitivity to the needs as well as the expertise of educators is repeatedly demonstrated in the care with which they shepherded this project. I thank them both.

The members of the Education Core Team at Search Institute deserve praise for listening repeatedly to updates on the progress of the book and stories from the authors, and for being supportive in the process. Sandy Longfellow, manager of the Information Resource Center at the institute, supported the book by gathering many bits of information and references, often with very short notice. In addition, I also wish to acknowledge my colleagues in the National Initiatives Division who excused me from meetings, punted for me when I could not appear, and extended deadlines in the name of finishing a resource that will play a part in all of their work as well.

And special thanks is due a friend and colleague, Grace Hall, former director of Human Resources at Search Institute, whose enthusiasm for my writing helped me through deadlines and whose ability to provide dinners, lunches, and good humor sustained me throughout the process.

JUDY TACCOGNA

Part I

How You Teach Makes a Difference

Introduction

Rising above the Challenges of Change

Making Your Teaching Count
with an Asset Mind-Set

JUDY TACCOGNA, ED.D.

Education Director

Search Institute

Minneapolis, Minnesota

The multiple contributors to this hands-on resource well appreciate the daunting charge laid at your and other educators' feet: to help *all* students meet academic standards in the face of an environment of change—change not only in students' needs and cultural demographics, but also in academic expectations and the very nature of schooling itself. Despite these unrelenting pressures, asset-building educators are convinced that we can all—youth and adults, students, teachers, and staff—rise above the challenges of change by maintaining focus on the true bottom line: fostering the academic, social, and emotional growth of the *whole* child.

This book is designed to help you as an educator do just that, no matter what your content area or grade level is, and regardless of your classroom diversity or administrative responsibilities. This resource shows you, through several different paths, how you can foster the growth of each of your students by teaching in a way that intentionally supports their academic, social, and emotional growth.

When you infuse into your teaching what researchers at Search Institute have identified as *developmental assets* (see Appendix A: Lists of the 40 Developmental Assets on page 261) while also providing sound learning opportunities, you can create optimal situations for your students to learn academic knowledge and skills as well as to develop as whole people. What we offer you here, through a wide range of specific examples from multiple asset-building educators, is insight into how to blend asset building with your teaching and with what is required of you. What we're talking about is a way of thinking, an attitude—not another program.

What This Book Offers You

What this unique resource offers you is five guiding principles we've synthesized from the common themes of our contributors' classroom examples to help you embrace the asset mind-set. These principles of infusing developmental assets represent some universal strategies for connecting asset-building efforts to classroom content as well as to the process of teaching (see Handout 1.1: Principles for Infusing Assets into Your Curriculum and Instruction on page 14). By incorporating these principles into your instructional thinking, you're more likely to provide asset-rich teaching.

More specifically, we provide you three paths to facilitate your use of all the contributors' examples to help you think about how you, too, can relate asset building to what you do in your classroom. For each path, we've provided a chart (see Appendix B: Charts of What's in This Book on page 269) that highlights each contributor's approach.

Paths to What's in This Book

Path	Appendix (chart)	Page
Particular assets that contributors address in their content areas and teaching practices	Appendix B.1: Assets Promoted by Contributors' Practices	271
Asset-rich strategies that contributors use to support the needs of *diverse students*	Appendix B.2: Asset-Rich Strategies for Supporting Student Diversity	272
Established *instructional strategies* that contributors use to enhance asset building	Appendix B.3: Connecting Asset Building to Instructional Strategies	276

Each chart enables you to easily find lessons that support what may most interest you. Herein lies part of the beauty of this book: we offer you the choice to think about asset building in a way that works for you. Immerse yourself in the examples—keeping in mind the five guiding principles for infusing assets—via one or all three of the paths, in whatever order suits you.

When you can infuse building assets into the heart, the process, and the content of your classrooms, the chances are greater that you will achieve educational results and foster the development of capable and caring individuals. Infusing assets into your processes of teaching and learning will also build bridges that enable you and other teachers and administrators to move from one change agenda to the next *and* keep the ultimate goal of nurturing youth in view.

The asset framework provides a common language for you and other school personnel (as well as those in the community at large) working in varied roles with students of diverse backgrounds and current situations. The asset framework advocates for the potential strengths and common needs that research indicates are present in most young people across many cultural backgrounds.

No New Curriculum Required!

We've designed this book to help you as a teacher or administrator to frame, as asset-rich strategies, the best of the educational approaches currently producing results, rather than give you a specially created "asset curriculum" to deliver. We elaborate on the process of *infusing* assets into what already exists and is good in teaching.

One of Search Institute's first publications specifically designed for educators, *Great Places to Learn: How Asset-Building Schools Help Students Succeed*[1] identifies fives areas of schooling you and almost every other educator and school in America deal with:

- Curriculum and instruction (what's taught and how it's taught);
- Organization (the structure of your school's building and the school day);
- Cocurricular programs (after-school and before-school programs, previously called *extracurricular* programs);
- Community partnerships (relationships with families, neighbors, volunteers, and community organizations and businesses); and
- Support services (health care, counseling).

This book, *Powerful Teaching: Developmental Assets in Curriculum and Instruction*, focuses on just one of those five schooling areas—curriculum and instruction. Here, you can draw energy—and real lesson plans and handouts—to tackle the formidable task of enhancing learning for diverse students from the knowledge that implementing effective instructional practices also helps build developmental assets in all students in a classroom at the same time. By looking at what you already have that is good, you can intentionally direct asset building to permeate everything you do—from the way you interact with students personally, to how you contribute to your school's environment, to how you structure the lessons in your own classroom.

That's much different than "teaching assets" for six weeks and being done with it. Infusing assets also underscores the idea that asset building is for *all* students *all* the time, not just when problems crop up in your classrooms or school. Using the asset lens enhances everything you do. It especially helps you become more aware of and address preconceived attitudes about diverse youth that may be insidiously buried in a "no problems here" attitude.[2]

Amidst continuous change, the teacher is still the key to unlocking the possibilities for success for any child or adolescent or even an adult in school. Certainly a teacher is not the *only* person responsible in the awesome process of nurturing the growth of a young person, but you can potentially influence a young person more than many of the other adults in each of your students' lives. Capturing a clear vision of the needs of diverse learners and orchestrating circumstances to nurture their success is part of both the art and science of teaching.

So this book is specifically for you—the asset-building teacher who wants to make a deeper difference on a daily basis for the variety of youngsters in classrooms, and the administrator who wants to facilitate that happening (see "Who Should Use This Book?" below). We provide you with a resource to help you look at everything you do as a teacher or administrator through an asset lens: to help you intentionally make the potentially asset-rich elements of both your content and your instruction come alive daily with your students.

Who Should Use This Book?

If you work in any kind of teaching role with youth, read on! We've designed this resource especially for classroom teachers (for youth and for future teachers) and school or district administrators, but you may readily adapt the ideas to your particular domain if you work with youth in other kinds of teaching roles.

- **Counselors or prevention specialists**—to engage classroom teachers in asset building;
- **Staff development personnel**—to help individual teachers or districtwide groups become asset builders in classrooms;
- **Content specialists**—to enhance work with students or small groups requiring special assistance;
- **College or university professors**—to train teachers, counselors, administrators, and other educational professionals to be asset-building educators from day one;
- **Learning center teachers and leaders**—to provide asset-rich instruction to children;
- **Cocurricular program instructors and directors**—to infuse assets into programs to consistently complement efforts in your affiliated asset-building school; and
- **Youth-serving organization leaders**—to view your work through the asset lens.

What's in This Book

This book explores asset-rich teaching in *six subject areas*, as well as in sound, research-based *instructional strategies* that are consistent with asset building. It helps you "go deeper" into infusing asset building into some of the content and practices that you not only are already required to use, but that are also asset-building opportunities for all students.

With the perspectives and materials presented here, you can gain insight into how to analyze the content of what you teach to emphasize the asset elements. And you'll find how a variety of good instructional strategies are often full of asset-supportive opportunities to work with young people and nurture their learning. The book may also inspire you to make leaps beyond the examples discussed here to incorporate asset building and enhance your own curriculum area, the predesigned curricular program you teach, and your instructional strategies.

"Going deeper" as an asset builder implies just that. It involves embedding an asset approach into the very core of what and how you teach. It is to that deeper level that this book takes you. It enables you to see ways to connect asset building to your quality programs (your curricula, units, lessons) and practices (your instructional strategies and other approaches to teaching).

To get you there, we've organized the book as follows.

Chapter 1 presents the five principles of infusing asset building into your curriculum and instruction, synthesized from the major recurring ideas presented in the contributions of all 23 authors (see Handout 1.1: Principles for Infusing Assets into Your Curriculum and Instruction on page 14). You can now use these principles as prompts for infusing the asset approach into your own instructional work.

Chapter 2 examines research by Search Institute showing how schools can directly affect the level of development assets students report having, protecting them from a number of risky behavior patterns and promoting an array of positive results. It also delineates how teaching with an asset mind-set helps manage the ongoing changes asked of you, particularly in meeting the learning needs of all students in increasingly diverse classrooms. (See Appendix B.2: Asset-Rich Strategies for Supporting Student Diversity, another of the paths we recommend to use this book, on page 272.) In addition, this chapter elucidates how these strategies complement and support other well-regarded educational requirements.

Chapter 3 views through an asset lens examples of solid, research-based instructional strategies that teachers are using and for which districts are advocating today. These strategies illustrate how good teaching is, in itself, asset rich. In addition to presenting an overview of many asset-consistent strategies, the chapter explores two in more depth: cooperative learning and differentiation. Appendix B.3: Connecting Asset Building to Instructional Strategies (another path we recommend to use this book, see page 276) pulls together the threads of all of the asset-rich instructional strategies described throughout the book, allowing you to see how various contributors apply an asset lens using the same established instructional approach.

Chapters 4 through 8, the heart of the book comprising our contributors' inspirational examples (see Appendix B.1: Assets Promoted by Contributors' Practices on page 271), focus upon six key subject areas. First are the core areas of language arts, social studies, mathematics, and science. Health education and the visual arts follow, both representing content areas that offer particularly natural connections to building assets. We have provided recent demographics for each contributor's school if available.

Finally, Chapter 9 provides insights into curricular and instructional applications beyond the scope of a single classroom—ideas designed to inspire broader applications of the asset approach as part of the vision of a whole school, district, or state department of education. At a school level, a history teacher describes how an asset focus plays into transitioning students from middle to high school. At a district level, a superintendent outlines a graduation project that supports students over time. And beyond an individual district, the chapter includes examples of how teachers and administrators have infused assets into county frameworks or state standards. In addition, it suggests how to infuse asset building into the supervision and instructional improvement process of a school or district, ultimately widening the impact of asset building by ensuring that it is embedded in the framework of teaching itself.

Just how you decide to jump in to "go deeper" is up to you. We've suggested three paths you might take to incorporate asset building into your teaching or instructional program: through the assets themselves, ways to support student diversity, and asset-rich instructional strategies.

Beyond using these entrance points, we hope you'll see the examples highlighted here as only the beginning of the possibilities. Explore the ideas in your own content if that is represented, but also look at others. You'll find many ideas are adaptable to a number of content areas. And in the spirit of continued growth for asset-building educators, we hope you share the new applications you create with others interested in combining the best of the instructional world with the benefits of building assets to enrich the academic, social, and emotional lives of each of your students.

Notes

1. Starkman, Neal, Scales, Peter C., and Roberts, Clay. (1999). *Great Places to Learn: How Asset-Building Schools Help Students Succeed*. Minneapolis: Search Institute. *Great Places to Learn* includes scores of brief stories that illustrate how various school personnel have created asset-rich ways to connect with young people and help their communities connect with them within the school community. For more on these stories, see Starkman, Neal. (2001). *Ideas That Cook: Activities for Asset Builders in School Communities*. Minneapolis: Search Institute. This resource provides the recipe for success in producing each idea, in addition to presenting many new activities for building assets in diverse environments.
2. Mane, Nandini. (1993). Children and Hate: Hostility Caused by Racial Prejudice. In Varma, Ved., ed., *How and Why Children Hate: A Study of Conscious and Unconscious Sources*. London: Jessica Kingsley Publishers, 119.

Chapter 1

Principles for Infusing Assets into Your Curriculum and Instruction

# The What and How of Teaching

JUDY TACCOGNA, ED.D.

Education Director

Search Institute

Minneapolis, Minnesota

It often seems it's not so much *what* you teach, but *how* you teach it that matters in whether students learn. The educators who helped create this resource provide unique perspectives on asset building within their curricular areas and their instructional practices; they have also, as a collective group, helped crystallize five principles of infusing developmental assets—principles that make a difference in how they teach (see Handout 1.1: Principles for Infusing Developmental Assets into Your Curriculum and Instruction on page 14).

We identified these five principles from common themes in our contributors' examples about:

- The *how* of what they describe; and
- The connections they make with the urgent issues and contemporary instructional practices of education.

These principles serve not only those of you who teach in the content areas in which our contributors provide examples, but others in different areas as well, because the principles represent some universal strategies for connecting asset-building efforts to classroom content and to the process of teaching. They provide an overarching lens for synthesizing and incorporating the asset mind-set.

Principle 1: Connect Personally to Your Students

Research indicates that adult support is associated with students' higher grades, school engagement, IQ and math test scores, and high school completion rates.[1]

Principles for Infusing Developmental Assets into Your Curriculum and Instruction

Principle 1: Connect Personally to Your Students

- Build relationships.
- Create personalized environments.
- Consider how each student can connect personally with the content through your understanding of her or him.

Principle 2: Build on Youth's Interests

- Incorporate your students' ideas into lesson planning and classroom procedures.
- Use youth as resources within lessons and in classroom procedures.

Principle 3: Apply an Asset Lens to Programs, Units, Lessons, and Materials You Already Know

- Analyze existing lessons and units as well as programs (commercial and local) for ways to emphasize building assets.
- Find ways to highlight the asset elements inherent in curriculum materials you're already using.
- Choose materials with assets in mind.
- Choose materials that are well researched in their own domains.

Principle 4: Apply an Asset Lens to the Instructional Strategies That Meet Diverse Learning Needs

- Attend to diverse needs through your choices of practices and materials.
- Honor the strengths and validate the identity of learners through your choices of instructional practices (e.g., cooperative learning, differentiation, etc.).
- Choose instructional strategies that are well researched in their own domains.
- Emphasize the asset-rich elements of those well-researched instructional strategies.

Principle 5: Capitalize on the Power of Sound Instructional Practices and Content to Build Interpersonal and Cultural Competence

- Build developmental assets along with interpersonal and cultural competence skills through your choices of instructional practices.
- Recognize that some instructional strategies you already use build interpersonal and intercultural competence as well as assets.
- Incorporate traditions of many cultures into your instruction.

Connecting personally with students to accomplish curricular goals is advocated by our authors more often than any other strategy.

Andrea Godfrey Brown, a language arts teacher (see "Serving Up John Grisham: Developing Reading for Pleasure" on page 85), fosters relationships by allowing and guiding students through a more adult experience in book talks over breakfast. This involves students differently, closing the chasm often felt between student and teacher in more traditional settings. Brown emphasizes that making personal connections gets back to the emphasis in the asset model of building relationships with youth. She considers relationships critical to the success of her classroom, not only in terms of inspiring students to read for pleasure, but also in communicating high expectations and motivating students to achieve, complete homework, and bond to school—all part of what helps them mature.

For Amy Almendinger, another language arts teacher, establishing personal connections with students allows her and school guidance counselors to collaboratively create an environment in which students can talk about sensitive issues in the context of classic theater: specifically, teen suicide, depression, and family communications (see "From Tragedy to Hope: Addressing Real-Life Issues in *Romeo and Juliet*" on page 117). Stephanie Karno, also in language arts, motivates her students to collect interview information about themselves for their college essays with asset-based prompts (see "Compelling College Candidates: Creating Meaning in Preparing Applications" on page 126). Her interest in making evident her students' personal stories opens doors that positively affect her ability to engage students throughout the rest of the year.

Jonathan Miller-Lane, a social studies teacher, builds relationships and thereby assets by shifting the role of the teacher in a Socratic seminar discussion to one of equality with students. His mental mapping activity opens doors to more personalized connections as well (see "Liberty and Justice for All? Examining Perceptions, Assumptions, and Involvement in Civic Life" on page 145).

Helene Louise Perry stresses getting to know her middle school math students well—what they like, where they live, what makes them tick—to ensure designing lessons that hook them with relevant content. Using a simulated real-life setting of an amusement park, she helps students build the confidence they need to hypothesize and estimate answers as much as to motivate and reinforce expectations (see "There Is No Such Thing as a Stupid Question: Role Playing to Succeed in Math" on page 171).

Health education consultant Colleen Mahoney advocates that it is fundamentally teacher-student relationships and classroom environment more than the curriculum that promotes learning in health classes (see "Capitalizing on Strengths and Creating Solutions: Leaping the Hurdles in Health Education" on page 193).

Several teachers promote projects that tie students to significant adults in the school over extended periods of time. Such relationships enhance the projects and the opportunity to provide positive adult role models. Kristine Willett helps each of her elementary art students to create her or his unique, cumulative portfolio of the assets at each grade level (see "A Masterpiece Show: Visualizing the Assets in

Art" on page 215). The on-going creations enable students to develop a long-term commitment to building assets as well as a long-term relationship with a significant adult in their lives.

History teacher Steven Henderson's transition program for incoming high school students helps new 9th graders focus first on making personal connections to increase greater academic success during the coming school year and beyond (see "Taking the First Step: Linking Supports for High School Success" on page 235). Superintendent Dennis J. Tulli's graduation project connects students with advisers during all four years of their high school experience (see "The Graduation Project: An Asset-Rich Journey" on page 247).

Principle 2: Build on Youth's Interests

Contemporary instructional strategies, including many our authors cite, involve attending to and incorporating students' interests into the content and processes of our teaching and learning. That in itself supports building assets by using youth as resources and engaging them in learning that plays on their unique interests.

Some approach youth interests from a *content* point of view: The graduation project in Dennis J. Tulli's district focuses on an area of interest to the youth. Both Kristine Willett and art teacher Jaime L. Shafer (see "Gaining Cultural Insights through Art" on page 223) integrate many student interests into the art projects they lead. Helene Louise Perry changes the content of math problems she gives to her middle school students to reflect their personal interests, streets in their neighborhoods, and interactions in their social lives. Stephanie Karno captures student interests in getting into—and paying for—college as a motivating factor in learning to create a good application essay. And the issues of being a teenager are reflected in the connections Amy Almendinger makes between the literary characters of Romeo and Juliet and the mental health and communication issues contemporary teens face.

Other teachers incorporate student interests through the *process* of instruction. Brainstorming opportunities appear in a number of the lessons, enabling students of all ability levels and cultural backgrounds to introduce ideas in a nonjudgmental context. Engaging youth in learning communications skills occurs readily in the classroom of Joyce Arnason and Cheri Schaney through their use of various technologies of high interest to students (see "Ready, Set, *Assets in Action*: Producing a Video for Youth" on page 138).

Focusing on student interests through content or process does not mean that student interests drive the curriculum solely. Rather, each emphasis builds in some ways to involve students within the context of the curricular content they need to learn and the standards they need to achieve. Focusing on their interests helps you craft units and lessons that engage and motivate them more solidly because you have incorporated those interests into the learning opportunities.

Our contributors also promote attending to youth's interests to implement a particular teaching strategy. For example, one of the ways to differentiate curriculum and instruction is to design assignments to address differing interests of individuals or groups of students in the class. When differentiating, you can alter the content of your lessons, the processes involved, and/or the products you require students to produce depending upon a particular student's readiness for learning the particular skill or content, the student's interests, and her or his learning profile (the way he or she learns).[2] Once you are clear about the skills and understandings a student must achieve to meet expectations or to achieve a content or process standard, embedding the interests of that student in required projects or assignments raises her or his level of engagement in the task and motivation to learn. In turn, the student is able to find more "hooks" on which to hang relevant information. This process of designing instruction builds assets through its attention to the needs, interests, and learning styles of youth.

Research in the field of positive youth development indicates that youth feeling valued and having useful roles are associated with, among others, higher self-esteem; greater sense of personal control and optimism about the future; greater perception of safety at school; increased social skills; higher levels of moral reasoning; decreased school failure; higher levels of thinking; and increased academic performance.[3]

Including student interests is one way to act on using youth as resources in classroom settings and attain some of the outcomes just listed. For example, you can ask youth to contribute as knowledge sources in assignments or learning opportunities. Involving youth in decision making, planning and leading discussions, and facilitating group work contributes to learning the content in indelible ways, enhances a student's connection to school, and often raises self-confidence.

Social studies teacher Jonathan Miller-Lane's Socratic seminar fosters dialogue that incorporates individual interests and differing points of view. Cooperative learning opportunities reinforce student interests when you, the teacher, consider them in determining groups appropriate for each learning task. Communications teacher Jan Mitchell's cooperative learning activities capitalize on students' interests as well as their decision-making skills (see "The Work Team Project" in "Negotiating at the Bargaining Table: Three Leadership Projects" on page 101).

Special education reading teacher Karen Kupfer Johnson illustrates involving youth as resources when she coaches middle schoolers to read to kindergartners (see "Service Circles of Reading: Gaining Competence and Self-Confidence" on page 99). She cites higher self-esteem and increased skills as two of the results. Principal Dave Guile embraces a similar approach to this in including incoming 5th-grade students in planning his new elementary school's naturescape (see "Designing a Naturescape: Cultivating Asset Growth" on page 181).

Principle 3: Apply an Asset Lens to Programs, Units, Lessons, and Materials You Already Know

Principles 3 and 4 are related. Although both suggest applying an asset lens to what you already know and do in teaching, principle 3 focuses on curriculum and principle 4 on instruction. For our purposes here, we include as curriculum anything that presents content: programs, lessons, units, or materials created by you, your district, or a commercial enterprise. Many of the curricular materials schools currently use are asset rich.

Our contributors highlight the asset-building aspects of the programs, units, lessons, and materials they're already using. Colleen Mahoney illustrates with two examples how the asset model connects so naturally to the content requirements taught in health, one of the earliest content areas to embrace asset building. Standards in health education address information and behaviors, such as communication skills and resistance skills, that young people must learn and use to be safe and successful.

One of the ways to build the health concepts of growth and development throughout a life cycle is reflected in H. Wallace Goddard's idea for creating a folklore record of an older generation (see "Celebrating Folklore: Collecting and Publishing a Community's Stories" on page 114). Although completed as a writing assignment, the process of the activity builds cross-generational understanding and enhances the assets of young and old alike.

Karla McComb's district infuses assets into the locally created elementary school substance abuse and violence prevention program (see "Kids Are the Core" on page 206). Program advocates infuse assets by analyzing existing lessons for each grade level and flagging those related to the targeted assets. Consultant-trainer Dee Lindenberger (see "Powerful Strategies for Bullying Prevention" on page 203) illustrates how you can connect assets to an existing program. Assistant Principal Georgia Teppert reinforces concepts and behaviors learned in health classes through a leadership club (see "Leaders of Tomorrow: Making Health-Positive Choices" on page 210), providing opportunities for students to practice the skills learned within the curriculum.

Other examples of viewing curriculum content through an asset lens include Amy Almendinger's lesson that connects literature curriculum with the guidance curriculum. She addresses commonalities between the two areas as well as identifies asset features of each, in addition to teaching decision-making skills and social competencies.

That example of integrating two curricular areas and adding an asset focus is similar to Brenda Duffey's approach as well (see "Trekking Cross-Country: Cultural Empathy and Quality Decisions" on page 163). She designs her unit on a cross-country trip to integrate language arts, social studies, mathematics, and science in ways that highly engage learners who lag behind their peers in education.

Needs for new support systems, such as Steve Henderson's transition program, or updated materials, such as textbooks or other supplementary books, also provide opportunities to create or select programs and materials that already have asset-rich elements. Often teachers use materials or content that has garnered previous success in a particular content area. Selecting quality materials that have credibility within a discipline enhances the attractiveness of connecting assets to them. It also illustrates for other teachers that building assets can, indeed, firmly connect to rigorous academic content, rather than represent affective fluff.

Explicit appearance of the developmental assets language in materials is not the key criterion, however. Rather, it is how you adapt and use quality materials.

Even the need for a new school offers a way in which looking at what you already have through an asset lens can play out, as it did with Dave Guile. Envisioning an entire school built on the asset principles is intriguing. A goal up front for Dave Guile and his planning team of teachers was to include asset development. The curriculum maps they created serve to remind teachers that looking at all they do through an asset lens is an expectation of school staff. The backward-planning process enabled them to be intentional about infusing assets from the beginning of their planning work.

Principle 4: Apply an Asset Lens to the Instructional Strategies That Meet Diverse Learning Needs

Many of our contributors also talk about several instructional practices that professional journals, educational books, and professional development programs routinely promote. Many schools and districts contend, in fact, that staff proficiency in delivering instruction using these practices is so important that they mandate comprehensive programs to help classroom teachers and administrators understand and implement them regularly with students. Staff development programs in differentiation of curriculum and instruction, curriculum integration, cooperative learning, higher-level questioning and thinking strategies, and inductive approaches, such as the Socratic method, are common. And workshops abound about school restructuring strategies that enhance learning, such as peer tutoring, peer coaching, looping, school-within-a-school, and extending school schedules and services.

Accommodating various ability levels in the same class is an ongoing challenge for most teachers. And the manner in which many school districts are requiring their teachers to learn and deliver their content varies widely, as Principal Stan Paine describes (see "Doing Away with Disengagement: Asset-Rich Strategies for K–12 Instruction" on page 53). Most, if not all, of these strategies, however, are actually asset rich, which can reassure you and other teachers of their value. These strategies often require you to identify strengths and weaknesses, select developmentally appropriate materials and approaches, attend to varying learning styles, use redundancy throughout the year to reinforce learning, base instructional decisions on the latest brain-based research, and hold high expectations for all students.

Joyce Arnason and Cheri Schaney's group work placed students of varying disabilities together. One of the results has been that students come to appreciate their strengths and differences more after the project and are able to listen better to the ideas of others. This authentic project not only addressed a variety of learning styles and needs, it capitalized on several approaches that are less typical in many high school classrooms: high levels of active participation of students, learning activities that involved physical movement, and high-interest technological media.

Helene Louise Perry sees the challenges of her struggling middle school math students as opportunities for learning, both for her and her students—hallmarks of an asset approach. She first analyzes what her students need and then shores up their self-esteem by beginning instruction where they are and reinforcing what they do know. Preassessing to determine students' strengths and weaknesses is a solid asset-rich platform on which to begin. Strength-based teachers teach from what students know, not just to remediate students' weaknesses.

Perry's use of an organizer helps students navigate through steps of an investigation, obtain the proper materials, and complete appropriate prior work. This strategy builds self-esteem, helps with planning, and increases students' feelings of personal power and control.

In teaching language arts, Pamela N. Widmann uses accelerating and compacting, two strategies for differentiating instruction to meet needs of gifted children (see "Creative Writing with an Asset Theme" on page 131). By recording verbatim the story her class creates, she also ensures all students' voices are heard. Eliciting suggestions from everyone includes students with diverse needs in more subtle ways, as well.

You and other educators who wish to focus on building assets for and with your students can often do so most comprehensively in your classrooms by using well the research-based, effective strategies you are already being asked to learn and use. So asset building is not just one more thing for a busy teacher to do—it is inherent in good teaching. The better we teach, the more thoroughly we can build assets.

Principle 5: Capitalize on the Power of Sound Instructional Practices and Content to Build Interpersonal and Cultural Competence

Many educationally sound instructional strategies accommodate diversity well. Add to that the way in which a teacher enhances those practices by highlighting assets and you have opportunities that are much more inclusive and strategies that build both interpersonal and cultural competence.

When you expect cross-cultural communication and sharing as part of the process of learning, the number of opportunities for your students to learn interpersonal and intercultural communication skills rises dramatically. When you intentionally weave opportunities into regular classroom learning activities, cross-cultural listening, interacting, and appreciating become a part of what's expected day to day at school. As such, you can build skills and understandings fundamentally deeper and different from those gleaned by only periodic exposures of youth to a variety of cultures or by special cultural days, months, or festivals alone.

For example, the philosophical underpinnings of Jan Mitchell's partnership project focus on developing other-centeredness. The need to learn skills necessary to maintain a long-term partnership with someone else in class forces students to learn and use effective listening and interpersonal communications skills. Partnerships that involve students of different genders, cultures, language proficiencies, or socioeconomic backgrounds help students break down any preconceived notions about people unlike themselves and decrease prejudice. Further, a skill needed to build effective interpersonal competence as well as cultural competence is the ability to take the opposite point of view in a conflict, as Jan Mitchell exemplifies in her legislative process activity.

Jonathan Miller-Lane addresses diversity and cultural competencies in two particularly significant ways in his work. He helps keep it foremost in students' minds throughout the year by posting their consensus definition on the classroom wall and empowering them to accomplish their individual plans for ensuring that cultural competence is greater within their school. During the Socratic seminar, he insists on wait-time, an admonition to "allow for silence to be a member of the group." This empowers *all* students to participate, especially those who need more time to do so (e.g., for students learning English).

Another opportunity to build cultural and interpersonal competence is described in the interactive headband activity developed by the health educators at the Comprehensive Health Education Foundation (see "Labeling and Stereotyping: Do You Really Know What It Feels Like?" on page 159). It provides a powerful experience for students in understanding the effects of stereotyping and labeling.

Attending to diversity in curriculum and instruction is much like enunciating high expectations to students. You don't "do" high expectations. Rather, you continuously send messages about your expectations through how you do many things. Similarly, you don't "do" diversity, but you attend to addressing varying needs of diverse students through everything you select to use with students and do in your classroom, either explicitly or implicitly.

Our contributors model attending to the needs of diverse students and building intercultural communication skills in their classrooms most strongly through the instructional strategies they use. Addressing those needs through curriculum content is also useful.

For asset-building educators to more fully address building assets for and with *all* youth, examination of long-standing curricula and programs that do not reflect the backgrounds and needs of increasingly diverse student populations is needed. Consistently incorporating materials that present balanced viewpoints, works by authors of both genders and of various races or ethnicities, and content that includes history of a variety of cultures and belief systems is also necessary for us to fully support the range of youth in our schools and communities.

Just *How* Do You Infuse Assets?

The 40 developmental assets identify responsibilities, opportunities, values, and skills that contribute to youth being more healthy, responsible, caring, and successful. The framework does not tell us, however, exactly which practices are effective in building any particular asset. To determine that, we must use our collective good judgment based on *related* research and our wisdom about what works in nurturing children and adolescents in educational settings.

The infusion process, as many intentional asset-building educators in schools throughout the country demonstrate repeatedly, and as you can see from our contributors, involves three steps:

1. Begin with describing the elements of what you do or what the program includes.
2. Next, identify the specific assets that those practices or information are likely to support.
3. Distinguish how you can more intentionally focus on the asset elements already in your curriculum, add asset elements that are compatible, emphasize a particular element more explicitly, and/or adjust your instruction to more directly support students' gaining or strengthening an asset.

One tool that may be helpful in analysis is Handout 1.2A: Increasing the Asset-Building Power of Curriculum and Instruction (on page 23). Side one provides space to analyze curriculum content or a program; side two focuses on instructional practices or strategies. (For a partially completed sample of side two, see Handout 1.2B: Sample Use of Handout 1.2A on page 25.)

Viewing your role, your curriculum planning, and your delivery of instruction through an asset lens helps support youth without adding a single new program for you to implement. Incorporating an asset approach into your teaching will also assist you in addressing a number of contemporary educational issues and some of the latest research—school change and reform, contemporary instructional strategies and expectations, and student diversity. Further, the five principles we've developed here will help you in any teaching role, even outside of a K–12 school setting—in after-school programs, cocurricular activities, youth-serving organizations, or higher education—to infuse assets into the learning situations that you supervise in your varied roles.

Look closely at the sound curricula and effective instructional practices already surrounding you in your schools and the educational research literature. Then, using an asset lens, determine for yourself, in your particular educational context, how best to enhance learning opportunities for the young people you touch. Give them each opportunities to acquire the knowledge, skills, and understandings about academic disciplines as well as about diverse people and relationships that will contribute to their growth as healthy, caring, and responsible individuals.

Notes

1. Scales, Peter C., and Leffert, Nancy. (1999). *Developmental Assets: A Synthesis of the Scientific Research on Adolescent Development.* Minneapolis: Search Institute, 27.
2. Tomlinson, Carol Ann. (1999). *The Differentiated Classroom: Responding to the Needs of All Learners.* Alexandria, VA: Association for Supervision and Curriculum Development.
3. Scales and Leffert, *Developmental Assets*, 53–54.

Increasing the Asset-Building Power of Curriculum and Instruction

Take some time to think about each category of the developmental assets: Are you building assets in what and how you teach? Are you intentionally building them? How are you doing it? Which assets aren't you building?

This chart provides space in which you can analyze the curricula or programs you teach (side one) and the instructional practices or strategies you use (side two) to infuse assets more completely in your classroom or school. In the "Features" column, list elements of the curriculum content or the instructional strategy you are analyzing. In the center column, itemize the assets that support that content or practice. In the right-hand column, brainstorm ideas for increasing the asset-building impact of the content or the practice. (For a partially completed sample of side two, see Handout 1.2B.)

Features of the Curriculum Content	Developmental Assets That Support Content	Ways to Increase the Potential for Building Assets

SIDE ONE

Features of the Instructional Practice	Developmental Assets That Support Practice	Ways to Increase the Potential for Building Assets
_____	_____	_____
_____	_____	_____
_____	_____	_____
_____	_____	_____
_____	_____	_____
_____	_____	_____
_____	_____	_____
_____	_____	_____
_____	_____	_____
_____	_____	_____
_____	_____	_____
_____	_____	_____
_____	_____	_____
_____	_____	_____
_____	_____	_____
_____	_____	_____
_____	_____	_____
_____	_____	_____
_____	_____	_____
_____	_____	_____
_____	_____	_____
_____	_____	_____
_____	_____	_____
_____	_____	_____
_____	_____	_____
_____	_____	_____

SIDE TWO

Sample Use of Handout 1.2A

This handout illustrates how to complete side two of Handout 1.2A: Increasing the Asset-Building Power of Curriculum and Instruction and most effectively analyze your instructional practices in an asset framework:

- *First, describe the features or component parts of an instructional strategy. This sample case highlights one component of cooperative learning.*
- *Next, using your professional judgment (without stretching the possibilities too far), list the assets that each component might strengthen or build. (Your own list may differ slightly depending on the context in which you created your cooperative group.)*
- *Last, enter your ideas for how to emphasize building one or more of the assets. Pull out the essence of the asset as well as the strategy components, and emphasize both concurrently. Avoid skimping in explaining why you're asking students to operate in a particular way.*

Features of the Instructional Practice	Developmental Assets That Support Practice	Ways to Increase the Potential for Building Assets
Cooperative Learning	5. *Caring School Climate*	■ *Explain well to students your*
Positive interdependence:	15. *Positive Peer Influence*	*rationale (interdependence among*
Groups and assignments are	21. *Achievement Motivation*	*group members is an advantageous*
structured so group members	22. *School Engagement*	*skill to learn; it points out and builds*
perceive they need to depend	26. *Caring*	*on each member's capabilities) for*
on one another to "sink or swim"	30. *Responsibility*	*structuring groups as you did for*
together.	33. *Interpersonal Competence*	*the cooperative learning activity.*
	34. *Cultural Competence*	■ *Reemphasize and relate the assets*
	36. *Peaceful Conflict Resolutions*	*to previous class discussions and*
	37. *Personal Power*	*practices that build assets.*
		■ *Reinforce the need for good com-*
		munication within groups to help
		students help each other to "swim
		together."
Cooperative Learning	33. *Interpersonal Competence*	■ *More purposefully assign groups*
Reduces prejudice and enhances	34. *Cultural Competence*	*to include diverse ethnicities as well*
cross-cultural communication		*as abilities.*

SIDE TWO

Chapter 2

*Asset Building to Support
What's Already Required*

The Developmental Assets Connection

MEETING THE DEMANDS OF EDUCATIONAL ISSUES AND EXPECTATIONS

JUDY TACCOGNA, ED.D.

Education Director

Search Institute

Minneapolis, Minnesota

Promoting the development of healthy, caring, and responsible youth involves all that teaching and a school are about—the affective *and* the academic. There's much behind those simple few words. What is so significant and meaningful, though, is that we know definitely from research that developmental assets make a difference. To better ensure that you understand how valuable teaching through an asset lens is, it's important to consider how well an asset-rich instructional approach facilitates rising above the challenges of change, in addition to complementing and supporting other highly valued educational recommendations.

The Developmental Assets

So what are these assets that can be of so much benefit to students in schools? As a result of research in the late 1980s and early 1990s, Search Institute has identified 40 relationships or experiences that influence children and youth in protecting them from a number of risky behavior patterns as well as in promoting an array of positive results (e.g., being successful in school, maintaining good health, valuing diversity, and overcoming adversity). Called *developmental assets* (see Appendix A: Lists of the 40 Developmental Assets on page 261), these 40 relationships or experiences fall into two broad groups:

- External assets—those that are provided by others for young people; and

- Internal assets—the skills and values youth develop that provide the internal compass for navigating life successfully and positively.

Each of those broad groups is, in turn, divided into four categories that pull related assets together. The names of the external categories represent how others in an asset-rich community—families, schools, congregations, youth organizations, neighbors—provide resources, structures, and opportunities through which young people grow: Support, Empowerment, Boundaries and Expectations, and Constructive Use of Time. Similarly, the names of the internal categories reflect that those assets develop within the young person, often with the help of nurturing adults— teachers and administrators like you—in their environment: Commitment to Learning, Positive Values, Social Competencies, and Positive Identity.

Results from Search Institute's *Profiles of Student Life: Attitudes and Behaviors* survey, designed to measure the number of these developmental assets youth in grades 6–12 experience, reveal that they do protect young people.[1] To date, more than 1.5 million young people have taken that survey. Those youth who report having more of the developmental assets (see Handout 2.1: The Power of Assets on page 31) tend to be less involved in high-risk behaviors (e.g., problem alcohol use, illicit drug use, early sexual activity, and violence). In addition, possessing more developmental assets also promotes positive attitudes and behaviors, including success in school (see "Thriving Behaviors of Students" on page 32).

Success in Schools

Great Places to Learn: How Asset-Building Schools Help Students Succeed,[2] one of Search Institute's first resources for educators, highlights the fact that building relationships, creating supportive school environments, and connecting developmental assets to programs and practices are the three primary ways to build assets in schools. As you review the list of the 40 developmental assets, you can probably identify those assets that you as a teacher or administrator already feel you influence.

Schools can actually directly affect 22 of the assets (see Handout 2.2: Percentage of Youth Who Report Experiencing the Developmental Assets That Schools Can Most Directly Affect on page 33). And 13 of these assets are more directly related to academic achievement (starred on Handout 2.2). Keep in mind, though, that focusing on either those 13 or the 22 contributes to supporting many other assets as well, since the assets are all interrelated. The level of assets most students report having, however, is less than desired. And that's why we've developed this resource—to help you foster an increase in those assets.

Charts in *Great Places to Learn* illustrate how asset-rich strategies probably already exist in your school's educational practices within each of the 13 assets most directly connected to academic success (see examples Handout 2.3: Building the Assets Most Directly Connected to Academic Success: School Engagement on page 34 and Handout 2.4: Building the Assets Most Directly Connected to Academic Success: Achievement Motivation on page 35). Many strategies that current

The Power of the Assets

On one level, the 40 developmental assets represent common wisdom about the kinds of positive experiences and characteristics that young people need and deserve. But their value extends further. Surveys of more than 200,000 students in grades 6–12 reveal that assets are powerful influences on adolescent behavior. Regardless of gender, ethnic heritage, economic situation, or geographic location, these assets both promote positive behaviors and attitudes and help protect young people from many different problem behaviors.

Promoting Positive Behaviors and Attitudes

Our research shows that the more assets students report having, the more likely they are to also report the following patterns of thriving behavior:

Protecting Youth from High-Risk Behaviors

Assets not only promote positive behaviors, they also protect young people: the more assets a young person reports having, the less likely he or she is to make harmful or unhealthy choices. (Note that these definitions are set rather high, suggesting ongoing problems, not experimentation.)

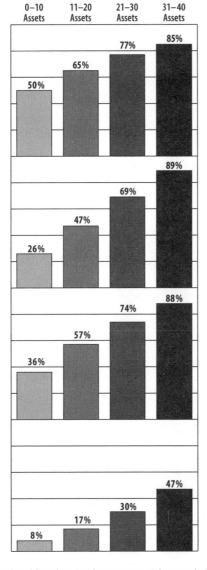

Exhibits Leadership
Has been a leader of an organization or group in the past 12 months

Maintains Good Health
Takes good care of body such as eating foods that are healthy and exercising regularly

Values Diversity
Thinks it is important to get to know people of other racial / ethnic groups

Succeeds in School
Gets mostly A's on report card (an admittedly high standard)

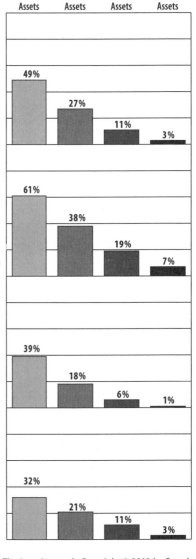

Problem Alcohol Use
Has used alcohol three or more times in the past 30 days or got drunk once or more in the past two weeks

Violence
Has engaged in three or more acts of fighting, hitting, injuring a person, carrying a weapon, or threatening physical harm in the past 12 months

Illicit Drug Use
Used illicit drugs (marijuana, cocaine, LSD, PCP or angel dust, heroin, or amphetamines) three or more times in the past 12 months

Sexual Activity
Has had sexual intercourse three or more times in lifetime

Thriving Behaviors of Students

Success in school is one of the thriving behaviors, or "markers of developmental success," measured as "getting mostly A's on report cards" in Search Institute's *Profiles of Student Life: Attitudes and Behaviors* survey.[1] As you saw in Handout 2.1: The Power of the Assets, young people with 31–40 assets report doing appreciably better in school than others with fewer assets. The number of developmental assets is positively correlated with students' self-reported grades. The effect is even stronger for the most vulnerable youth (those with several developmental deficits, such as experiencing abuse or violence, too much time at home alone, and too much television); in other words, vulnerable youth surveyed reported receiving fewer A's and experiencing fewer assets.

Search Institute researchers have found that several specific assets cluster and meaningfully predict those self-reported grades as well: achievement motivation, school engagement, time in youth programs, time at home, and personal power. Each of these specific asset connections is also significant for three of the six racial and ethnic subgroups of students surveyed—African American, Asian American, Hispanic/Latino, Multiracial, American Indian, and Caucasian.[2] Depending upon the racial/ethnic group of the student, this cluster of assets explains from 19 to 31 percent of the variation in grades that different students get, over and above demographic variables such as age, gender, and socioeconomic status.

This explanation of assets compares favorably to that of other variables, such as family or peer relationships, which affect academic success.

Institute researchers are seeing the same pattern (more assets associated with higher grades) when surveying actual as well as self-reported grades. Further, more research is currently under way to determine whether and how asset building affects student achievement more directly as evidenced by other indicators of academic success, such as standardized test scores. To date, early returns show promise in making that link.

In addition, indications exist that higher asset levels may also help decrease traditional gender differences in grades. For example, in another Search Institute study, boys with more assets have grades in English more similar to those of girls, and girls with higher numbers of assets have grades in mathematics closer to those of boys.[3]

Notes

1. For more information on thriving behaviors, see Benson, Peter L., Scales, Peter C., Leffert, Nancy, and Roehlkepartain, Eugene C. (1999). *A Fragile Foundation: The State of Developmental Assets among American Youth*. Minneapolis: Search Institute, Appendix D, 173–182; and Scales, Peter C., Benson, Peter L., Leffert, Nancy, and Blyth, Dale. (2000). The Contribution of Developmental Assets to the Prediction of Thriving Outcomes among Adolescents, *Applied Developmental Science*, 4(1): 27–46.
2. Scales et al.
3. Leffert, Nancy, and Scales, Peter L. *The Impact of Developmental Assets on Adolescents' Academic Achievement*. Manuscript submitted for publication.

educational literature emphasizes or that your own district embraces are consistent with the asset approach and reinforce the notion that infusing assets into teaching begins with looking at the good work your school's already doing.

Embracing School Change

Change has been the name of the game in schools for the past two decades at least! Managing it has been overwhelming both for school administrators and classroom teachers. From the early 1980s on, ensuring that the practices schools use are based on sound research has been gaining momentum on a par with communities' and with states' increasing concern about the quality of education delivered to their youth. Infusing assets into your teaching facilitates effectively managing all this change as well as supports these other highly regarded educational recommendations.

Effective Schools Research

The "effective schools process" is embodied in a school-change framework that emerged in response to *A Nation at Risk*, the 1983 report of the National Com-

Percentage of Youth Who Report Experiencing the Developmental Assets That Schools Can Most Directly Affect

Assets Schools Can Most Directly Affect	Percentage of Youth Experiencing Asset
21. Achievement Motivation*	67%
15. Positive Peer Influence*	65%
22. School Engagement*	61%
18. Youth Programs*	58%
24. Bonding to School*	54%
12. School Boundaries*	53%
23. Homework*	53%
10. Safety	51%
9. Service to Others	51%
16. High Expectations*	49%
33. Interpersonal Competence*	47%
36. Peaceful Conflict Resolution	45%
3. Other Adult Relationships*	45%
35. Resistance Skills	42%
6. Parent Involvement in Schooling*	34%
32. Planning and Decision Making	30%
14. Adult Role Models	30%
5. Caring School Climate*	29%
8. Youth as Resources	28%
7. Community Values Youth	25%
25. Reading for Pleasure*	23%
17. Creative Activities	20%

N = 217,277 students grades 6–12 in public and private U.S. schools surveyed during the 1999–2000 school year.

*Assets that research suggests are most important to academic success.

Building the Assets Most Directly Connected to Academic Success: School Engagement

School Engagement: 61% of students report having the asset.

Area	Strategies
Curriculum and instruction	■ Develop integrative and interdisciplinary curricula. ■ Use team teaching with adequate common planning time. ■ Initiate projects that involve more than "skill and drill". ■ Implement exploratory programs that keep students interested. ■ Use student-led activities and group learning.
Organization	■ Arrange large schools into small "houses" or teams so that more intimate learning communities can foster interpersonal connections. ■ Use adviser-advisee or teacher-based guidance programs to foster close teacher-student relationships.
Cocurricular programs	■ Offer a variety of clubs and after-school activities based on inclusion more than interscholastic competition.
Community partnerships	■ Engage businesses and other community organizations to provide internships and experiential education that connects students to the "real" world. ■ Invite community people into school as resources.
Support services	■ Have extensive articulation programs to ease building transitions from elementary to middle school and middle school to high school. ■ Maintain a low student-to-counselor ratio.

Building the Assets Most Directly Connected to Academic Success: Achievement Motivation

Achievement Motivation: 67% of students report having the asset.

Area	Strategies
Curriculum and instruction	■ Provide ungraded units and courses to stimulate learning for its own sake. ■ Use heterogeneous grouping whenever possible and minimize tracking. ■ Add "authentic" assessment, e.g., student portfolios. ■ Evaluate students' personal progress, not only their standing relative to their peers.
Organization	■ Use flexible scheduling that allows greater depth of content and more opportunity for teacher aid to individual students.
Cocurricular programs	■ Provide tutoring alternatives. ■ Offer after-school homework programs.
Community partnerships	■ Offer experiential education, including service learning.
Support services	■ Offer ways of engaging students as leaders in the community (such as youth members of school boards or community planning boards).

mission on Excellence in Education.[3] That framework prompts constant updating of the research about schools that effectively teach the curriculum to *all* students. Based on the individual and collective effective schooling research efforts of Ronald Edmonds, Larry Lezotte, and others, seven characteristics emerged describing schools that meet the standards of effectiveness: safe and orderly environment, high expectations for success, instructional leadership, clear school mission, opportunity to learn and student time on task, frequent monitoring of student progress, and home-school relations (see "The Correlates of Effective Schooling" below).[4] Building developmental assets aligns well with many of these correlates because many of the advocated schooling practices are also consistent with the asset model. Handout 2.5: The Correlates of Effective Schooling and the Developmental Assets on page 37, shows where several assets are supported by educational practices embedded in each correlate.

The Correlates of Effective Schooling

The individual and collective research of Ronald Edmonds, Larry Lezotte, and others identifies seven characteristics that effective schools have in common. These correlates represent the recommended ways to achieve high and equitable levels of student learning.[1] The research behind each of these correlates is well documented in a research synthesis produced by the Northwest Regional Educational Laboratory in Portland, Oregon.[2]

1. Safe and Orderly Environment
- Effective schools are relatively safer, cleaner, more orderly, and quieter.
- Adults care about the work of creating a safe and orderly environment.
- The environment conveys a sense of importance about the teaching/learning of essential skills.

2. High Expectations for Success
- A climate of expectation exists in which staff believes and demonstrates that *all* students can attain mastery of essential school skills.
- They do not expect that any significant number of children of any race or social class will fail.

3. Instructional Leadership
- The principals of effective schools are the instructional leaders in their buildings.
- Principals are much closer to the day-to-day instructional program, closely monitor pupil progress, and provide systematic feedback.

4. Clear School Mission
- There is a clearly articulated school mission through which the staff shares an understanding of a commitment to the instructional goals, priorities, assessment procedures, and accountability.
- The staff accepts responsibility for students learning the essential skills.

5. Opportunity to Learn and Student Time on Task
- Teachers allocate a significant amount of classroom time to instruction in the essential skills.
- Students are engaged in whole class or large group learning activities that are planned and teacher directed.

6. Frequent Monitoring of Student Progress
- Progress is measured frequently.
- A variety of forms of assessment are used.
- The results of assessment are used to improve individual student performance.

7. Home-School Relations
- Parents understand and support the basic mission of the school.
- They are made to feel that they have an important role in achieving that mission.

Notes
1. Association for Effective Schools, Inc., *Correlates of Effective Schools.* Web site accessed September 25, 2002: www.mes.org/correlates.html. This 501(c)(3) nonprofit is located in Styvesant, NY.
2. Cotton, Kathleen. (1995). *Effective Schooling Practices: A Research Synthesis—1995 Update.* Portland, OR: Northwest Regional Education Laboratory (NWREL). This synthesis update is based on the original 1984 *Effective Schooling Practices: A Research Synthesis*, written by Robert E. Blum and others at NWREL for use in their "Onward to Excellence" school change and improvement process implemented by more than 2,000 schools across the country.

The Correlates of Effective Schooling and the Developmental Assets

Effective schools research defines seven characteristics evident in schools that meet the standards of effectiveness.[1] This matrix illustrates that numerous assets in Search Institute's developmental asset framework connect to the seven correlates of effective schooling.

DEVELOPMENTAL ASSETS	CORRELATES OF EFFECTIVE SCHOOLING						
	Safe and Orderly Environment	High Expectations for Success	Instructional Leadership	Clear School Mission	Opportunity to Learn and Student Time on Task	Frequent Monitoring of Student Progress	Home-School Relations
5. Caring School Climate	■	■	■		■	■	
6. Parent Involvement		■					■
8. Youth as Resources	■			■	■		
10. Safety	■			■			
12. School Boundaries	■			■			■
14. Adult Role Models	■	■		■			■
15. Positive Peer Influence	■				■		
16. High Expectations		■	■		■	■	
17. Creative Activities				■			
18. Youth Programs				■			
21. Achievement Motivation		■	■	■	■	■	
22. School Engagement		■	■		■	■	■
23. Homework		■				■	
24. Bonding to School	■		■	■			
25. Reading for Pleasure			■	■			
32. Planning and Decision Making			■	■		■	
33. Interpersonal Competence	■	■	■			■	■
34. Cultural Competence	■	■	■			■	■

1. Association for Effective Schools, Inc., *Correlates of Effective Schools*. Web site accessed September 25, 2002: www.mes.org / correlates.html. This 501(c)(3) nonprofit is located in Styvesant, NY.

Elements of School Change

You can see in Handout 2.5 that elements of the assets show up throughout the seven practices evident in effective schools, but just how might you think about asset building as supporting change itself? Michael Fullan, dean of the Ontario Institute for Studies in Education at the University of Toronto, and a highly regarded researcher and lecturer on educational change, contends there are four critical points to remember about change:[5]

1. Reculturing is more than restructuring.
2. The way to reculture is to change actions of individuals, not to restructure systems.
3. Change is mandatory; growth is optional. But you don't have to change all at once.
4. Don't be afraid to start where you are with what you've got.

From an asset perspective, then, dealing with change goes beyond just structuring your classroom or school differently. Building assets involves attending to the culture of your classroom and your school.

Second, reculturing schools and classrooms using the asset framework first necessitates individually building relationships person to person, creating supportive environments, and connecting to programs and practices already on your plate that are known to be good. Only then can you and others collectively begin to create change on a larger scale.

Yes, dealing with educational change on your plate is mandatory. And while looking at new expectations through an asset lens is optional, regarding such expectations as an opportunity to infuse stronger asset-consistent approaches into your work may foster your own professional growth and enhance asset-building opportunities for your students—all *while* you incorporate the mandated change. Asset building can begin with your committing to relating to your students in ways that work with their strengths, validate them as individuals, and nurture their growth. This strength-based approach is fundamental to many education change agendas.

Get started with what you've got. Here's how one middle school teacher did just that:

Already overwhelmed with required changes when she attended a developmental assets workshop, a middle school teacher decided she could at least commit to one small thing that would add an asset approach to her work without much planning or other time impact. She determined that she would stand at her classroom door and greet each student by name with a friendly comment each period as they reported to class.

Several months later a phone message appeared that the mother of one of her students, Sam, had a question. Puzzled, the teacher called. Sam's mother wanted to know what the teacher was doing differently because a formerly disengaged Sam was suddenly so much more interested in English than he had been, and he seemed to be doing better as well. The only thing the teacher could come up with was her daily greeting of the students by name!

Being greeted by name every day was a small but evidently very meaningful change for Sam that enabled him to perceive class differently, connect in a new way with a significant adult, engage more with his learning, and become motivated to achieve. For the teacher, focusing in a very easy way on engaging students in learning lightens a piece of her workload due to the change in relationship she fostered. Seemingly unrelated to higher achievement, the greeting strategy certainly promotes the conditions for it.

Change boils down to the need to shift thinking and systems person by person before other individuals can change and incorporate behaviors; then it involves accumulating the critical mass of people in the same school culture moving collaboratively in a common direction over time before the change is really incorporated into the fabric of the school.

Turning Points 2000

Similar to the admonitions of effective schools research and Michael Fullan's recommendations, *Turning Points: Preparing American Youth for the 21st Century*, a key report by the Carnegie Corporation of New York in 1989, reads like a list of asset-building suggestions.[6] Based on this report, which describes what was needed to reform middle-level education, the Carnegie Corporation provided a series of grants to implement the recommended changes in 225 school systems throughout the country.

During the ensuing 10 years, researchers studied what those schools were learning about the changes, and in 2000 they produced a second report with revised recommendations.[7] While these recommendations all fall under the overarching goal of ensuring success for *every* student, the new report emphasizes teaching and learning as the drivers of change in all other related aspects of schooling (e.g., school organization, staff development). Again, very asset supportive.

Building developmental assets enhances accomplishing a number of the latest *Turning Points* recommendations (see Handout 2.6: *Turning Points 2000* Recommendations and the Developmental Assets on page 40). Although created for a middle school audience, the new recommendations have elements also applicable at the elementary and high school level.

The first of the new recommendations includes addressing adolescents' interests:

Teach a curriculum grounded in rigorous, public academic standards for what students should know and be able to do, relevant to the concerns of adolescents and based on how students learn best.

This doesn't mean you should build a curriculum solely on students' interests. Rather, you must look at the academic standards and find ways to move your students toward those using the context of their interests and concerns as hooks.

Turning Points 2000 Recommendations and the Developmental Assets

This chart illustrates that numerous assets in Search Institute's developmental assets framework connect to each of the Turning Points 2000[1] *recommendations. If your school requires you to implement the* Turning Points 2000 *recommendations, this chart shows which assets you may also be building. Similarly, if you are intentionally building assets in your class or school, the chart shows the assets on which you may want to focus while addressing the* Turning Points 2000 *recommendations.*

DEVELOPMENTAL ASSETS	*TURNING POINTS 2000* RECOMMENDATIONS						
	Relevant Content, Based on Learning Research, to Standards	Instructional Methods to Prepare All Students	Teachers Expert with Adolescents, Continuous Professional Development	Relationships Supporting Climate of Learning for Adults	Democratic Governance of Staff	Safe, Healthy Environment Toward Improved Academics and Caring and Ethical Citizens	Parent and Community Support Learning and Healthy Development
3. Other Adult Relationships			■	■		■	
5. Caring School Climate	■		■	■		■	
6. Parent Involvement				■			■
7. Community Values Youth						■	■
8. Youth as Resources	■	■			■	■	■
9. Service to Others	■	■					■
10. Safety						■	
11. Family Boundaries							■
12. School Boundaries						■	■
13. Neighborhood Boundaries							■
14. Adult Role Models			■	■	■	■	■
15. Positive Peer Influence						■	
16. High Expectations	■	■	■			■	■
17. Creative Activities							■
18. Youth Programs							■
20. Time at Home							■
21. Achievement Motivation	■	■	■	■		■	■
22. School Engagement	■	■	■			■	
23. Homework							■
24. Bonding to School	■			■		■	
25. Reading for Pleasure		■				■	■
26. Caring		■				■	
27. Equality and Social Justice		■				■	
28. Integrity						■	
29. Honesty						■	
30. Responsibility		■			■	■	
31. Restraint						■	
32. Planning and Decision Making				■	■	■	
33. Interpersonal Competence	■	■		■	■	■	■
34. Cultural Competence	■	■		■	■	■	■
35. Resistance Skills						■	■
36. Peaceful Conflict Resolution		■		■	■	■	■
37. Personal Power					■	■	
38. Self-Esteem		■				■	

1. Jackson, Anthony W., and Davis, Gayle A. (2000). *Turning Points 2000: Educating Adolescents in the 21st Century.* A report of the Carnegie Corporation of New York. New York: Teachers College Press, 23–26.

"Based on how students learn best" brings into play two other educationally sound areas: the brain research that schools today emphasize so much and multiple intelligences, a framework that provides a useful lens for your teaching, much as the asset approach does. Recent brain research has provided us with insights into what is actually happening in the brain during the processes of growth and learning. That helps inform us about ways to revamp the approaches and strategies we use to add relevance to what we are teaching and thus better ensure that the learning stays with students longer and hooks their prior knowledge into new ideas they are gaining (see "Brain-Smart Teaching" on page 42).

Harvard University psychologist Howard Gardner's acclaimed and influential work on multiple intelligences similarly affirms the benefit of finding the strengths of students and building from them.[8] In contrast to focusing only on the traditional verbal and mathematical areas of intelligence, Gardner's research in the early 1980s identified seven forms of intelligence: linguistic, logical-mathematical, visual-spatial, bodily-kinesthetic, musical, interpersonal, and intrapersonal.[9] Since then, he has defined another, naturalist, and proposed a possible ninth area, existential.[10] Implementing classroom activities that use various intelligences increases the chances of engaging your students and their learning by hitting on how each one learns best.

Tailoring content and instruction to how your students learn best also opens the door for meeting the needs of all students, as *Turning Points 2000* addresses in its second recommendation:

> Use instructional methods designed to prepare all students to achieve higher standards and become lifelong learners.

You can obviously enhance equity of access, highlighted in the effective schools research, by your choice of instructional practices, including heterogeneous grouping, cooperative learning, and a variety of appropriate assessment strategies. And in so doing, you can capitalize upon student diversity rather than sweep it under the rug.

The many strategies involved in differentiating curriculum and instruction also contribute to preparing *all* students. You, as the teacher in the classroom, can modify the content, the process, and the product required in the learning unit to gear instruction to an individual student's needs. At the same time, you can use differentiation to infuse asset building into your teaching in a number of ways: using youth as resources, building other adult relationships in their lives, paying attention to the needs of and support for others, planning strategies to meet the needs of a variety of students, and demonstrating support for cultural and other forms of diversity.

But how does one support asset building and adhere to the third recommendation from *Turning Points 2000*?

> Staff middle grade schools with teachers who are expert at teaching young adolescents, and engage teachers in ongoing, targeted professional development opportunities.

Brain-Smart Teaching

Dee Lindenberger, M.A.
Education Consultant-Trainer
Marquette-Alger Regional Education Service Agency and
Michigan Strategic Alternatives in Prevention Education Association
Marquette, Michigan

One of the educational changes of the recent past is increased emphasis on basing instruction upon how young people learn. The alignment of the asset model with recent research about how the brain functions during learning reveals that instructional strategies that take such research into account are also usually asset rich.

Based on current neuroscientific research, brain-based instruction describes an approach to teaching that recognizes that how the brain learns is biologically driven. In the past 10 years, researchers have learned more about how the brain functions than in previous years altogether. These advances open tremendous opportunities for you to use strategies that promote teaching *with* the grain of your students' biology rather than *against* it.

Research in neuroscience points to many specific techniques teachers can use to get and maintain the brain's attention and to encode memory. The key qualities of an enriched, brain-friendly learning environment also align strongly with asset building. Both brain-based instruction and asset building advocate the following strategies.

1. Create a learning environment that is physically and emotionally safe.

The importance of safety is best understood in terms of how the brain functions in the presence of threat. Those threats may be clearly physical or subtler (e.g., social exclusion, public embarrassment, or a sarcastic remark from a peer or a teacher).

When we perceive danger, our brain does what it's designed to do: it goes into a survival mode known as *downshifting*. This process is similar to the body's reaction to hypothermia—blood flow to the nonvital extremities decreases and diverts to the body core to help us survive. In downshifting, blood flow and glucose consumption decrease in the upper brain areas and increase in the lower brain's fight-or-flight system. This phenomenon is important for educators to understand for two reasons:

- Areas of the upper brain, such as the frontal lobes, are critical for complex, higher-order thinking and problem solving. When a student is in survival mode, the reduced activity in the upper brain severely inhibits information retrieval and new learning.
- Exposure to threat triggers the release of stress chemicals that inhibit attention and, over time, kill neurons in the hippocampus (essential for memory formation and storage).

Three of the most effective strategies for increasing safety include teaching and modeling respectful communication and problem-solving skills, implementing comprehensive bullying prevention strategies, and regularly taking time for relationship-building activities (e.g., class meetings, cooperative learning, social activities/noncompetitive games). When you invest time to create a classroom environment that is safe and comfortable for all students, you are not only building assets, you are teaching in a brain-smart way.

2. Promote respectful and caring relationships.

Respectful and caring relationships (student to student and student to teacher) can answer some of your and other educators' most challenging questions: How can I reduce threat and stress, and increase safety? How can I increase motivation? How can I get students more involved in their learning experience and boost their creativity?

As respectful and caring relationships grow, so too will a sense of community and bonding. Your students will feel more supported and more likely to risk publicly offering what might be a wrong answer. Their active involvement in learning activities will increase, as will their creative thinking and problem solving; ultimately, learning will increase.

Research in both brain-based instruction and asset building clearly demonstrates that building relationships is not incidental to profound learning or healthy youth development: it is a fundamental component in both.

3. Provide opportunities for cooperation and active involvement.

Traditionally, a classroom teacher stands in front of the room and teaches (i.e., talks), and students sit in their seats and learn (i.e., listen). The question is, how much do students really learn in this passive role?

(continued)

Brain-Smart Teaching *(continued)*

Current brain research indicates that the average length of time an adult can pay attention when someone is lecturing is approximately 10–12 minutes; the time span is even less for children. Our brains are not designed for long periods of passive learning.

Activities that include cooperation and involvement capture the brain's attention and stimulate production of chemicals that promote learning. When interspersed throughout a lecture, even short activities that get students actively participating will serve as effective "state changes" to the brain and extend the period of time students can pay attention and increase their learning. For example, when you incorporate activities that require cooperation and participation into a service-learning or social justice project, you introduce another level of learning beyond the academics—being empowered to make a positive difference in the world.

4. Utilize activities that help students make learning personally relevant and meaningful.

Eric Jensen, a leading advocate of brain-based instruction, says, "We never really understand something until we can create a model or metaphor derived from our unique personal world."[1] Our brain is hardwired to seek meaning and relevance for things that have personal value to us, particularly things related to our well-being (physical, emotional, social, or economic). It's about relationships: we teach *people* first and *content* second.

If you are successful in relating to your students as individuals and in helping them find relevance in learning, they will be attentive and motivated because they have a vested interest in learning. The process of finding relevance is about helping your students answer two questions:

- "Why should I want to learn this?"
- "How does this relate to me as a human being?"

Your students need to see a real-life application for the information you're teaching. Field trips, bringing community members into classes, and simply framing a learning project through student interests help them find meaning. A variety of reflective activities such as journaling or writing, group discussions, or art projects promote introspection and internalization of that meaning. The more you can relate learning to your students' personal lives, reaching both their heads and their hearts, the more profound their learning experience will be—and the more humanely they will use their education.

Notes

1. Jensen, Eric. (1996). *Brain-Based Learning*. Del Mar, CA: Turning Point Publishing, 33. A former teacher (all education levels, elementary through university), Jensen cofounded SuperCamp, the nation's first and largest brain-compatible learning program for teens. He is currently president of the professional training organization Jensen Learning, Inc., in San Diego, CA.

I've heard it said, "Feed the teachers or they'll eat the kids!" It's true at any level of schooling. Sometimes in the chaotic weeks of managing many students a day as well as accomplishing all of the related support tasks, attending staff development opportunities seems interruptive and burdensome. Learning anything when one's brain is on overload is a feat in itself.

Reframed through an asset lens, however, mandated staff development can actually become golden opportunities to learn educationally sound ways to increase student achievement. And more than a few of these proven instructional practices are asset supportive, engaging students at higher levels, promoting interpersonal as well as academic skills, and increasing student motivation.

As part of staff development at Baylor School, an independent high school in Chattanooga, Tennessee, Jim Buckheit, headmaster, focuses on how collegial relationships can enhance the learning environment for staff members as well as for students. This asset-building work clearly supports *Turning Points 2000*'s fourth recommendation:

> Organize relationships for learning to create a climate of intellectual development and a caring community of shared educational purpose.

Buckheit works with his staff to translate the asset framework into language that reflects asset building for adults in the school. Creating a school environment that youth report as caring begins with creating an environment for adults in the school that models the goal. Through all-staff discussions, Baylor faculty members developed a list of what they needed to ensure support for growth of their own assets (see Handout 2.7: Professional Health Assets for Faculty on page 45). Their list exemplifies one way to create a climate conducive to learning by building relationships.

Part of organizing relationships also involves structuring buildings to make relationships more likely to develop and endure, no matter what the size of your school. Smaller-sized schools generally can more readily create an asset-building environment. Larger-sized schools often face more challenges to do so. But that doesn't mean that you can't build assets if you're part of a larger school. Larger schools can still organize in ways that enable individuals to connect meaningfully to smaller units within the school and set the stage for asset-building opportunities. Connecting young people across three or four years of their schooling to the same adults in an advisory group or team also provides better opportunities for building other adult relationships that carry over time.

Developing long-term relationships is about making decisions together, another asset-rich practice recommended in *Turning Points 2000*:

> Govern democratically through direct or representative participation by all
> school staff members, the adults who know the students best.

The *Turning Points 2000* authors emphasize that although decisions should focus "relentlessly on attaining the goal of success for every student . . . based on data drawn from various sources," those who know students best should be actively involved in the decision making. Governing a school democratically also models for students valuing individual opinions, resolving conflicts constructively, and using colleagues as resources.

The sixth recommendation from *Turning Points 2000* is nothing new to asset builders:

> Provide a safe and healthy school environment as part of improving academic
> performance and developing caring and ethical citizens.

"Healthy lifestyles and academic success are tightly interwoven—improvement in one leads to improvement in the other, both directly and indirectly," explain the authors. Much of what has been written to date about making schools more youth friendly deals with creating positive and supportive school climates or environments—from ensuring physical safety to using instructional strategies that promote classroom environments in which asking questions and making comments is a risk-free activity and increases exchanging ideas and the learning.

Turning Points 2000 concludes by advocating an exchange of ideas and learning beyond school:

Professional Health Assets for Faculty

Please read the lists and descriptions and respond by placing a mark in the middle (numbered) column as follows: "+" for an asset you have; "0" for an asset you don't have; "?" if you are unsure or don't understand the description.

EXTERNAL ASSETS		
Support	1.	**Colleague support** (You experience a high level of mutual respect, positive regard, and personal support from colleagues in similar roles.)
	2.	**Positive communication** (It is easy to engage colleagues and supervisors in open, honest exchanges.)
	3.	**Positive relationships outside department** (You feel known by and communicate easily with others not directly affiliated with you, e.g., with nonacademic administrators.)
	4.	**Sense of caring from parents, alumni, and trustees** (You feel a sense of positive regard and a desire to be helpful coming from members of key constituent groups.)
	5.	**Caring school climate** (You sense that you are personally valued by the school and that steps are taken to protect and promote your interests and well-being.)
	6.	**Supervisors knowledgeably involved with your teaching** (You see evidence that your supervisors understand your job and have some direct knowledge of your performance.)
Empowerment	7.	**School community values teachers** (You see evidence that parents, alumni, and trustees hold the profession in high regard and pay attention to you and your colleagues.)
	8.	**Administration listens to teachers** (The school's leaders consult with you and your colleagues and utilize you as resources in problem solving and decision making.)
	9.	**Colleagues call on each other as resources** (You and your colleagues consult with each other and utilize each other as resources in problem solving and decision making.)
	10.	**Safety** (You feel you can voice concerns and reveal difficulties without embarrassment, reprisals, or putting your position in jeopardy.)
Boundaries and Expectations	11.	**School expectations** (The school's expectations for you, its rules and sanctions relevant to you, and its criteria for decisions affecting you are clear and reasonable.)
	12.	**Department/Division expectations** (The guidelines for conduct and shared commitments among you and your colleagues in your department are clear and reasonable.)
	13.	**Community expectations** (The prevailing community norms and expectations placed on the school support your work and what you consider good educational practice.)
	14.	**Administrator conduct** (Supervisors and other administrators model in their own conduct what they expect of you and your colleagues.)
	15.	**Peer conduct** (Your colleagues model professional conduct and appropriate expectations toward you and toward one another.)
	16.	**High expectations** (You feel the expectations of you are appropriately high, and you sense tangible support for high achievement in your work.)
Impact on Broader Life	17.	**Culture** (Your professional involvement with the school enhances your quality of life by supporting or broadening your cultural opportunities.)
	18.	**Leisure** (Your professional involvement with the school enhances your quality of life by supporting or broadening your recreational opportunities.)
	19.	**Faith** (Your spiritual convictions are respected by the school, and your religious commitments are honored.)
	20.	**Home** (Your family commitments and the boundaries of your private life are respected and honored by the school.)

INTERNAL ASSETS		
Commitments	21.	**Professional goals** (You have explicit professional goals and a plan for your own continuing professional development.)
	22.	**Engagement** (You feel meaningfully engaged in your teaching and in the development of your curriculum.)
	23.	**Management** (You effectively manage your priorities, fulfilling your core duties and attending to the ancillary tasks associated with teaching.)
	24.	**Bonding** (Your own beliefs and values are aligned with those of the school, and you feel a philosophical commitment to the school and its mission.)
	25.	**Personal development** (You see yourself as a learner and regularly engage in developing yourself beyond your area of specialization.)
Values	26.	**Caring** (You see yourself as a contributor to a caring workplace; you are cognizant of and reach out to colleagues in need.)
	27.	**Social justice** (You are interested in the political and social implications of the school's mission and the role it plays in the broader community.)
	28.	**Integrity** (You voice your own beliefs and values, when appropriate, whether they are dissonant or consonant with those of your colleagues or the school.)
	29.	**Honesty** (You are truthful in your professional relationships and provide candid feedback to colleagues and administrators.)
	30.	**Responsibility** (You accept a fair share of responsibility for the broad work at the school and for the problems the school experiences.)
	31.	**Health** (You practice habits of self-care and self-management, e.g., diet, rest, exercise, moderation.)
Competencies	32.	**Planning and time management** (You are able to budget your time, set priorities, plan ahead, and adhere to a plan.)
	33.	**Interpersonal skills** (You demonstrate interest in others and practice effective communication: thoughtful expression, empathic listening, respectful negotiating.)
	34.	**Cultural skills** (You demonstrate openness to diverse viewpoints and experiences; you are able to practice "code switching" to facilitate communication across cultural boundaries.)
	35.	**Personal boundaries** (You are able to empathize with a situation or problem another person is experiencing without taking it on as a personal burden.)
	36.	**Conflict resolution** (You demonstrate respect, careful listening, and a blame-free, problem-solving approach to disagreements and conflicts.)
Professional Identity	37.	**Power** (You have a sense of adequate control over what happens to you at school and the ability to influence decisions that are important to you.)
	38.	**Self-esteem** (You feel positive about being a teacher and about being a member of this school community.)
	39.	**Sense of purpose** (You have a sense of personal mission and a career plan or life plan for fulfilling that mission.)
	40.	**Positive view of future** (You are optimistic about where the school and the profession are headed.)

Comments (e.g., anything missing? anything unclear? reactions to the exercise?):

_____

_____

_____

_____

Involve parents and communities in supporting student learning and healthy development.

"Schools and families must collaborate to establish continuity (for example, similar high expectations) and communication between home and school; to monitor and support students' schoolwork and academic progress; to create opportunities outside the school for safe, engaging exploration; and to improve the school itself through parent and community involvement on site," write the Carnegie researchers. Similarly, in asset-attentive communities, schools, families, and neighborhoods also work to support consistent boundaries, promote positive adult role models, and communicate to youth the value they bring to the community.

Teaching the Diverse Faces of Change

One of the numerous challenges facing educators—changing demographics—places a huge expectation at your classroom door: providing effective learning situations for *all* children in an increasingly diverse society. A particularly urgent issue many of you currently face, for example, is supporting students struggling to master English as a second language in addition to classroom content.

One of our objectives in this book is to illustrate the fact that good instruction is both asset supportive and meets the needs of diverse students. Historically, many educators have viewed diversity as racial and ethnic, and perhaps addressed it less than adequately by simply presenting discrete units about many races or cultures. We know one of the key issues in classrooms today is addressing a wider array of students of diverse races, cultures, religions, socioeconomic situations, gender, sexual orientation, innate abilities, language proficiencies, and learning styles. The nature of good instruction itself affords us the opportunity to do that.

In addition, valuing diversity is another of the thriving behaviors Search Institute identifies (see "Thriving Behaviors of Students" on page 32). On the institute's *Attitudes and Behaviors* survey, valuing diversity refers to "placing a high importance on getting to know people of other racial/ethnic groups."[11] The original aggregate sample of data from 100,000 youth during the 1996–1997 school year, as well as a newer aggregate sample from 1999–2000 that represents a more diverse sample of 217,000 young people, both indicate that the power of the assets is evident across all cultural and socioeconomic groups.

Survey results also indicate, however, that the reported presence of the cultural competence asset goes down across middle and high school, with males in particular noting the asset less. As 6th graders, 48 percent of youth surveyed indicated having the asset, but by 9th grade, the percentage falls to 39 and then holds steady through graduation.

In the developmental assets framework, cultural competence is defined as having knowledge of and comfort with—valuing and appreciating—people of different cultural, racial, or ethnic backgrounds. The survey questions regarding cultural competence do not address how youth relate to others of a different ethnicity or race than their own. Nor do they inquire about how youth view (e.g., accept, are proud of) their own cultural heritage. While the institute recognizes that its survey's inclusiveness merits improvement, well-founded efforts to develop the cultural competence asset will undoubtedly pay off in enhancing the broader definitions of such competence.[12]

As teachers and administrators, you can be influential in shoring up this thriving indicator of valuing diversity and in addressing the cultural competence asset by incorporating instructional strategies and content that build interpersonal and cross-cultural skills. Many school districts make available curricula and strategies for building multicultural skills or for reducing prejudice that are very consistent with asset building.

In addition, the work you and your schools do to improve your students' interpersonal skills in general is related to building cultural competence. Strategies such as the following all contribute: facilitating interracial friendship ties, bringing diverse youth together in task-related settings (e.g., learning groups of various kinds), fostering skills in empathizing, and building social skills in a variety of school contexts and programs.[13] By incorporating such attention to building interpersonal skills, increasing cultural competence, and valuing diversity, you will contribute to the developmental success of your students as well as improve the chances for success for all young people from diverse backgrounds.

Our contributors illustrate a number of ways they attend to the needs of diverse student populations. Appendix B.2: Asset-Rich Strategies for Supporting Student Diversity charts where our authors use strategies that emphasize diversity issues while building assets and using good instructional approaches (see page 272). Referencing their examples allows you to investigate building assets and support your own students' diversity as well.

Jumping In to "Go Deeper"

Embracing the asset mind-set begins with the basics: building relationships and creating supportive environments. Relating well to students in the classroom is a key to hooking them into learning, motivating them to achieve, and encouraging growth of the whole child or adolescent. And one of the effective schools correlates tells us that without a school environment that is both physically and emotionally safe, young people do not learn as well: "In the effective school, there is an orderly, purposeful, businesslike atmosphere which is free from the threat of physical harm. The school climate is not oppressive and is conducive to teaching and learning."[14] Only when those two prerequisites are in place can teachers really move forward to effectively foster learning.

But "going deeper" means using that asset mind-set in the course of everyday teaching. It means incorporating building assets into both the content and the process of instruction so that the norms for teaching in your school reflect positive support for student learning, growth, and development. Our contributors take you deeper in the chapters that follow.

Notes

1. Benson, Peter L., Scales, Peter C., Leffert, Nancy, and Roehlkepartain, Eugene C. (1999). *A Fragile Foundation: The State of Developmental Assets among American Youth*. Minneapolis: Search Institute. Also, Scales, Peter C., and Leffert, Nancy. (1999). *Developmental Assets: A Synthesis of the Scientific Research on Adolescent Development*. Minneapolis: Search Institute.

2. Starkman, Neal, Scales, Peter C., and Roberts, Clay. (1999). *Great Places to Learn: How Asset-Building Schools Help Students Succeed*. Minneapolis: Search Institute. *Great Places to Learn* includes scores of brief stories that illustrate how various school personnel have created asset-rich ways to connect with young people and help their communities connect with them within the school community. For more on these stories, see Starkman, Neal. (2001). *Ideas That Cook: Activities for Asset Builders in School Communities*. Minneapolis: Search Institute. This resource provides the recipe for success in producing each idea, in addition to presenting many new activities for building assets in diverse environments.

3. National Commission on Excellence in Education. (1983). *A Nation at Risk: The Imperative for Educational Reform*. Washington, DC: Government Printing Office.

4. Association for Effective Schools, Inc., *Correlates of Effective Schools*. Web site accessed September 25, 2002: www.mes.org/correlates.html. This 501(c)(3) nonprofit is located in Styvesant, NY. Downloaded on September 25, 2002.

5. Fullan, Michael. (March 21, 1994). Presentation to the Association for Supervision and Curriculum Development's national conference, Chicago, IL. See also Fullan, Michael. (2001). *Leading in a Culture of Change*. San Francisco: Jossey-Bass.

6. Carnegie Council on Adolescent Development. Task Force on Education of Young Adolescents. Carnegie Corporation of New York. (1989). *Turning Points: Preparing American Youth for the 21st Century: The Report of the Task Force on Education of Young Adolescents*. Washington, DC: Author.

7. Jackson, Anthony W., and Davis, Gayle A. (2000). *Turning Points 2000: Educating Adolescents in the 21st Century*. A report of the Carnegie Corporation of New York. New York: Teachers College Press, 23–26.

8. Campbell, Linda, and Campbell, Bruce. (1999). *Multiple Intelligences and Student Achievement: Success Stories from Six Schools*. Alexandria, VA: Association for Supervision and Curriculum Development, 5.

9. Gardner, Howard. (1985). *Frames of Mind: The Theory of Multiple Intelligences*. New York: BasicBooks.

10. Gardner, Howard. (1999). *Intelligence Reframed*. New York: BasicBooks.

11. Benson et al., *A Fragile Foundation*, 86–87, 91.

12. Scales and Leffert, *Developmental Assets*, 187–188, 190. Additional information on the cultural competence asset may be found in this same resource on 174–176, 181–183, and 187–190.

13. Ibid.

14. Association for Effective Schools, Inc., *Correlates of Effective Schools*. (See note 4.)

Chapter 3

Infusing Assets through Instructional Strategies

■ *Our contributors confirm that building assets for and with students in a classroom has as much to do with instructional practice as it does with content (Principle 4). In fact, their ideas demonstrate how intentionally infusing asset-building strategies into your instructional approaches not only supports assets but also makes more meaningful and relevant many of the staff development tasks and instructional improvement imperatives that you face as a teacher or administrator.*

To help you tap into the instructional suggestions cited throughout this book, Appendix B.3: Connecting Asset Building to Instructional Strategies (on page 276) charts the major strategies our authors use, the assets they support, and where in the book to find examples illustrating how they use a particular strategy in an asset-rich way. Because instructional strategies that support asset building are threaded throughout the content chapter examples, this chart helps you find those discussed in content areas other than your own that may be adaptable to your unique context.

In this chapter, our first contributor, Stan Paine, provides an overview of many of the current, asset-consistent instructional approaches that you see on Appendix B.3. We then focus more deeply on two (differentiation and cooperative learning) to give you a feel for how to use the infusion process described in Chapter 1 to analyze a strategy and enhance its asset-building qualities.

Doing Away with Disengagement

ASSET-RICH STRATEGIES FOR K–12 INSTRUCTION

STAN PAINE, PH.D.

Principal (grades K–5)

Centennial Elementary School

Springfield, Oregon

Why do students in one class appear ready to fall asleep, while those in another nearby can barely contain themselves until they are called upon to participate? Why do some students chronically pay little attention to the instructor, or even cut class, while others are deeply engrossed in class activities and don't want to miss a single moment? What makes one student grow more disengaged from school over time while another becomes more interested? The answer likely lies, in part, in the instructional strategies a teacher chooses to deliver the curriculum to the students and with the level of engagement—the active participation and thinking—that the instructor creates through the questions and activities he or she asks and provides.

The content that different teachers teach has long been similar—governed traditionally by textbooks and increasingly by state standards. But the manner in which teachers deliver content to students varies widely from one teacher to the next. I suggest that this is true at all levels of education. These variations in instructional delivery can make a significant difference, not just in academic achievement, but also in other learning outcomes such as attitudes about school and commitment to learning as well as a number of the developmental assets.

In the following pages, I identify a number of instructional strategies both elementary and secondary teachers use that have strong potential for helping to build student assets. Some of the strategies also have applications in the newer teaching and learning paradigms in higher education. First, I focus on strategies for initial subject matter instruction. Then I describe asset-related approaches for helping students process and integrate learning; methods for practice, remediation, enrich-

SCHOOL DEMOGRAPHICS
Centennial Elementary School
Springfield, Oregon

Students: 467

Grades: K–5

Gender:
Male	51.10%
Female	48.90%

Race and Ethnicity:
Black/African American	2.00%
Hispanic/Latino	13.80%
Asian/Pacific Islander	1.40%
American Indian	1.80%
White/Caucasian	81.00%

Socioeconomics:
Free/Reduced Lunch	90.00%

ment, and motivation; and ideas for structuring programs or courses, assigning students and staff, and extending school services. I define each strategy, provide examples of its use, and relate briefly how the strategy can help build developmental assets in students of any age.

Strategies for Initial Instruction

For generations, educators have explained variations in student achievement in terms of differences in students' abilities. Teachers taught what needed to be taught, and some students did well while others did poorly. That's just the way it was.

The arrival of the standards-based movement in education has greatly accelerated a shift toward trying to help *all* students do better—to help more students reach the standards. The instructional paradigm for education has shifted from providing the same input to all students and allowing the outcomes to vary, to that of adjusting the input for some in an effort to help more students reach a standard.

Differentiated Instruction

This newer effort, commonly known as *differentiating instruction*[1] (providing more instruction—or a different type of instruction—to various students), holds great promise for accelerating student achievement and enhancing assets in those who traditionally have difficulty in school, as well as for meeting the needs of all students within a particular classroom.

How might you differentiate instruction in early reading, for example, for learners who have different backgrounds? One way is to provide a variety of programmatic approaches to meet differing needs. Our elementary school, like many sites, offers an array of programs to boost the skills of children at risk for reading failure:

1. An extended-day program for (half-day) kindergarten students whose early literacy skills lag behind those of their classmates;
2. A "double dose" of reading instruction daily for lower-performing primary grade students;
3. An alternative developmental reading program conducted at a more measured pace with greater structure and more controlled vocabulary;
4. Several special programs for fluency building and comprehension development;
5. The Junior Great Books program for literary enrichment;
6. Supplemental literacy instruction for English language learners;
7. Incentives to read outside of school; and
8. Extensive training and coaching for teachers and assistants to allow them to monitor and adjust children's reading programs as needed.

The differentiated support provided by these programs has allowed 93 percent of our school's 3rd-grade students, 90 percent of whom live below the federal poverty line, to reach the state reading benchmark by the end of 3rd grade.[2] Other examples of differentiating support include using homework clubs or study groups to assist students with their assignments, providing tutoring (through peer or adult volunteers) for difficult material, and using highlighting, outlining, or technology to make key material more salient to struggling learners.

How can differentiating programs build student assets? They can help students perceive teachers who take the time to help them as more caring. They can communicate higher expectations to students and help them see those standards as more attainable. The success students feel can even increase their commitment to learning and enhance their perceptions of themselves as successful learners. We know that our 3rd graders, many of whom struggled in learning to read, now see themselves as successful readers and capable learners. (See "Building Assets through Differentiation" on page 64 for more about the asset-consistent elements of differentiating classroom curriculum and instruction.)

Interdisciplinary Curriculum / Integrated Thematic Instruction

Interdisciplinary curriculum (sometimes called *integrated thematic instruction* at the elementary school level) involves using a concept, issue, problem, or topic (e.g., "interdependence" or "cycles of change") as a focus of study involving multiple subjects over a period of time.[3] The theme or topic serves as a common element, and various subject areas or subtopics are woven together with this common thread. Strategies such as project learning (learning through work over time on a defined project) and service learning (learning through activities that provide a useful service to others) are types of integrated thematic instruction.

Integrated instruction is highly engaging when you select the concepts or topics that you teach for their interest to your students or their relevance to your students' experiences. Using youth as resources in instructional planning is certainly asset consistent. If you choose well the broad topic and fold in student perspectives, integration also allows students to see connections among elements that might not otherwise be apparent and gain a wider understanding of both the broad areas and the focus topic. In addition, if you're juggling a crowded curriculum, you may find it more efficient to address two or more curriculum areas simultaneously through a common focus.

A cross-grade tradition at our school provides a good example of interdisciplinary project learning that provides both sound instruction as well as opportunities for growth in assets. Each year, our 2nd and 5th graders do a joint, hands-on study of the life cycle of the salmon (a topic of much interest in the Northwest). Objectives in reading, writing, math, science, and technology are all part of this study, which spans several weeks. At the end of the project, students release the newly hatched salmon into a nearby stream.

Younger children feel special when they teach their older peers the content they have learned. Fifth graders value the responsibility to show their younger buddies how to use technology to communicate the information they have learned. Both groups are empowered in the exchange.

A project in an area middle school illustrates another interdisciplinary service-learning project. Students interview local senior citizens about their life stories, write the stories, publish them in a book, and then give copies to the senior citizens and their families as well as the local library. This project involves much planning, organizing, word processing, and debriefing. Language arts, history, and technology skills are all part of the work, which leaves both students and senior citizens feeling good about the process and the service they provided—and about each other.

In addition to providing rich learning opportunities, both types of integrated thematic learning I've mentioned—project learning and service learning—have a powerful potential to increase the support and recognition youth receive for their participation in the project. Indeed, many such efforts—the culminating activities of project learning or the support of service-learning activities—would not take place in a community if an instructor and group of students didn't take them on. Such activities provide useful service to the community (e.g., releasing the salmon, validating the lives of senior citizens by telling their stories), enable other community members to see youth as positive resources, and help youth see themselves as valued members of the community who have something significant to offer. These activities also tend to engage students more highly in their learning activities than do many traditional learning methods, help youth develop a greater sense of caring about issues or caring for others, and help them learn the skills of working together to accomplish a goal.

All of these benefits contribute to a heightened sense of positive identity for youth. Imagine the difference in engagement, interest, and outcomes for students who are expected to learn primarily through traditional lecture and in-class discussion versus those who participate in active discovery and service projects that reach into their communities. The difference illustrates the tremendous opportunity you and other teachers have for developing assets through the thoughtful selection of instructional strategies.

Cooperative Learning

Cooperative learning addresses curriculum content by incorporating "positive interdependence between students, face-to-face interaction, [and] individual accountability for all students and interpersonal skills" into instructional activities.[4] You can apply cooperative learning to many instructional goals, such as discussing literature, digesting health issues, exploring science or social studies content, or pondering together the deeper meaning of any subject matter. It addresses a wide range of assets: it sets expectations for all students to participate in learning activities, provides incentives for positive peer collaboration in learning, promotes student responsibility for doing one's share of the work, and helps build social competencies. Students are more likely to be motivated to participate and to do well in learning activities when working closely with peers.

A recent project in our school provides an example of cooperative learning in action. Students studied cultural similarities and differences among themselves, their families, and their ancestors, following the theme "We are more alike than different." The teacher assigned students to teams, ensuring a variety of cultural backgrounds, and gave each team member a role (e.g., facilitator, timekeeper, recorder). Teams met to discuss their project and brainstorm ideas. As a homework assignment, each member interviewed a parent or grandparent using a series of prescribed questions. When interviews were complete, teams met again to organize their ideas, design presentations for the class, and create a poster board for Family Heritage Night.

At the project's conclusion, the teacher led students in debriefing the process and identifying lessons learned. The teacher evaluated the students as a team and individually, using a scoring guide based on participation in all activities and specific contributions to the final product. Participation was enthusiastic, the projects were inspiring, and students were able to see and begin to apply the idea that they were, indeed, more alike than different. (For more details on the connections between cooperative learning and developmental assets, see "Sinking or Swimming Together: Assets and Cooperative Learning" on page 68.)

Higher-Level Questioning/Thinking Strategies

In considering how to keep students engaged in the classroom, Benjamin Bloom's[5] classification of cognitive educational objectives, developed in the mid-1950s, is still worth using. These objectives range from recognition and recall to synthesis and evaluation—from activities requiring little thought to those involving a great deal of complex thinking to complete. While objectives at the lower end of the taxonomy have their place, you should challenge students to operate at the middle and upper ranges of thinking so that they stretch and grow as learners. Use questioning strategies that prompt that stretching.

The Great Books and Junior Great Books programs[6] provide excellent examples of programmatic approaches that encourage higher-level thinking in reading comprehension. At our school, students read selections (often classic literature for youth) chosen for their multiple interpretations and then engage in a teacher-facilitated discussion of *shared inquiry*. We have seen students who had little to say in traditional discussions become engaged, enthusiastic participants in lively, shared inquiry discussions, passionately expressing a point of view.

Similar to shared inquiry is the classical pedagogy of the *Socratic dialogue*. (See "Liberty and Justice for All? Examining Perceptions, Assumptions, and Involvement in Civic Life" in Chapter 5 on page 145 for an example of such a lesson.) Christopher Phillips has given Socratic dialogue new life in his book for adults, *Socrates Café*, as well as in his children's book, *The Philosophers' Club*.[7] Phillips argues for the importance of giving young people who often ask "Why?" interesting, important, and even serious questions to ponder—questions without "right answers" but that engender plenty of opportunity for thinking and sharing ideas; questions that empower young people and provoke them to think and express their voice.

Instruction that engages students at these higher levels of Bloom's taxonomy infuses asset building by setting high expectations and creating positive peer examples. Such instruction certainly motivates students intrinsically and engages them thoroughly in learning. And it helps students increase their self-esteem and confidence—assets that will serve them well in further learning and in life.

Inductive Approaches

What is it about the inductive approach—about starting with specific details and moving to the general case—that is so engaging, so intriguing that it often leaves students with a seemingly insatiable appetite for more discussion, or at least a continuing desire to discuss the issue after class ends? In addition to the Socratic method, I'm thinking of approaches such as *guided discovery* and asking *leading questions*.

If you have taken a law class (e.g., an introduction to law and education) and have deliberated legal cases, you perhaps experienced the sense that "this class is different" or "class time flies by." I believe this reaction is due to the fact that inductive approaches are highly engaging (high on Bloom's taxonomy) and do not make the "correct answer" immediately apparent. Rather, learners discover plausible answers through thoughtful analysis and dialogue with others. As with other higher-level thinking approaches, inductive methods have tremendous power to engage and motivate students as well as to enhance their perceptions of themselves as thinking, capable learners—indeed, as "smart kids."

Skills Instruction

You can often teach skills, whether basic skills (reading, math algorithms), advanced skills (computer use, second language learning), or social skills (carrying on a conversation, problem solving) through a format involving instruction, demonstration, practice, and feedback. Skills instruction is usually quite effective in establishing the targeted skills in both core academics as well as interpersonal skills when you match them to your students' prior skill level, monitor their progress, and infuse corrective processes.

Our school's focus on learning math facts and the "Math Stars Hall of Fame" (for students who have mastered those basic math facts) provides practice, feedback, and motivation for learning math. Our use of the Second Step Program[8] (a research-based curriculum that teaches and reinforces interpersonal skills using photographs and discussions of realistic school situations) provides instruction, demonstration, practice, and feedback in showing empathy, managing anger, and solving problems peacefully. These and other examples of skill-building approaches help develop students' assets by incorporating high expectations, enhancing engagement and motivation for learning, creating a range of social competencies, and fostering confidence and self-esteem.

Strategies for Processing and Integrating Learning

Once you have introduced new material, you will need to develop learning further to help students develop a more complete understanding of the content. Good instruction helps each student process new information and integrate it into what he or she already knows. Several approaches work well for this purpose, while also strengthening developmental assets.

You might want to preview content by preteaching vocabulary or introducing an *advance organizer*. This helps students organize information for use in later discussions or projects. Or, you might review content to connect or transfer the learning through a gamelike quiz bowl. You can also summarize learning using a K-W-L *closure*[9] technique (What do I **k**now? What do I **w**ant to know? What do I need to **l**earn?) or through written reflections in learning logs, both of which can help students distill new knowledge into its essential elements and make clear connections to previous knowledge or a future focus. You might also engage students in *metacognition* (thinking about their thinking) on the topic, or facilitate their articulating what they now know about what they've studied and reflecting on where, when, and how they might apply that knowledge.

All of these approaches validate your learners by taking into account where each is in the learning process and building on that—an instructionally sound process of listening to students and structuring learning to push them beyond where they are. That's bound to increase their motivation and engagement because you've been sensitive to their learning needs and expected them to progress. Using these approaches also contributes to building your students' assets by strengthening their understanding—and their confidence in themselves as capable learners—by communicating high expectations, empowering their success, and enhancing their commitment to learning.

Strategies for Practice, Remediation, Enrichment and Motivation

Once you have introduced and reviewed or otherwise processed curriculum material, look for ways to:

1. Provide practice, remediation, and/or enrichment related to the knowledge or skills taught; and
2. Motivate students to work with the material to meet standards and to reach the next level of understanding.

Here, too, a thoughtfully selected instructional strategy or program can help build assets simultaneously.

Peer-to-Peer Strategies

At our school, peer tutoring and peer coaching strategies[10, 11] work well for these purposes. We use both same-age and cross-age peer procedures, as well as mentoring and buddy programs, to provide extra practice, help, or opportunities and to motivate students to stay involved with the material. Like many other schools, we use peer coaching to practice math facts and spelling words and to build oral reading fluency and comprehension. Middle school, high school, and college students, as well as parent and senior citizen volunteers, tutor children who need extra help to learn the material. We also involve 5th graders as resource buddies for primary students to build motivation for reading and writing. The 5th graders help their partners and enhance their own learning when they become the leader or teacher. Peer learning builds assets both for the helper and the younger student.

Remediation and Enrichment Approaches

In working with children at risk for reading failure, we have developed several programmatic academic interventions to help them succeed. An extended-day kindergarten program, *double dosing* (reteaching lessons in various settings) with primary reading students, and afternoon or after-school literacy lab and fluency-building activities can provide the extra help that at-risk readers need.

For students needing enrichment, the Junior Great Books groups and after-school book clubs help extend their literacy interests. To further enrich instruction and engage students, using community resources, role playing, and dramatic reenacting of literary or other stories work well. Collaborations, competitions, and gamelike formats (e.g., keeping score; competing against another team, time, or a criterion; and celebrating outcomes) can help engage even reluctant learners and make practice or extension activities more fun for all. Such strategies can raise expectations for learning, make standards seem more attainable, enhance student success, and cement commitment to further learning.

Staffing, Structure, and Extended Services

In your own classrooms, you as teachers and instructional supervisors have access to many strategies that you can implement for enhancing asset development and promoting student learning. They are part of your everyday world.

Other asset-building strategies, though, involve cross-classroom collaboration to work effectively. Three such approaches that also support asset building very well are looping, school-within-a-school structures, and extended school schedules and services. (See "Taking the First Step: Linking Supports for High School Success" on page 235 about a high school transition program that illustrates well a cross-classroom strategy.)

Looping

We use looping (sometimes called *multiyear assignments*) extensively to create stronger learning communities. When we use this strategy for staffing and assigning students to classes at the elementary level, a teacher moves from one grade level to the next so that students spend two years with the same teacher. The teacher then typically moves back to the original grade level to begin a new two-year cycle with a new group of students the following year.[12] At the secondary level, we may intentionally schedule students to have the same teacher for the next level in a particular subject area (e.g., English, math) the next year.

Teachers, students, and parents at our elementary school unanimously express their pleasure with looping. Teachers like getting to know students and parents better. Students and parents like feeling comfortable and knowing the teacher's expectations and instructional style (and having the teacher know them) from the beginning of the second year.

Looping also makes a difference academically. Oregon, which has benchmark outcomes, requires state assessments in elementary schools at grades 3 and 5. Teachers who loop with their students into an assessment year (i.e., from 2nd to 3rd grade or from 4th to 5th grade) report that students perform better on those assessments.

In our experience, looping definitely helps build young people's relationships with other caring adults and gives them a head start academically and emotionally in year two of the loop. It also fosters positive communication between school and home, increases parent support for their child's school effort, clarifies classroom and school behavior boundaries, helps develop a positive peer culture, and builds greater school engagement—all asset enriching.

School-within-a-School Structures

In recent years, a number of schools have adopted a school-within-a-school organizational structure.[13] In this model, a larger organization is divided into two or more smaller units. For example, a 750-student middle school in our district became three parallel systems of 250 students each. Similarly, a 450-student elementary school was organized as three wings of 150 students each.

Although the building in each case serves the same number of children, students, parents, and staff, all perceive a much smaller, more nurturing learning environment. Students experience more contact with fewer teachers and peers, rather than less contact with more staff and other students. Often, the school climate seems safer and more caring, attributes that foster students' bonding with school and engaging in learning more.

Extended School Schedules and Services

Unless we challenge some of the basic assumptions upon which traditional educational systems are based, our efforts to do better will be like trying to improve an obsolete product—like trying to build a new and improved covered wagon to transport goods. What are some of those assumptions? That students:

1. Need three months away from school in the summer to help out on the family farm;
2. Go home after school to a mother who is waiting to give them warm cookies and help with their homework; and
3. Get all the learning they need during school hours and are not interested in extending their school day, week, or year.

In reality, these assumptions apply to very few students anymore. We must confront them head-on to address what in fact is true for many children: unmet needs for learning and nurturing.

Our school and others in our district collaborate with several organizations to provide safe places and structured opportunities for students to learn (e.g., homework club, reading-improvement programs, and interest groups) during times when they might otherwise not be in school. Funding for these opportunities comes from the school district, park district, parents, federal programs (Title 1 and 21st Century Schools programs), and local businesses (most notably the Burger King Academy program).[14] For example, working with the park district, we extend supervision and nurturing through school-based child care from 7:00 to 8:00 A.M. and from 3:00 to 6:00 P.M. each school day. With 21st Century Schools grant monies and bilingual program funds, we offer Saturday classes in English and Spanish for both children and adults. With funding from Title 1 and a local bank, we provide a summer school program and access to our school library to encourage students to read for pleasure in the summer. Such services extend our entire community's asset-building efforts by increasing opportunities for building positive relationships with other caring adults, positive adult role modeling, a sense of caring in our community, increased safety for youth during nonschool hours, and additional creative and athletic program opportunities.

The instructional strategies and collaborations that you select or establish can make a big difference in the development of each of your students' knowledge and skills and in cultivating their strengths. As educators and asset builders, let us recommit ourselves to those instructional approaches that bring out the best in our students, both as learners and as people.

We can do no better, and they deserve no less.

Notes

1. Tomlinson, Carol Ann (1999). *The Differentiated Classroom: Responding to the Needs of All Learners.* Alexandria, VA: Association for Supervision and Curriculum Development.
2. Oregon Department of Education. (2002). *Statewide Assessment Results 2002: Percent of Students Meeting Performance Standards, Reading and Literature and Mathematics.* Salem: Oregon Department of Education. Web site accessed November 14, 2002: www.ode.state.or.us/asmt/results/index.htm.
3. Jacobs, Heidi Hayes (ed.). (1989). *Interdisciplinary Curriculum: Design and Implementation.* Alexandria, VA, Association for Supervision and Curriculum Development.
4. Johnson, David W., Johnson, Roger T., Holubec, Edyth J., and Roy, Patricia. (1984). *Circles of Learning: Cooperation in the Classroom.* Alexandria, VA: Association for Supervision and Curriculum Development.
5. Bloom, Benjamin S. (1956). *Taxonomy of Educational Objectives. Handbook I: Cognitive Domain.* New York: David McKay.
6. Great Books Foundation. (1992). *An Introduction to Shared Inquiry.* Chicago: Author.
7. Phillips, Christopher. (2001). *Socrates Café: A Fresh Taste of Philosophy.* New York: W. W. Norton. Phillips, Christopher. (2001). *The Philosophers' Club.* Berkeley, CA: Tricycle Press.
8. Committee for Children. (1997). *Second Step: A Violence Prevention Curriculum.* Seattle: Author.
9. This technique uses Ogle's K-W-L model in the context of Madeline Hunter's closure strategy. Ogle, Donna. (1986). K-W-L: A Teaching Model That Develops Active Reading of Expository Text. *Reading Teacher,* 39:564–570. For more about closure, see also: Hunter, Madeline. (1982). *Mastery Teaching: Increasing Instructional Effectiveness in Secondary Schools, Colleges and Universities.* El Segundo, CA: TIP Publications.
10. Greenwood, Charles R., Maheady, Lawrence, and Delquadri, Joseph. (2002). Classwide

Peer Tutoring Programs. In Marc R. Shinn, Hill M. Walker, and Gary Stoner (eds.), *Interventions for Academic and Behavior Problems. II: Prevention and Remediation*. Bethesda, MD: National Association of School Psychologists, 611–650.

11. Fuchs, Douglas, Fuchs, Lynn S., Mathes, Patricia G., and Simmons, Deborah C. (1997). Peer-Assisted Learning Strategies: Making Classrooms More Responsive to Diversity. *American Educational Research Journal*, 34(1):174–206.

12. Grant, Jim, Johnson, Bob, and Richardson, Irv. (1996). *The Looping Handbook: Teachers and Students Progressing Together*. Peterborough, NH: Crystal Springs Books.

13. Goodlad, John I. (1984). *A Place Called School: Prospects for the Future*. New York: McGraw-Hill.

14. Title 1 is a program funded under the Elementary and Secondary Education Act (Title I) of the U.S. Department of Education, administered by the Office of Elementary and Secondary Education (OESE); Web site accessed November 14, 2002: www.ed.gov/offices/OESE. The 21st Century Community Learning Center Program is a funding stream of the U.S. Department of Education; Web site: www.ed.gov/21stcclc/. For information on the Burger King Academy program, see the Web site accessed November 14, 2002: www.burgerking.com/Community/Bkacademics/.

Building Assets through Differentiation

JUDY TACCOGNA, ED.D.

Education Director

Search Institute

Minneapolis, Minnesota

Differentiation of curriculum and instruction within a classroom is a philosophical approach that holds great promise both for addressing the needs of students in our increasingly diverse schools and for building developmental assets. It may, in fact, be a way of thinking that your district is discussing widely or for which you've noticed K–12 professional organizations are offering resources and training opportunities.

Such differentiation happens when you as the teacher adjust the content, process, and/or products of a lesson or unit to meet a variety of student needs. Often associated with meeting the needs of academically talented youth, differentiation is an approach that is useful much more broadly—that taps into the strengths and interests of *all* levels of student and builds developmental assets in the process.

What It Is and What It Is Not

Like asset building, differentiating curriculum and instruction is not a program or a strategy in and of itself. Rather, it is a way of thinking about teaching that takes a variety of student differences into consideration. It is not embodied in a particular instructional strategy but uses many of them. It is a way of looking at the strengths and needs of children and adolescents with careful planning, playing on their profiles and interests to help them grow in understanding and skills. It represents a refinement of already good teaching—an artful orchestration of a number of instructional strategies in ways that best meet the needs of given learners.

Carol Ann Tomlinson, a leading proponent of differentiation and professor at the Curry School of Education, University of Virginia in Charlottesville, talks about a number of principles of differentiation,[1] four of which are particularly consistent with the asset approach:

- The teacher attends to student differences;
- The teacher modifies content, process, and/or products;
- All students participate in respectful work; and
- The teacher and students collaborate in learning.

Tomlinson further explains that you can differentiate instruction in three ways: by modifying content, process, and/or products. Within those areas, the adjustments you choose to make depend on three key sets of information about each of your students: readiness (level of skills and understandings), interests (curiosity or passion for a particular topic), and learning profile (how a particular student learns).

The fact that you attend to the variety of needs, interests, and learning styles in your classroom to provide targeted instruction for your particular classroom of students supports a number of the assets. You set high expectations for all—you expect all students to make progress from where they are, to understand more than they did when they began the year, as well as to move toward the academic standards. You enhance your students' engagement and motivation because you have aligned required instructional content with their interests, to say nothing of the fact that you use youth as resources for their own learning.

As part of a differentiated classroom routine, you no doubt build in many points at which your students need to take responsibility for their own learning, whether that is individually or within a group. In particular, the degree to which you need to know your students individually to learn about their interests and learning profiles opens you to collaborating more with them. In turn, the fact that students are involved in their learning and in classroom decisions about it underscores that collaborative, guide-on-the-side approach and helps you become a positive adult role model for them. Assets everywhere!

In her book *The Differentiated Classroom: Responding to the Needs of All Learners*, Tomlinson compares in a concise chart a traditional classroom with a differentiated classroom.[2] Handout 3.1: Infusing an Asset Mind-Set into a Differentiated Classroom expands her original overview with ways in which asset building is supported by each of her key descriptors of a differentiated classroom. For example, in a traditional classroom, coverage of texts and curriculum guides drives instruction; in a differentiated classroom, student readiness, interest, and learning profile shape instruction; and in an asset-building classroom, the focus on readiness, interests, and the student learning profile means no student is invisible, making instructional planning and delivery more personally supportive to each student. Handout 3.1 also represents another approach to analyzing an instructional strategy for its asset-rich qualities.

If you are truly attending to your students' needs by differentiating your curriculum and instruction, you are also building assets! The bottom line: it therefore takes no more time to build assets in your classroom than it does to learn and implement good instructional approaches that are consistent with asset building, approaches that your school or district often already requires or encourages. It merely means intentionally overlaying the asset language and mind-set onto instructional approaches that you find support building assets.

Notes

1. Tomlinson, Carol Ann. (1999). *The Differentiated Classroom: Responding to the Needs of All Learners*. Alexandria, VA: Association for Supervision and Curriculum Development, 9–14.
2. Ibid., 16.

Infusing an Asset Mind-Set
into a Differentiated Classroom

Traditional Classroom	Differentiated Classroom	Asset-Building Classroom
▪ Student differences are masked or acted upon when problematic.	▪ Student differences are studied as a basis for planning.	▪ Student strengths are highlighted as a basis of the planning process and as part of creating a supportive classroom environment.
▪ Assessment is most common at the end of learning to see "who got it."	▪ Assessment is ongoing and diagnostic to understand how to make instruction more responsive to learner needs.	▪ Assessment is ongoing and diagnostic to understand how to make instruction more responsive to learners' needs, motivate them more highly, and generate more student engagement and bonding to school.
▪ A relatively narrow sense of intelligence prevails.	▪ Focus on multiple forms of intelligences is evident.	▪ Multiple forms of intelligence are honored to engage students in learning and to motivate and facilitate higher achievement levels; creative activities are encouraged and incorporated into lessons where possible.
▪ A single definition of excellence exists.	▪ Excellence is defined in large measure by individual growth from a starting point.	▪ Individual strengths are honored and plans are created to support growth in weaker areas, to maintain motivation and engagement, and to foster achievement.
▪ Student interest is infrequently tapped.	▪ Students are frequently guided in making interest-based learning choices.	▪ Individual student interests and strengths are honored and using youth as resources is incorporated into instructional planning and decision making about content and learning pathways.
▪ Relatively few learning profile options are taken into account.	▪ Many learning profile options are provided for.	▪ Diverse learning styles are recognized and seen as strengths; the teacher provides multiple pathways to success based on varying learning modalities and multiple intelligences.
▪ Whole-class instruction dominates.	▪ Many instructional arrangements are used.	▪ Multiple instructional strategies are used to acknowledge and support different student interests, readiness levels, and learning styles as well as to increase student engagement and achievement motivation.
▪ Coverage of texts and curriculum guides drives instruction.	▪ Student readiness, interest, and learning profile shape instruction.	▪ The focus on student readiness, interests, and learning profiles means no student is invisible, making instructional planning and delivery more personally supportive to each student.
▪ Mastery of facts and skills out of context are the focus of learning.	▪ Use of essential skills to make sense of and understand key concepts and principles is the focus of learning.	▪ Instruction is contextual, heightening student engagement and motivation, and promoting student applications of communication and decision-making skills. Such instruction usually also happens in classrooms where adults are providing good role models and building relationships with students.

Traditional Classroom	Differentiated Classroom	Asset-Building Classroom
■ Single-option assignments are the norm.	■ Multi-option assignments are frequently used.	■ Options in assignments not only promote a better match between learner needs and instruction, they also increase engagement and level of success for students, contributing to students' sense of personal power, self-esteem, and life purpose.
■ Time is relatively inflexible.	■ Time is used flexibly in accordance with student need.	■ Flexibility in the use of time focuses on student needs, promoting greater chance for success, higher achievement motivation, and deeper student engagement in learning.
■ A single text prevails.	■ Multiple materials are provided.	■ The variety of materials provided reinforces the individuality of students as people as well as learners and often allows students to be used as resources in the classroom.
■ Single interpretations of ideas and events may be sought.	■ Multiple perspectives on ideas and events are routinely sought.	■ Using students as resources (e.g., in soliciting their ideas, involving them in problem solving and cooperative learning) and honoring their differing perspectives is usual; these practices increase student engagement and provide opportunities for improving and using interpersonal, decision-making, and conflict-resolution skills.
■ The teacher directs student behavior.	■ The teacher facilitates students' skills at becoming more self-reliant learners.	■ Teachers capitalize on opportunities regularly to build student responsibility, increase interpersonal and cultural competence through skill building, and foster independence in planning and completing assignments (both as homework and in class).
■ The teacher solves problems.	■ Students help other students and the teacher solve problems.	■ Opportunities for students to serve as learning resources and problem solvers are built into instruction within the classroom and across the school.
■ The teacher provides whole-class standards for grading.	■ Students work with the teacher to establish both whole-class and individual learning goals.	■ Both group and individual goals are emphasized, building achievement motivation, student engagement, bonding to school, and sense of purpose.
■ A single form of assessment is often used.	■ Students are assessed in multiple ways.	■ Students are seen and assessed as individuals in multiple ways that define and highlight their growth, strengths, and needs.

Sinking or Swimming Together

ASSETS AND COOPERATIVE LEARNING

JUDY TACCOGNA, ED.D

Education Director

Search Institute

Minneapolis, Minnesota

One of the instructional strategies contributor Stan Paine recommends—cooperative learning—oozes with asset-building opportunities. Research indicates that the strategy actually reduces prejudice, enhances intergroup understanding, and builds skills for cross-cultural communication.[1] Because its capacity to increase learning as well as build cultural competence is particularly strong, cooperative learning is a good strategy to use to illustrate the process of infusing developmental assets into instruction. When implemented with fidelity to its well-researched components, cooperative learning is a highly engaging and instructive way to help young people learn curricular concepts and master essential skills of cooperation and collaboration, increasing their ability to work on teams as students and, later, as adults.

Not every group opportunity in a classroom is a cooperative learning experience, though. Cooperative learning is much more than small-group discussion or math problem solving or project collaboration.

To capture fully the benefits of a cooperative learning group experience, you need to structure group selection carefully. Intentionally grouping students to ensure balanced representation of ability level, race, ethnic group, gender, language proficiency, and opinion better promotes positive intergroup relationships.

The Components of a Cooperative Learning Group

According to researchers David W. Johnson and Roger T. Johnson at the University of Minnesota's Center for Cooperative Learning in Minneapolis, a cooperative learning group must have the following five components: positive interdependence, individual accountability, face-to-face promotive interaction, social skills, and group processing.[2]

Positive Interdependence

Group composition as well as assignments must be structured so that group members perceive that they need to depend on one another to fully accomplish the assignment and succeed—that it's "sink or swim" together. Mutual learning goals help accomplish this: "Learn the assigned material and make sure all of your group knows it as well." Dividing the resource materials among group members makes sharing imperative, and assigning specific complementary roles to each group member (e.g., reader, questioner, "rephraser," reporter) differentiates tasks. Some or all of the rewards for working in the group need to be joint rewards as well (e.g., "If all of your group scores at 90 percent or above, each of you will receive five bonus points."). This component certainly supports building the positive peer influence and interpersonal competence assets.

Individual Accountability

Although the working environment is a group, the individual still is accountable for her or his own performance. Although Johnson and Johnson link group and individual accountability, Robert Slavin, another leading researcher on cooperative learning from Johns Hopkins University in Baltimore, Maryland, contends that grading in cooperative groups should be based on individual performance and kept separate from any rewards for group performance.[3] Ways to assess individual learning need to be built into the process as well, to ensure accountability and also to help the group know who needs what kind of help to succeed. Such methods include giving an individual test, judging individual performance against a rubric, randomly calling on one student to represent the group's answer (meaning all must be prepared to answer well), or having each person explain the answer to a partner so that the teacher as well as group members can monitor learning. Requiring students to take responsibility is built in.

Face-to-Face Promotive Interaction

This type of group interaction involves members promoting each other's success in positive ways to ensure that the group meets its learning goals. This aspect of cooperative learning reinforces the need for improving social-competence skills, including the ability to help one another, share information and materials effectively, and provide good feedback to one another. Face-to-face promotive interaction also involves constructively challenging each other's ideas to promote thinking at higher cognitive levels and making better decisions.

Social Skills

Not all students come to class with the interpersonal and small-group skills essential for a successful cooperative learning group. Before expecting a group to perform well cooperatively, teachers need to ensure that students have the appropriate skills, including how to listen, communicate, build trust, share resources, resolve conflict, and take leadership roles—elements that are all evident in the social-competencies category of developmental assets.

Group Processing

Reflecting on how group members work together is an integral part of group members' learning. Groups need to be able to identify the skills they are or are not using, know how to decide whether they are working effectively, and provide effective feedback to others. Groups need to incorporate decisions about how to perform better during subsequent activities. In fact, evidence shows that groups that actively reflect cooperatively improve more in their interpersonal skills and also achieve more than cooperative groups that do not reflect on their process.[4]

Even at the university level, researchers working to improve physics education tout using cooperative learning groups to improve problem-solving skills. They found that group-derived solutions to problems were "significantly better than those produced by the best problem solvers" and that even the "individual problem-solving performance of students improved over time at approximately the same rate for students of high, medium, and low ability."[5]

Building Conflict Resolution Skills through Academic Controversy

Cooperative groups, notably, often foster more controversy and conflict than other instructional approaches because students must collaborate and work together. On the other hand, structuring cooperative groups well forces students to understand multiple points of view, build open-mindedness, and improve the ability to restate another's position on an issue.

One of the most intriguing strategies for teaching people to address group controversy—as well as to teach content that includes controversial issues—is called *academic controversy* or *constructive controversy*. According to Johnson and Johnson, academic controversy is the "instructional use of intellectual conflict to promote higher achievement and increase the quality of problem solving, decision making, critical thinking, reasoning, interpersonal relationships, and psychological health and well-being."[6]

An academic controversy lesson is structured in five stages:[7]

1. You, the teacher, divide students into groups of four, with two sets of pairs. Each pair is responsible for one position on an issue. You can either provide the content or have students conduct research to dig it out. Each pair prepares a persuasive presentation and a series of arguments to use in supporting their views to the opposing pair.
2. Each pair presents their case—no arguing allowed at this point!
3. Students all openly discuss the issues, clarify both positions, defend their own positions, and refute claims as needed. Students should also take notes on and know the opposing position. Pairs then separate to prepare new arguments and represent their own positions.
4. At this point, the pairs are asked to reverse positions and present the opposing point of view as forcefully as possible. Students can use their own notes, but not the opposing pair's notes or resources.
5. Both pairs then drop all advocacies and, as a group of four, reach a synthesized consensus. Students may write a report or present their joint position and rationale.

Johnson and Johnson[8] validate that this strategy produces powerful outcomes in building advocacy positions, listening, assuming another person's point of view, collaborating, coming to consensus, and decision making. They further attest that academic controversy results in greater achievement and retention, more involvement and motivation to learn, attitude changes, enhanced liking and social support among participants, higher self-esteem, greater social competence, more accurate perspective taking, and increased ability to cope with stress and adversity.[9] They advocate as well that "with the implementation of cooperative learning and academic controversy in the classroom, the stage is set to create a caring learning community."[10] Is that not exactly what we as asset-building educators want to do?

Building Cultural Competence

The great need to address the increasing diversity of students, as the makeup of schools today changes, is another reason to strongly consider using cooperative learning in your instruction. Research shows that it improves intergroup relationships in terms of cross-cultural issues as well as across other socioeconomic factors. In addition, the *Harvard Education Letter* reports that according to Slavin, most studies of cooperative learning also show equal benefits for low-, average-, and high-achieving students.[11]

Robert Slavin and Robert Cooper at Johns Hopkins University report that cooperative learning affects relationships among various kinds of groups.[12] Their work, as well as other studies, reveals that cooperative learning groups increase academic achievement and enhance intergroup relationships.[13] "They [cooperative groups] have great potential to facilitate the building of cross-ethnic friendships and to reduce racial stereotyping, discrimination, and prejudice. When students work cooperatively, they have the opportunity to judge each other on merits rather than stereotypes."[14] Although cross-ethnic relationships are not the norm in the desegregated schools Slavin and Cooper studied, the researchers note several studies that show a rise in numbers of cross-ethnic friendships among students who worked in various cooperative-group formats.[15] Another researcher, Evelyn Jacob, also notes that the elements of cooperative learning contribute to better relationships among diverse student groups.[16]

Inasmuch as cooperative learning groups are teacher assigned to include youth of difference races, sexes, innate abilities, language proficiencies, and strengths, they provide opportunities for young people to work collaboratively with, depend upon, and become comfortable with people of many unique strengths, needs, and backgrounds. The personal relationships students develop within cooperative groups and through particular structured activities, such as an academic controversy, promote candid discussions and increased understanding of likenesses and differences.

If you and other teachers set such expectations, you send a clear message that you support interracial, multiability, mixed-gender contact in groups—that you appreciate and embrace diversity, and expect it as a norm. Clearly, cooperative learning is an effective way to advance academic learning and to strengthen many of the assets.

Notes

1. Slavin, Robert E., and Cooper, Robert. (1999). Improving Intergroup Relations: Lessons Learned from Cooperative Learning Programs. *Journal of Social Issues*, 55(4):647–663.

2. Johnson, David W., and Johnson, Roger T. (September, 1994). *Cooperative Learning, Cooperative Schools, Academic Controversy, and Peer Mediation: Innovations in Cooperative Learning*. Minneapolis: University of Minnesota. Paper presented at the European Conference on Curriculum, University of Twente, Enschede, The Netherlands, 6–9. Johnson, Roger T., and Johnson, David W. *An Overview of Cooperative Learning*. Center for Cooperative Learning at the University of Minnesota, Minneapolis, 1–4; Web site accessed May 15, 2002: www.clcrc.com/pages/overview paper.html.

3. Slavin, Robert E., as referenced in Walters, Laurel Shaper. (May–June 2000). Putting Cooperative Learning to the Test. *Harvard Education Letter*, 16(3):5. Cambridge, MA: Harvard Graduate School of Education.

4. Johnson, Roger T., as referenced in Walters, Putting Cooperative Learning to the Test, 4. (See note 3.)

5. Heller, Patricia, Keith, Ronald, and Anderson, Scott. (1992). Teaching Problem Solving through Cooperative Grouping. Part 1: Group versus Individual Problem Solving. *American Journal of Physics*, 60(7):627–636.

6. Johnson, David W., and Johnson, Roger T. (1995). *Creative Controversy: Intellectual Challenge in the Classroom*, 3rd ed. Edina, MN: Interaction Book Company, 4–7.

7. Johnson and Johnson, *Cooperative Learning*, 13–14. (See note 2.)

8. Another reference that talks about intellectual controversy is Johnson, David W., and Johnson, Roger T. (1989). *Cooperation and Competition: Theory and Research*. Edina, MN: Interaction Book Company.

9. Johnson and Johnson. *Academic Controversy*, 1. Johnson and Johnson. *An Overview of Cooperative Learning*, 6. (See notes 7 and 2, respectively.)

10. Johnson and Johnson. (September, 1994). *Cooperative Learning*, 15.

11. Slavin, as referenced in Walters, Putting Cooperative Learning to the Test, 6. (See note 3.) Walters also acknowledges that cooperative learning may not be as beneficial for the very highest level of gifted students.

12. Slavin and Cooper, Improving Intergroup Relations, 648.

13. Lopez-Reyna, N. A. (1997). The Relation of Interactions and Story Quality among Mexican American and Anglo American Students with Learning Disabilities. *Exceptionality*, 7:245–261, as referenced in Slavin and Cooper. Improving Intergroup Relations, 648.

14. McLemore, S. D., and Romo, H. D. (1998). *Racial and Ethnic Relations in America*, 5th ed. Boston: Allyn and Bacon, as referenced in Slavin and Cooper, Improving Intergroup Relations, 648.

15. Slavin and Cooper, Improving Intergroup Relations, 649, 653–658.

16. Jacob, Evelyn. (1999). *Cooperative Learning in Context: An Educational Innovation for Everyday Classrooms*. SUNY Series, The Social Context of Education. New York City: State University of New York Press, 13–14.

Cooperating to Build Assets

JAN MITCHELL, M.A.

Communications Teacher (grades 9–10)

Marshalltown High School

Marshalltown, Iowa

To help you see just how you can implement the components of cooperative learning in your classroom through an asset lens, Jan Mitchell describes the details of three examples from her high school communications classes. (You can read more about their context within her language arts classes in "Negotiating at the Bargaining Table: Three Leadership Projects" in Chapter 4, page 101.)

Cooperative learning invites asset building. It generates belonging because it gives students membership and participation in an interactive group with a common task or goal in which they learn to build personal support systems. In my high school communications classes, I use three particular activities to build skills essential to academic progress as well as to support growth in assets for young people: "Five-Square Puzzle"[1] stresses building interpersonal skills as students learn about group process; the "Candy Distribution Challenge" focuses on learning negotiating, consensus-building, and problem-solving strategies; and the "Consensus Construction" project stresses skills needed to come to good agreements. All three are riddled with asset building as well.

The Five-Square Puzzle: Insights into Interpersonal and Cultural Competence

Interpersonal competence involves the ability to build and maintain relationships with coworkers, friends, and family. Your students' ability to work well in cooperative learning groups and to demonstrate competence in relating across cultures requires the same skills they need to build healthy relationships in their personal (and work) lives.

The five-square exercise (see Handout 3.2: Five-Square Puzzle on page 74) exposes students to the idea that healthy group relationships don't just happen. Well-functioning groups evolve because group members use other-centered communication, see distinct parts and how they fit into the whole, and share ownership of the outcome.

To set up the exercise, I distribute kits with copies of the rules and puzzle pieces cut from card stock or foam board to groups of five. Group members distribute three puzzle pieces having the same letter (A, B, C, D, or E) to each person, who joins in the process of assembling those pieces to make five six-inch squares for the group.

SCHOOL DEMOGRAPHICS
Marshalltown High School
Marshalltown, Iowa

Students: 1,641

Grades: 9–12

Gender:
Male	52.7%
Female	47.3%

Race and Ethnicity:
Black or African American	3.5%
Hispanic or Latino	17.0%
Asian / Pacific Islander	2.0%
American Indian	0.5%
White / Caucasian	77.0%

Socioeconomics:
Free / Reduced Lunch	33.4%

Five-Square Puzzle

The five-square puzzle illustrates well for students how healthy group relationships don't just happen. Through this cooperative learning activity, students gain insight into building the assets of interpersonal and cultural competence, and what group process is all about.

Materials Needed

1. Puzzle pieces made from card stock or foam board, with the letters A, B, C, D, or E marked on the back. See patterns below.
2. Card with rules printed on it to place in full view of the group.

Object of the Process

1. The group (five members) has the task of using the puzzle pieces to form five six-inch squares.
2. Group members should also watch the process to observe what happens as the group reaches barriers to a solution.

The Process

1. Explain the process.
2. Review the rules.
3. Group members assign selves as A, B, C, D, or E.
4. Distribute the packet.
5. Distribute puzzle pieces to A, B, C, D, or E.
6. Each member of the group tries to assemble pieces of the puzzle to make one of the five six-inch squares.

7. Members may give pieces to others but may not take any from others or signal what others are to do.
8. When all squares are assembled, debrief the process.

Communication Concepts

1. Communication is other-centered.
2. Group process involves seeing parts and how they fit into the whole.
3. Everyone has ownership of the whole.
4. Perception of others' needs is vital to group communication, whether performing a group task or making a group decision.
5. Group process involves helping others stay open to the best solution, even when they think they have the answer. (They are usually sitting on a part that doesn't fit the whole.)

The Rules

1. No member may speak.
2. No member may ask for a piece or in any way signal for one.
3. Members may give pieces to others.

Configuration for the six-inch squares (not drawn to scale):

*These little triangular pieces should be the same size and, when put together, equal the size of the C square in the top row.

The rules restrict natural instincts: No one may speak. No member may ask for a puzzle piece or in any way signal for one but may give pieces to others. Although the pieces can form a variety of six-inch squares, the answer to the puzzle is a specific configuration of squares and forces students, through trial and error, to find the less obvious combination.

Because group members are not able to ask for help or signal for a puzzle piece, someone may sit with an incorrectly formed square oblivious to the fact that it contains pieces that others need. Or, some in the group may see the solution but get frustrated because one member sits with the first square formed and has stopped working for the group.

When groups do find the solution, I ask that they write observations of what happened when they noticed barriers to a solution and speculate about what they could have done to make the group process work better without violating the rules. Most suggest that group members who "hogged the squares" need to think of the whole group.

Our debriefing of the group process leads to two key concepts:

- Perception of the needs of others is vital to group success; and
- Group process involves helping everyone stay open to the best solution even when some members think they have the best ideas.

The activity provides insight into interpersonal skills needed for healthy relationships. Students who can work well in cooperative learning groups recognize that self-centered and possessive behaviors create barriers to successful group process. By trying to see and meet others' needs and genuinely sharing interest in a learning group's success, students develop skills in the classroom that also enhance relationships outside of school.

The Candy Distribution Challenge: Skills for Resolving Conflicts

Interdependent work groups inevitably disagree as they work to resolve complex tasks. The candy distribution project (see Handout 3.3: Candy Distribution Challenge on page 77) grew out of my need to equip students with tools to negotiate solutions to problems within cooperative learning teams. Rather than let students muddle through poorly functioning groups, I use this negotiations project to help them learn to listen and respond to one another with greater awareness of each other's needs.

The challenge starts with a bag of individually wrapped candies—peppermints, butterscotch disks, miniature Tootsie Rolls, and others. I choose six or seven kinds, depending on my class size, ensuring that each student gets an average of 2.5 pieces. Then I separate the candies out so that I have only three of one kind, five of another, seven of another, and so on. I purposely provide the fewest of the kind that I believe will be most popular and most of the kind that no one will want.

When I initially present the idea of negotiating for candy, the students only know that they can choose among the kinds I have to offer. They don't know that the number of pieces varies according to kind.

I ask students to set up individual plans for the candy distribution. They record their first, second, and third choices on index cards and hand them to me. These choices determine a portion of the points for the exercise after the candy distribution is over.

I then randomly divide the students into five or six collective bargaining units and give each unit an information sheet about the amounts of candy and the rules. Their task is to prepare a proposal about how to distribute the candy fairly within the rules to all members of the class. Before the bargaining units finalize their proposals, however, I present information about skills and behaviors involved in the negotiation process. I include profiles of consensus-building and consensus-blocking behaviors that I have constructed from observation and experience, along with sample phrases to use when communicating for agreement (see Handout 3.4: Profile of a Consensus Builder and Consensus Blocker on page 78).

A table in the center of the room is the negotiation table. As each group finishes its distribution proposal, I ask them to determine the order they want for rotation of representation in the negotiation board meetings. A representative from each group takes a chair at the table for the first bargaining session, while the other students and I sit around the outer edge of the room to observe. I score the communication process by giving plus points for any communication at the board table that is consensus building and negative points for consensus-blocking behaviors.

The bargaining goes on through several class periods, with new representatives rotating in every 20–25 minutes. The bargaining group has to work through the difficulty of deciding which students should get the coveted, but least available, candy pieces and which students will get any leftover third pieces at the expense of others who can get only two.

The challenge arises from conflicting perceptions of fairness. Often tensions occur between negotiators whose bargaining unit believes a random plan is fairest and other negotiators who want to manage the process by calculating points for each student's candies piece by piece.

The actual distribution takes a variety of forms. Sometimes students agree to a draw-out-of-a-hat random plan. Other times, they engineer the solution so that everyone knows how each specific piece will be distributed and what points given.

Creativity also plays a part. One class needed a compromise to pull conflicting philosophies together and used a rock-paper-scissors tournament to determine who should receive each piece of candy. Another class arranged to drop the candy pieces randomly on the asphalt track around the football field, and at the sound of a whistle, students ran from the 50-yard line in all directions in search of the pieces they wanted.

The candy distribution project tests each student's ability to interact with others and work through conflict. Representatives to the negotiations board have a personal responsibility to promote their groups' plans while meeting standards of civility and fairness. The cooperative learning culture is at its best when the students at the negotiation table listen to each other to hear what other groups and individuals need and engineer a solution that works for all.

Candy Distribution Challenge

Materials

Sixty-three pieces of seven types of candy: Tailor the number (and kinds) of candy according to the size of your class, averaging 2.5 pieces per student.

  3 Cadbury chocolate eggs
  5 miniature Tootsie Rolls
  7 root beer
  9 Rolos
  11 butterscotch
  13 strawberry
  15 peppermint

The Rules

Note: Students choose first, second, and third choices of candy without knowing the number of each available.

1. All pieces must be distributed.

2. Each person must receive no more than three pieces.

3. Each person must receive no fewer than two pieces.

4. All people who have no more than four letters in their last name are guaranteed three pieces.

5. Absent students must be counted for candy distribution.

6. No person shall receive more than two pieces of the same kind of candy.

7. All persons will serve as a representative at the negotiation board meeting in a rotation sequence determined by the bargaining unit.

8. Final agreement is reached when consensus occurs.

9. Anyone who is argumentative will be withdrawn from the exercise and awarded no points and no candy.

Points

Award toward a goal of 50 points as follows:

For speaking during the negotiation board meeting, you will gain:

- +2 points for each observable consensus-building contribution

- 0 points for contributing neither consensus building nor consensus blocking

- -2 points for each observable consensus-blocking behavior

Following negotiations:

- 5 points, if consensus is reached resulting in everyone in the class getting candy

- 0 points for failure to reach consensus and no one getting candy

If, with the final distribution plan, you get one or more of your choices, you will gain:

- 8 points for your first choice

- 5 points for your second choice

- 3 points for your third choice

Profile of a Consensus Builder and a Consensus Blocker

Profile of a Consensus Builder	Profile of a Consensus Blocker
■ Focuses on the group task: "we" agenda	■ Focuses on what interests self: "my" agenda
■ Uses energy to find what will work	■ Uses energy to find reasons ideas will not work
■ Is open-minded, willing to learn and grow	■ Is closed-minded, unwilling to take risks that lead to growth
■ Communicates with respect for all ideas	■ Vocalizes strong opinions
■ Listens to understand others' needs	■ Listens to find points to argue
■ Listens for similarities	■ Listens judgmentally
■ Questions for understanding	■ Questions to intimidate
■ Uses the language of mediation: *"So you're saying that ..."* *"Would you consider ..."* *"What are our options?"*	■ Uses the language of polarization: *"You can't be serious about ..."* *"But wouldn't it be better to ..."* *"Here's why my idea is best ..."*
■ Responds to pull the group together	■ Ignites disagreement
■ Uses open gestures	■ Uses closed or power gestures
■ Recognizes and participates in give-and-take of decision making	■ Works to persuade others to accept her or his ideas
■ Works for a decision that is agreeable to all	■ Works for immediate decisions to get things done

The Language of Communicating for Agreement

"So you're saying that ..."

"Would you consider ..."

"What do you see as our options right now?

"Tell me, so that I can understand ..."

"Would/Could you agree that ..."

"Can you help me to understand ..."

"We agree, then, on ..."

Consensus Construction: Developing Planning and Decision-Making Skills

When I ask students to use high-level skills in group settings, I find that they need frequent, regular debriefing of group processes. I work at giving them concrete experiences because the process seems invisible to them—they don't know what there is to see.

To teach consensus building, I use a whole-class construction project to facilitate talking about invisible planning and decision-making skills, making them more obvious through a tangible reference. This hands-on activity is designed to help students learn communication skills for cooperative learning.

Pleading for a Common Goal

The first part of the activity involves distributing plastic building pieces similar to Lego blocks, along with written goals that match the color of each piece. The students with blue pieces have a different goal from those with red pieces, and so on. The goals are conflicting rather than compatible: to build a tall structure, to build a wide structure, to build an object with no two consecutive pieces of the same color, and to build a statue in the shape of a recognizable animal. However, I don't tell the students that the goals conflict, only that they will contribute pieces to a single structure the entire class is building rather than to a creation within their own group.

Each color group formulates a strategy to reach its goal, and members sit together to observe as each student adds pieces to the unplanned class structure. Each color group gets one turn at a time; members rotate within their groups to give everyone a turn. My rules allow each student the choice of adding two pieces or adding one new piece and moving two pieces already placed on the structure.

In a short time, students complain that the task is unrealistic because they can't meet their goals. When I ask how they want to solve that problem, they plead to be allowed to focus on a single goal that they can achieve together. Getting them to want to work on a unified goal is the point of the activity.

The Value of Common Vision

We move then to a second phase of construction in which I ask class members to brainstorm possible recognizable shapes that they could build from the pieces. I lead them to select one as a class and to discuss the details so that they all can envision the structure before they build it.

When the students seem to achieve consensus, they come forward one by one to contribute to the structure, two pieces at a time. Students who have a detailed, specific plan naturally take on supervisory roles as each member of the construction crew walks forward. The students coach each other so that each addition to the structure fits the collective vision.

The results reflect their process. Three examples from one semester show how varied the results may be:

- The final product conforms to the plan.

- The incongruity of the finished product reflects an inability to come to a true consensus.
- The final product mirrors a lack of vision and distraction by an agenda other than group consensus.

In the first scenario, the class decided on a statue of me. (I don't know why, but that's how it was.) They discussed in detail the color: my skirt and shoes (blue), my blouse (red), my arms, legs, and face (yellow), and my hair (green). Then someone observed that there were students who had colors that wouldn't be used if they didn't add more green or red. So they decided to put me on a multicolored pedestal of four levels. They formed a mental picture and then built it, student by student, piece-by piece. The final product conformed to their plan.

The second class brainstormed several ideas but couldn't find energy in any of them. One student suggested a compromise that would combine the ideas of a sunset, teeter-totter, and a tree together in a park, but couldn't convince two students who were holding out for a free-form sculpture in the form of a gigantic hand. They reached consensus by adding a free-form sculpture to the park. They built the structure they had agreed to, but the incongruity of the finished product showed their inability to come to a truly unified decision.

The third class showed little interest until someone asked, "Does this Lego set have wheels?" From then on, a large faction of the class pursued building two cars that could crash into one another. The cars took on monstrous shapes, with gaps between towering pieces that rose above the base in unrecognizable images. The students' energy during construction was not directed toward building a structure that matched a shared vision but toward getting it done so that they could crash the cars together. The end result mirrored the group's lack of vision and the fact that they were distracted by their own agenda.

Cooperative learning thrusts students into interdependent situations that demand complex skills. As they plan and make decisions together, they may be distracted by conflicting agendas, they may compromise and settle for a mediocre plan, or they may interact in ways that produce a unified, shared vision and succeed at achieving their goal. But through all, such learning opportunities reinforce development of a number of the internal assets in particular. At the same time, the students are building not just unique products, but skills that enhance their success both at school and in later life.

Notes

1. Kester, Kyra, et al. (July 1996). Five-Square Exercise. *Applied Communication Guidelines*. Washington State Department of Instruction. Kester and the Washington State Department of Education document their source as: Edited and adapted by Margaret M. Beilke, Ph.D., Central Washington University from *Communications and Human Relations Activities for Work Adjustment*, Utah State Board for Vocational Education, 1977; and *The Squares #, Human Relations Experiment Project*, by Dr. Donald O. Clifton, President. Selection Research Incorporated, University of Nebraska, citing Bavelas, Communication Patterns in Task Oriented Groups, *Journal of the Acoustical Society of America*, 1950, 22:725–730.

Part II

*Teach **What** You Know*

Chapter 4

Infusing Assets into Language Arts

Serving Up John Grisham

DEVELOPING READING FOR PLEASURE

ANDREA GODFREY BROWN, M.A.T.

Language Arts Teacher (grades 11–12)

Parkway South High School

Manchester, Missouri

I've read for pleasure my whole life, but today's high school youth rarely seem to curl up with a good book. Most 9th- through12th-grade language arts teachers are thrilled if their students read required texts at all. More typically, we're frustrated that our students aren't really reading: they're buying (or scanning on-line) commercially prepared study guides or summaries of the classics we assign. I kept questioning myself, "Could I get high schoolers to *choose* to read for pleasure?"

After a careful look at our existing required curriculum in the block schedule, I determined that I would have to create a very different course—and a complementary classroom environment—to invite 11th and 12th graders to join me in reading for pleasure. I decided to offer my students something I enjoyed, even if it wasn't great (read this with a British accent) literature.

I believe that the way to make adolescents better readers is, simply, to have them read. Period. It really doesn't matter what it is. Although many of my colleagues may raise an eyebrow, John Grisham is one of my own favorite reading-for-pleasure authors. Grisham novels don't have gratuitous sex, and profanity is rare. If I shared Grisham novels with my students, I reasoned, I'd also be modeling asset 25, reading for pleasure, that has been such a lifelong joy to me. I was ready to try something different in an effort to build readers.

Getting the school board to approve was simple since one reason we went to a block schedule was to give students the opportunity for more electives. I called my new course "John Grisham Novels and Social Issues" and sought classroom methods and activities that would promote my central asset, while building others

SCHOOL DEMOGRAPHICS

Parkway South High School
Manchester, Missouri

Students: 2,079

Grades: 9–12

Gender:
Male	50.0%
Female	50.0%

Race and Ethnicity:
Black / African American	13.8%
Hispanic / Latino	0.9%
Asian / Pacific Islander	4.3%
American Indian	0.2%
White / Caucasian	80.8%

Socioeconomics:
Free / Reduced Lunch	9.8%

as well. From Search Institute literature, I knew that asset building means building relationships.[1]

Essentially, I determined that we would talk about Grisham's novels the way adults talk about books: informally over a meal, instead of with students directing their conversation through me, the teacher, from uncomfortable desks. The students would drive both the directions the conversations took as well as the issues we investigated along the way. I saw that I had to be willing to be more of a "guide on the side than a sage on the stage," as I learned in a teacher's workshop I attended in the early 1980s.[2]

I chose to be less of a traditional teacher and more of a server by offering generous portions of something I like to read. I discovered my students are, in fact, quite hungry to read for pleasure, too.

Designing an Elective to Build Readers

Like many high school language arts teachers, I worried that maybe the traditional approaches in required courses were somehow contributing to a generation that simply doesn't *choose* to read books. We've all had those classes where we feel as if our job was reduced to mandating reading to get students to read. You know, a daily quiz to punish the ones who didn't read the assignment, punitive essay topics designed to "catch" the person who used a commercial summary to avoid the book, that paper-and-pencil test loaded with quotes to match to characters and obscure vocabulary words.

In designing my "Grisham Novels" course to build the reading-for-pleasure asset, I looked hard at what was working in my required courses. One element became obvious: I did my best teaching—and the students did their best learning—when I was teaching something I really liked.

I was fortunate because our district has an extensive list of approved texts for each grade level. For the most part, I am able to choose which novels, plays, and stories to teach. But let's face it, we don't have a lot of real choice in a traditional honors-level junior American Literature class. We have to teach the classic pieces, or the students don't stand a chance on the various high-stakes college-entrance exams they have to take.

Sadly, many of our students tell us that reading isn't all that pleasurable, no matter how many new ideas we try to incorporate. So, **precept 1** in designing an elective to build the reading-for-pleasure asset became: **Teach something you like yourself, even if your colleagues snicker at you.** (And some of them will.) Designing a course to build the reading-for-pleasure asset allows me to teach for pleasure, too.

Our district provides funds to high schools to purchase paperback books that we rotate and share. I had to choose which Grisham novels we would read before I ever met one elective student. I chose three books that deal with differing social issues as well as questions about traditional gender roles. *A Time to Kill* entails racism; *The Client*, juvenile justice and organized crime; and *The Runaway Jury*, the tobacco industry and large jury awards to plaintiffs.

After my first students read each book, I asked them three questions about the choices:

1. What worked well for you with this novel?
2. What did not work well?
3. What do I need to know?

I discovered my first precept for building readers needed refining. When we got to *The Runaway Jury*, the students reported that it was a runaway bore. Good to know.

The next year, based on my first students' recommendations, I ordered *The Street Lawyer*. It deals with the plight of the homeless in America, and the students loved it. **Precept 1 revised: Teach something you and the students both like.** I needed to see that even though "Grisham Novels" was an elective course, the young people choosing it should still have a voice about what we read. After all, I was trying to get them to read for pleasure; it was important that they had a pleasurable experience.

I elicit feedback about every book. Asking students my three questions after every book empowers and involves them in an adult way. This means students have to think for themselves and make their own judgments. That first year, when I'd already spent my allotted funds and the students reported that they didn't like one of the books I'd ordered, we scoured the public libraries and bookstores and found ways to get the books they wanted. **Precept 2 (probably obvious): Listen to the students and incorporate their ideas into the next part of the work.**

Talk about Books the Way Adults Do

In school, we ask young people to talk about and deal with books in a way that is unique to the educational institution. And whether we like to admit it or not, students often rebel by not reading what we assign. Then they go us one better. Because they think reading isn't fun (pleasure), they're not doing any outside reading either. We lose both ways because we're not developing lifelong readers.

In designing "Grisham Novels," I was determined to ask young people to talk about books the way adults do. We adults often talk about books over a meal, discussing what most interests us. **Precept 3: Help students deal with and discuss books as adults do, and apply the ideas to current social issues.**

To be fair, this third precept (I have eight. See "Andrea Godfrey Brown's Precepts for Designing an Elective to Build Readers" on page 89.) is the toughest part of designing an elective that promotes reading for pleasure because, darn it, we work in schools! The institutional mentality often doesn't promote reading for pleasure, at least in a majority of my experiences. For each book, I wanted a culminating discussion over a meal, composed of questions that the students themselves wrote. I couldn't imagine how I'd pull it off.

The food part was actually easier to set up than the discussion part. At first, I was reluctant to take high school youth to a restaurant because I've seen how they act in the lunchroom, so we had potluck breakfast. (My class is from 8:00 to

9:30 A.M.) The custodial staff removed our student desks, replacing them with long tables arranged in a U shape. I promised the custodians our leftovers; it was a good deal for us all because they had to break it all back down before the 9:30 bell. (I think there's another precept here: Be good to the custodial staff.)

Later, after experiencing at school the meal discussion working so well, I requested a local pancake house five minutes from school to save us tables, which we rearranged upon our arrival. The students ordered their own food, and I insisted on one check with the gratuity added in. (The corollary to the custodian precept: Be good to the server and the greeter.)

You may be wondering, "What about students who can't afford breakfast out?" We have a special fund at school for just this kind of situation. Or, I may buy a student's meal, or he or she may opt to meet me over lunch in my classroom. I watch carefully when I first talk about this to see if anyone seems uncomfortable and initiate a conversation accordingly. If taking students out to breakfast just isn't an option, though, do the potluck thing. Either way, you're treating young people like adults, and the payoff is huge.

I discovered that my students discussed the books in depth. They listened actively. They built on the ideas of others. They learned to disagree and move past it. I didn't have to cajole them, and I only had to redirect the conversation occasionally. Sometimes multiple conversations were going on at once (not too unlike most dinner parties I've been to). For the most part, I enjoyed a cup of coffee while they talked about the book we'd just read. It was amazing.

We got lots of stares at first. Most of the public thinks high school young people are monsters. They were astonished that these youth were talking about books. I can't tell you how many times I was stopped on my way out while other customers shared their delight at seeing well-behaved high school students discussing a novel. "Were these 'regular' kids?" many wanted to know. "Yes," I told them proudly, "and they're here because they want to be." Almost without realizing it, I was building the community-values-youth asset by changing the public's image of young people.

Going out for breakfast raises lots of eyebrows within the school community, as well. There are two distinct opinions. One is that I'm completely crazy to take high schoolers anywhere in public. The other one implies that I have some special privilege: "Why do *you* get to take kids out to breakfast, and I have to stay here?!" I've learned over time that there's no answer these people will really hear.

Being a more experienced member of the faculty has made a difference. I'm lucky to have a principal who trusts me and is supportive. I also keep him informed. If your boss knows of the good things that are going on in your classroom or department, when questions do arise, he or she already has some answers. It's a practice that has worked for me.

Initially, even though the students were providing their own transportation, I had to fill out all the paperwork for a one-block (class period) field trip. Later, after I proved myself, I sent out one of those reverse permission letters covering the

---

Andrea Godfrey Brown's Precepts for Designing an Elective to Build Readers

1. Teach something you and the students both like.
2. Listen to the students and incorporate their ideas into the next part of the work.
3. Help students deal with and discuss books as adults do, and apply the ideas to current social issues.
4. The students drive the discussions.
5. Evaluate differently than in traditional core courses.
6. Student as worker, teacher as coach.
7. Teach students how to take the risk to create diverse groups that can accomplish tasks and are not just the same old friends working together.
8. Make personal connections to the reading.

---

whole semester: It requests parents to sign the bottom portion of the letter if they object to their son or daughter going to Uncle Bill's Pancake House for our book talk. A quick e-mail to the attendance office, copied to my administrative liaison, took care of the rest.

Relationships Matter

Even with food in hand, getting youth to talk about books as adults do takes quite a lot more planning and consideration. I begin each class session for the first six weeks with some kind of warm-up activity to build relationships. Remember, before we can make readers out of adolescents, we need to build relationships.

On the first day, I have students make a name tent. On the side that faces the majority of the class, they print their name in big letters. In each of the corners, they draw four things they're passionate about. Sometimes I say, "Even if you're passionate about shopping or talking on the phone or sleeping, try to think of some other things to draw."

Of course, I always draw my rendition of a book and, in sharing (you should, too), am certain to mention how much I love reading for fun in the summer and on vacations. (Insert teacher grinning with a glint in her eye.) Then I go around the room and have each person share their four passions. Taking time to get to know each other on day one sets an important tone. Plus, it helps me learn my students' names sooner because I have a connection. "Marcie is the girl who loves horses," I tell myself.

Don't fall victim to the worn-out excuse for not doing this getting-to-know-one-another activity: that high school young people won't like it because such team-building activities are too infantile or touchy-feely. Your students may resist a little at first, but they will come around, especially if *you're* having fun with it, too. Be yourself, and only do those activities that you feel comfortable doing. The main point is: warm them up to you and to each other. Relationships matter.

How Can You Be Sure Students Are Reading?

I typically ask students to read 50 or 60 pages for the next class meeting, since we meet every other day. This may sound like a lot, but Grisham novels read fast. (That's one of the other reasons I chose them.) Some students stick to that schedule; others go faster.

I often ask the students to write down a debatable question or two from several reading assignments. Yes, I have to teach the difference between open- and closed-ended questions, but that's not a problem. Then we discuss the questions. The discussions are informal.

Remember, we're aiming to discuss books here as adults do. I insist that folks listen to each other, but I do let them engage in a little of what my high school English teacher called *side talking*, as long as they're discussing the current Grisham novel and not what they're wearing to homecoming.

Keep in mind the discussion questions are not *my* discussion questions; they're *the students'*. This helps the discussion. Students like hearing their own questions. They like answering them, too. I do edit their questions occasionally, adding in connections I see, just as I do for the more formal discussions I facilitate in core courses.

Precept 4: The students drive the discussions.

The other way I make sure my students are reading is to make discussions part of the course points: Don't talk at all, no points. Turn in your discussion questions, get points. On day one, I tell students that to get an A, they have to do everything I ask them to do, not pick and choose which assignments they can afford not to do.

The key, I've discovered, is making every assignment worth zero to four points, which in my head corresponds to A, B, C, D, F, with A being four points. The truth is, the points are not what matters because at the end of the semester, we don't have some huge number of points.

Gradually, I wean my students off of points as they start to understand that we're here to read and enjoy ourselves. Eventually, most start working because they're invested in what we're doing—they're enjoying reading and talking about books—and not because an assignment is worth a lot of points.

I still keep track of my four-point assignments in my grade book. Maybe someday I'll figure out how to give that up, but in Missouri, that's not an option. We have to turn in grade books at the end of the year, and empty pages are frowned upon.

Precept 5: Evaluate differently than in traditional core courses.

How Can You Get All Students Talking?

What also happens is that the students realize how much more fun it is when everyone "plays." The warm-ups help build trust. Stronger readers look out for weaker ones. Participation is infectious. The more reluctant students often come around by the end of the semester because a classmate insists through good-natured ribbing or by inviting that person into her or his next investigation group.

Investigations are critical to the students' learning in "Grisham Novels." This work, whatever shape it may ultimately take, involves researching social issues central to each book's plot lines. Also, I want students to get to know each other as team members. Asking students to inquire about an area linked to the book we're reading and discussing provides follow-up opportunities for group work and developing relationships further.

Several years ago, I trained to be a Critical Friends Coach[3] with the Central States Coalition of Essential Schools in Kansas City, Missouri. I've implemented many of the Critical Friends methods in my classrooms because they help me increase student learning. **Precept 6** for designing "Grisham Novels" is directly out of the work of the Coalition of Essential Schools: **Student as worker, teacher as coach.**[4]

One activity that helps students know one another as teammates is "Compass Points" (see Handout 4.1: Compass Points: How Do I Work with This Group? on page 92), which I learned during my Critical Friends training. Using the Keirsey Temperament Sorter II[5] (an assessment tool similar to the more familiar Myers-Briggs Type Indicator), this activity allows students to analyze how their personalities shape the way they work in this specific class.

Collaborative work "works" because students have a decision-making role in choosing their groups. But they do so armed with knowledge, instead of working with someone because the two are friends or they happened to have known each other's names on the first day. Students choose with whom to work based on real information—and in my experience, they rarely choose inappropriately. The activity also helps preempt anyone not doing her or his part, the great downside to group work.

Here's how "Compass Points" works: I paste the four main compass directions (north, east, south, and west) around the room. Then I read a brief description of each one, which is tied to how a person would function in the group. I give my students several minutes to think over how *they* function in this group of "Grisham Novels" (as distinct from how they might function in their personal lives or in another class), and ask them to move to that part of the room.

Their next task is to answer together with their other *compadres* the questions associated with each of the four compass directions. I ask the students to chart their responses on a big piece of paper and then report to the rest of the class.

After every group reports, I facilitate a discussion that includes asking:

- How did you know you were in the right group?
- How would you decide what percentage of each compass point would make the most effective group?

As we work through their responses, students begin to see the value in creating groups that are diverse and differentiated. I've found that projects are always better when they consider creating groups based on compass points than if they work with their best friends or with other young people who are just like them. I have had students remark, "I never realized why it took me so long to get a project done. We didn't have any 'Norths'!" Sometimes groups choose to incorporate at least one of each directional point in their groups. But I've also had all the "Easts" band

Compass Points: How Do I Work with This Group?

North

"I need to get the work done now."

I am product driven.

West

"Answer my questions before I can proceed."

I need to know who, what, when, why, where.

East

"I need the 'Big Picture.'"

I like to envision and express.

South

"I want everyone to share her or his thoughts."

In order to work, I need to know everyone is supported.

together, only to face the too-many-visionaries and not-enough-workers syndrome. Still, learning happens then as well. **Precept 7: Teach students how to take the risk to create diverse groups that can accomplish tasks and are not just the same old friends working together.**

Community Investigations

From this point on, the very curriculum of "Grisham Novels" is all about student-driven investigations and the opportunity to work in varying teams of their own creation. Each of the three novels we read in concert and their own choice novel all involve some kind of investigation and project.

We brainstorm lists of possible investigations on the white board with a student doing the writing. After combining like topics and voting as many times as students want, we reduce the list. Then I give students some think time. Sometimes I let them read our current novel for a half hour. When we revisit the topics, I have each student put her or his name under the topic of greatest interest. From there, they can create other smaller groups.

One time, I had students who wanted to investigate what real defense lawyers did while we read *A Time to Kill*. After some days of initial research, they began to tackle developing plans. In frustration, one girl commented, "This is going nowhere. What we really need is some defense lawyer to come in here and just talk to us and let us ask him or her questions!"

Now, you're probably thinking, "Why didn't the teacher see that ahead of time and just arrange for a guest speaker? I've done it myself tons of times."

And that's just the problem.

The teacher does all the work, and the students sit passively, daring us to teach them or entertain them or pass them because they showed up for class. *This* time *they* saw the need. *They* had their classmates write down questions. *They* figured out whom to call and saw the value of networking. The youth made the contacts, faxed the directions and the questions, let the front office know we were expecting a guest, met him the day of his presentation, facilitated the event, and wrote a thank-you note. Student as worker, teacher as coach!

Another issue in *A Time to Kill* is the insanity defense. One group of students wondered if they could arrange a field trip to the St. Louis Psychiatric Rehabilitation Center. They followed up with a phone call (it's really wonderful if you have a phone in the classroom and a phone book, too). "No way," they were told.

Not about to take no for an answer, one young girl asked if she and a classmate could come instead so that they could report back to the class. "That'd work," she was told. Again, she made the arrangements. She rescheduled her work and athletic commitments. (I've seen students do this when they get hooked on something in school, but even I had to ask myself, "Do you understand how huge that is?")

Because these two girls were so deeply interested in his work, the psychologist they'd been talking with and who showed them around the new assisted-living apartments asked if they'd like him to come and talk to the class himself. He even read *A Time to Kill* before he arrived. He really helped us dispel misconceptions we all had about the insanity defense that day.

I've had youth arrange field trips to the St. Louis City Workhouse (a medium-security prison), watch jury selection and opening arguments for a murder trial, bring in a counselor from a rape crisis center, and set up mock trials for *A Time to Kill*. Their only limitation—and yours—is what they are willing to do. I've discovered that students appreciate the chance to behave like responsible adults.

The only time I direct more of the project-investigation is when the students read a novel of their choice and multiple groups are reading different novels. For this book, students do a marketing project (see Handout 4.2: Marketing Your Choice Book: "Grisham Novels" Final Project on page 95).

Making Personal Connections

While students are working on their investigations before the final book talk that we hold when all have finished reading, I try to have some other kind of activity during the 90-minute class that also gives the students a chance to respond to the book on a more personal level. One that works well with any book is "Placemat," another activity I learned from Critical Friends training.[6]

I pass out newsprint and markers and ask the students to *draw* how the main character from the novel fits into her or his community. They are to refrain from writing words, though I'm lenient on this point, allowing just a few. The drawing takes some time. Let students talk as they draw. The results are amazing.

Once, a young boy who was very intelligent, but always in trouble with most of his teachers and all the administrators, drew a remarkable picture of a puzzle with one piece missing. Above the puzzle was a piece that obviously wouldn't fit. He eloquently explained how Jake, the main character in *A Time to Kill*, didn't exactly fit into his southern community of Clanton, Mississippi, because of his beliefs. The drawing was powerful and accurate, and the other students gave him approval in a way that no adult could at that point in his life.

I also have students do varied writing activities that capture their personal responses. Our school does an excellent job of teaching the analytical essay in response to literature, so I don't have to duplicate those efforts. I've had students turn a section of the novel into a dramatic scene and then deliver a great acting performance. I've asked them to write an opinion piece, or write and deliver point/counterpoint minispeeches about which was better, the book or the movie, when we're reading *A Time to Kill* and *The Client*. One aspiring filmmaker produced a short film.

Often I have students write a short personal essay in class in response to a particular question. I might ask, "What connections are you making with this book?" When I read their personal reflections, I always take the time to jot a comment back to them. This written dialogue has become a central part of my course. **Precept 8: Make personal connections to the reading.**

Sometimes I'll notice that a student needs more information. I can point them

Marketing Your Choice Book: "Grisham Novels" Final Project

For our last project, you and the members of your same-choice Grisham novel group will attempt to sell the public on this novel.

Part One

Everyone will create a large-size book cover. It must include:

1. Front cover with graphics, title, and author;
2. Front inside flap with a short, enticing summary that doesn't give away too much;
3. Back inside flap with a short "bio" of Grisham; and
4. Back cover with both real critical reviews and those authored by your classmates.

Part Two

You may choose one of the following, or design one of your own with my permission:

1. Jay Leno–style interview with a main character or characters, or Grisham himself;
2. Oprah-style interview with Grisham;
3. Grisham reads Grisham on a college campus;
4. Original movie trailer;
5. Game show;
6. Dramatic oral interpretation; or
7. Your own creative idea that would make someone want to read your book.

Presentations will be held during final exams.

in that direction as I respond. Simply, this kind of back-and-forth exchange helps me connect with young people. Some need more of that connecting than others, but I've found that adolescents need a reason to read that connects both of us personally. If they're just "students," we're not having that adult conversation I want. We have to establish enough of a relationship to talk honestly about issues together. I can do this one-on-one as I respond to their writing.

To help students make more personal connections beyond the classroom, such as with the topic of homelessness, one central issue in *The Street Lawyer*, I ask them to consider raising money and donating it to a variety of charitable institutions in our area, regardless of what else they've already chosen to investigate. Once they realize, through research on their own, that children comprise a sizeable percentage of the homeless, they're on board.

Recently, they raised more than $1,500 in three weeks by selling doughnuts and hot chocolate before school and going around the lunchroom with donation cans during lunch. One person wrote letters asking local businesses to donate as well. They did, too. The class also decided to "adopt" one of St. Louis's 100 Neediest Cases, a program sponsored by the *St. Louis Post-Dispatch* and United Way of Greater St. Louis. With the money the students raised, we were able to pay off one individual's gas bill, get new winter coats for her children, and give her $200 cash. The rest of the money went to the Salvation Army Hope Center for Children in St. Louis. When I had the youth evaluate the experience, most of them wrote about how good it felt to take on that kind of initiative and responsibility. Another girl used the experience as the basis for a *Newsweek*-style "My Turn" essay in another class.

Serving Up Readers

Because "Grisham Novels" is an elective for juniors or seniors, no other prerequisites exist. The only "qualification" is that the student is willing to read. Boys and girls have signed up in equal numbers, but it's not uncommon to end up with a class of readers at all different levels. I frequently have students who are diagnosed with learning or multiple disabilities, including hearing impairment. Within the same class, I've also had gifted students. Still, so far, students—and colleagues—have responded very positively to the course.

After the first year, the word was out. Since then, students have told their friends about it, promoting the class for me: "Is that the class where you eat breakfast and talk about books?"

My colleagues helped talk it up, too, despite their early jokes about teaching pop culture lit and not the real thing, the classics. I save them the time now and make the jokes myself, but they have been great about encouraging other students to sign up for the course, and each year it has grown.

Brendon,[7] a recent senior in my class, wrote me: "This class was a bunch better than I even thought it would be. And for the first time since early middle school, I read for pleasure."

I once overheard another student Jake[8] complaining to Todd[9] that he was behind in his reading. Todd said, "Jake, I have three words for you: Books on Tape! I listen to these books in my car and while I'm at work." It turns out that listening to books has been a strategy Todd had used for years. He had internalized a technique that worked for him and was comfortable sharing it.

Chris,[10] a senior with multiple learning disabilities, earned his first A in an English course. He put it this way, "John Grisham made a reader out of me!"

The thing I keep coming back to is this: serve adolescents up with generous portions of books that they will want to read. Let them select what they want to ingest, whether by author, as in this case, or by individual book. Give them some latitude. Don't chew it up for them.

Notes

1. Scales, Peter C. (Oct. 1999). Care and Challenge: The Sources of Student Success. *Middle Ground*, 3(2): 19–21; Scales, Peter C. (1999). Reducing Risks and Building Developmental Assets: Essential Actions for Promoting Adolescent Health. *Journal of School Health*, 69: 13–119; Scales, Peter C., and Judy Taccogna. (2000). Caring to Try: How Building Students' Developmental Assets Can Promote School Engagement and Success. *NASSP Bulletin*, 84(619): 69–78.

2. Taylor, T. Roger. (July 1981). *Teaching the Gifted and Talented*. Aspen, CO.

3. Rice, Richard, and Okerstrom, Jeanette. (July 25, 1998). *Critical Friends Coaches Training*. Cedar Creek Conference Center, New Haven, MO.

4. Coalition of Essential Schools. The Common Principles. Web site accessed September 11, 2002: http://www.essentialschools.org/pub/ces_docs/about/phil/10cps/10cps.html. The Coalition of Essential Schools is a national network of schools and regional centers, with a national office in Oakland, CA, that provides networking and professional development, conducts research, and advocates for public policies supporting its common principles of schooling.

5. Keirsey, David, and Advisor Team, Inc. (1978–2001). The Keirsey Temperament Sorter II. Web site accessed November 11, 2002: www.advisorteam.com/user/ktsintro1.asp.

6. *Critical Friends Coaches Training Follow-up*. (January 18, 1999). Golden Oaks Center, Kansas City, MO.

7. LeBeau, Brendon. Personal interview. May 18, 2001.

8. Bantel, Jake. Personal interview. Jan. 11, 2002.

9. Gwin, Todd. Personal interview. Jan. 11, 2002.

10. Bunch, Chris. Personal interview. May 18, 2001.

Creating Adaptations

Middle schools could also develop elective courses designed to entice students to read for pleasure. For example, the Harry Potter phenomenon is begging to be included. If the community objects, you could always choose something else—or forge ahead regardless, determined to promote asset 36, peaceful conflict resolution.

If your district curriculum can't include new elective courses, try what many teachers in my building have done: incorporate some kind of "choice" unit in your core language arts classes. You can select by authors or genres. Autobiographies are especially interesting.

Another idea I'm considering myself for the future is working with our district to start a Grisham book club for adult continuing education. What would really be cool is to figure out a way for high school seniors to join in and receive some elective credit. Mixing young adults and older adults would be powerful—and asset building—especially since I have adults asking if they can join "Grisham Novels" all the time.

Service Circles of Reading

GAINING COMPETENCE AND SELF-CONFIDENCE

KAREN KUPFER JOHNSON, M.ED.

Reading Specialist (grades 6–12)

Harrison Education Center

Minneapolis, Minnesota

Through her use of reading circles, Karen Kupfer Johnson has created an opportunity for two "opposite" grade levels of students: together, they work to improve skill development, as well as the assets reading for pleasure and interpersonal competence. In the process, she combines features of service to others.

To help my group of diverse middle and high school students who have learning or behavioral disabilities, or both, I have established volunteer service circles of reading that pair my students with kindergarteners from an adjoining regular education site. We are working to meet three literacy goals:

1. Increase functional personal reading levels;
2. Decrease nervousness while reading aloud in public; and
3. Make a difference in kindergarteners' listening vocabulary.

In addition to these content goals, this service-learning opportunity builds interpersonal competence and self-confidence for special education students, who often do not experience success either in content areas or in feeling that they can contribute to helping someone else academically.

Participants' Roles

Once each week we walk to a nearby kindergarten site a block away to participate in 30-minute service circles of reading. Each circle consists of an older reader (a middle or high school student), one supportive adult staff member, and small groups of kindergarteners from the regular education classroom. When we arrive, the kindergarten teacher divides the class into different small groups each week to ensure an equal number of readers for each older student. I choose stories that include a prosocial character, illustrate proactive problem solving, and contain vivid illustrations. Each reading circle participant has a role.

The Middle or High School Reader

The older reader is responsible for:

- Reading aloud to the kindergarteners;
- Asking predictive and clarifying questions, and
- Giving feedback to the kindergarteners about their responses.

The older students and I develop the predictive questions together during our pre-reading practice sessions, which I design to enhance the older readers' fluency and confidence before they read with kindergarteners. Typical questions include "What do you think will happen next?" or "Who will help him now?"

The Kindergartener

The younger student is responsible for:

- Listening carefully;
- Making predictions about what will happen next;
- Imagining the animated scenes; and
- Retelling portions of the story when prompted.

The Supportive Adult

The staff member is responsible for:

- Serving as a role model;
- Keeping participants on task;
- Clarifying vocabulary; and
- Displaying illustrations using a separate book.

Throughout the session, the older student and the adult ask predictive and clarifying questions based on the pictures and words in the story to engage active listening and build thinking skills on the part of both the older reader and the younger students. To close the circle of reading time, any of the participants can ask follow-up questions. Enthusiastic thank-yous are exchanged. We also close with a singalong or a call-response poem.

I observe my students during the groups and track their progress by logging their responses during the reading circle, including if or how they animate and intone action verbs, use emotional vocabulary to increase the group's attention and understanding, and make facial expressions that reflect the text content, such as smiling during humorous parts. I also log when the supporting adult does not need to cue or correct their pronunciation.

Between meetings, the middle and high school students follow up through journaling activities and discussions. Typical journal-writing prompts I use are "How do you think that your audience of children increased their vocabulary?" or "Explain how you served as a positive role model and leader in your group." Discussions topics include comparison of the story and real-life qualities of a hero, the power of reading literacy, and the importance of this service to other children to help us as students reach higher functional reading levels and to decrease anxiety about reading aloud.

The reading circles are highly enjoyed by all. The older students not only improve their reading skills—and desire to read—but also take pride in providing a service to others. At the same time, they succeed in beginning to shift from a sense of self-centeredness to more of a mind-set of other-centeredness.

Negotiating at the Bargaining Table

THREE LEADERSHIP PROJECTS

JAN MITCHELL, M.A.

Communications Teacher (grades 9–10)

Marshalltown High School

Marshalltown, Iowa

Education empowers us to get involved with others and our community. To help succeed in this, taking learning beyond the classroom walls is key. For me, teaching is an ongoing search for ways to involve youth in relevant, reality-based situations that provide the potential to improve not only communication skills but decision-making and problem-solving skills as well. Three leadership projects—the Partnership Project, the Work Team Project, and the Whole Class Project—are the result of that search.

Our communications course outline already included important components designed to help students develop specific skills in written and oral language—vocabulary study and directed instruction and practice for improving reading, writing, speaking, and listening—for a variety of purposes. I added leadership training to meet two needs:

- To give students the opportunity for directly applying communication skills; and
- To place asset building at the center of their projects.

Central to my approach is a belief that young people can gain developmental assets by meeting the needs of others. In each project, students participate through direct instruction, classroom practice, project implementation, and reflective written assessments. Direct instruction and practice build their interpersonal communication skills, which helps lead to healthy relationships with one another. Group decision making gives the students ownership as they develop complex skills involving other-centered communication, planning, and time management.

SCHOOL DEMOGRAPHICS
Marshalltown High School
Marshalltown, Iowa

Students: 1,641

Grades: 9–12

Gender:
Male	53.0%
Female	47.0%

Race and Ethnicity:
Black / African American	3.5%
Hispanic / Latino	17.0%
Asian / Pacific Islander	2.0%
American Indian	0.5%
White / Caucasian	77.0%

Socioeconomics:
Free / Reduced Lunch	33.4%

In my classroom, teaching and learning are reciprocal, participatory, and student centered. I personalize assessment by asking my students to rigorously reflect in writing evidence for their assertions.

The core objectives of the leadership-building communications course are no longer to develop effective communicators per se but effective communicators who:

1. Apply interpersonal skills to group interaction;
2. Know and are able to use procedures for group decision making; and
3. Adapt to the needs of a particular audience and situation.

The Partnership Project: Learning to Partner with One Other

To *effectively apply interpersonal skills to group interaction*, adolescents (as well as adults) often need help to shift from self-centeredness toward other-centeredness (sensing others and their needs). I designed the Partnership Project to help them begin to make that shift.

To guide the project, I define a partnership as:

> A process in which two or more parties cooperate and work together. This working together requires communication that leads to the development of shared commitment to a project, a respect for the needs of the partners, and a plan for contributions of all the partners to lead toward the implementation and the shared benefit of a successful project.

The Partnership Project presents the first opportunity within our class for two students to maintain a working relationship for an extended time. I first provide information about effective partner communication, including listening strategies and suggestions for observing the process. Then, after assigning partners, the student pairs start building their partnership through an activity that involves constructing a tower.

The Tower-Building Activity

I supply each team with eight 3-by-5-inch notecards and 30 inches of masking tape. Without using any other equipment, each pair builds a freestanding tower as tall as possible. I ask students to observe how they work together, to note whether they work as equals or slip into leader-helper roles, and to remember what they say to one another as they make decisions while erecting the tower. Afterward, I assign students to reflect in writing their experience communicating with their partners.

Building the tower with a partner gives students a concrete experience to facilitate talking about skills and competencies needed for building partnerships. While building the tower and reflecting on their particular experience, the students practice important social competencies—meeting the expectation of getting along with others while planning and making decisions together.

Developing Partnership Possibilities and Skills

After telling the class about Maslow's hierarchy of needs theory,[1] I ask each partnership to brainstorm project possibilities to meet one of the needs on Maslow's hierarchy for an individual or group outside our classroom, in the school, or in the community. Each partnership writes up the project idea as a proposal, including a goal statement and needs they plan to fulfill. For example, students might create a missing-person poster (need to know and understand), work on creative writing with younger children (need to know and understand, love and belonging need), or visit residents at nursing home (love and belonging need).

I intersperse class time for partnership planning with direct instruction about stages of listening, empathic listening, and interpersonal communications. We do a role-playing activity using scenarios in which students resolve partnership issues with "I" messages, an interpersonal communications technique for reaching solutions to potential conflicts within relationships.

Time-management skills become important in the partnership process, as well. To help partners with collaborative-planning skills, another teacher and I model timeline construction. This involves brainstorming a detailed to-do list, arranging it in sequence, distributing the tasks between the partners, and listing the target date for each item on the list.

Owning and Implementing Projects

Student partners make all the arrangements to implement their projects. While I monitor what they do by knowing their plan and keeping a copy of the timeline, they make all the contacts, obtain supplies (if needed), and arrange to be excused from part of the school day (if necessary). Sometimes a school principal, a business owner, or a community member will contact me with questions, but I am careful to transfer any necessary decision making and revision of plans back to the partners to preserve their ownership of the project. Unless an issue involves a legitimate concern about safety or a serious breach of trust, I don't intervene in their planning.

As students take control of their projects, they bring their own learning styles, skill levels, background experiences, and developmental assets to the planning. The decisions they make vary from partnership to partnership, naturally accommodating individual differences and needs. When students own the projects, they willingly invest energy to meet their goals and enhance their sense of personal power. When I am a guide from the side, the students often go far beyond my expectations.

Reflective Writing for Project Assessment

As a culmination of the project, each partner writes a reflective paper with this stated purpose:

> To reflect on your communication skills as you used them to build a partnership and as you worked with your partner to plan and implement a leadership project.

I ask that students refer back to the definition of partnership and analyze their roles as communicators and partners in planning and implementing their project. In addition to two pages of narration and reflection, the students provide one to two pages of artifacts to document that their role in the partnership and the project goal involved characteristics of good communication and leadership.

The reflective writing not only provides students with a vehicle for self-assessment, it also gives me a means to measure student achievement in skill areas not measured by tests. Through their own written observations of the process, students often best reveal the complex communication skills they've enhanced and the true quality of the project outcome. Their reflections also provide a differentiated assessment appropriate to the variety of students' skill levels and growth within the project experience. In addition, their writing creates readiness that bridges to skills in the next tier of instruction in the second leadership project.

As one Asian female student, who reacted to differences in work styles, put it:

> This was the first project that had ever required me to work and cooperate with a person so unlike myself. My partner's working habits and style were laid back and easy going. My working style usually includes precise and fast-paced working. At first, my partner was unwilling to make any decisions. In response, I tentatively made the decisions by myself and without the agreement of my partner. As the project progressed, I . . . discovered that while I needed to be the leader at times, I could also trust my partner to make the correct decisions.

English language learners who recently moved from Mexico reflected that the projects gave them opportunities to express their ideas. Wrote one boy:

> I always tried to give my few ideas that I had. Sometimes I don't know how to express my ideas. And because of that I felt a little nervous talking in English because I had not used to do that yet. I expressed my ideas and I cooperate doing everything we had to do.

The Work Team Project: Direct Instruction about the Assets

The focus on others' needs during the first project leads naturally toward conversations about needs of adolescents and the asset framework. I assign larger work teams (three to four students) whose first task is to select one of the categories of assets and teach their classmates about it. They use two asset-based publications (*What Teens Need to Succeed* and *Building a Better Me: 40 Ways to Build Your Own Assets*) and make team presentations to the class using visuals for support.[2]

This overview of assets gives a backdrop to their new projects: each team adopts a specific asset and designs and implements a project to build that asset for and with our city's youth. This second project also helps to develop effective speakers and listeners *who know and are able to use procedures for group decision making,* another core objective of the course.

The partnership skills from the first project remain important as students try to work cohesively as a team. In addition, I add another standard for them to achieve, using my synthesized definition for leadership:

> Leadership is the process of influencing yourself and others to reach a goal. It involves using skills, tools, and insight to inspire people to state their ideas, to believe their ideas, and to attempt their ideas. Effective leaders build trust, teamwork, responsibility, enthusiasm, integrity, and tolerance as they guide a group toward a common goal. The ability to communicate—especially to listen—and to understand others' needs allows for shared involvement toward a task. Good leaders help groups make good decisions, assess their strengths and weaknesses, and improve their group process so they can do excellent work.

To pre-assess group process, we start with the classroom activity "Five-Square Puzzle,"[3] which helps students see that self-centered and possessive behaviors block task completion while team-centered behaviors and openness provide the path to team success (see "Cooperating to Build Assets" on page 73).

The "Health-O-Meter" Analysis of Group Skills

The larger work teams need classroom time to brainstorm the possible asset-related projects, to weigh advantages and disadvantages as they arrive at a group decision, and to build a shared vision of their projects. To nudge them toward quality communication, I pull out my "Health-O-Meter," a chart of work team characteristics in three categories: healthy, in danger, and dying (see Handout 4.3: Group Process Health-O-Meter on page 106). I circulate among groups using the chart to reflect upon and build awareness of group skills as well as to monitor group process.

When the teams' project ideas begin to take shape, I ask each team to write its project plan in the format of a legislative proposal. Teams identify their group by asset goal and tell who will do what, when, how, and where. Copies are made for the entire class, and we then incorporate additional communication skill building by using a legislative format for each team to gain approval for its project.

Raising Assets for Youth Congress

An old parliamentary procedure unit[4] took new form and added value in using a legislative format for our "Raising Assets for Youth (R.A.Y.) Congress." During the congress portion of the class, the students represent their work teams as senators who need to persuade the other senators in the chamber to accept their project proposal. Not only do they learn parliamentary procedure during the senate meetings, but they must also prepare and coordinate persuasive speeches to convince their classmates that their project is worthy of the quality standards of the class, that there is a need for building that asset in our community, and that the project will provide the asset they have adopted as their goal.

The format helps students learn that you can refine decision making through opposition. The communication demands of a legislative format also help them

Group Process Health-O-Meter

To analyze and monitor group skills for quality communication, use this Health-O-Meter to chart how well your groups' team members are working together.

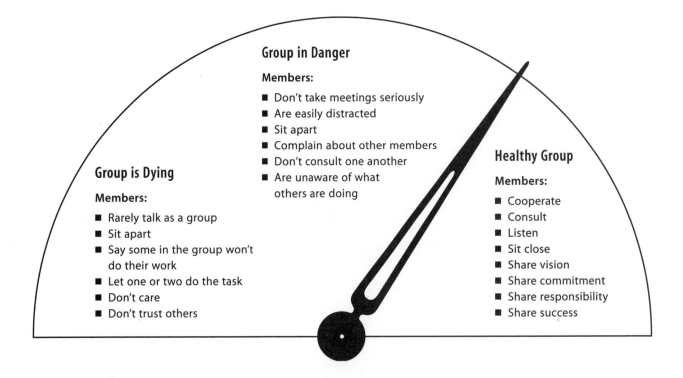

Group in Danger

Members:
- Don't take meetings seriously
- Are easily distracted
- Sit apart
- Complain about other members
- Don't consult one another
- Are unaware of what others are doing

Group is Dying

Members:
- Rarely talk as a group
- Sit apart
- Say some in the group won't do their work
- Let one or two do the task
- Don't care
- Don't trust others

Healthy Group

Members:
- Cooperate
- Consult
- Listen
- Sit close
- Share vision
- Share commitment
- Share responsibility
- Share success

practice and build skills in presenting persuasive arguments, posing and fielding questions, using critical and detailed listening, focusing thinking, clarifying ideas, solving problems to respond to areas of concern, and sensing group process enough to know when to make amendments or to call for a vote.

A simple checklist system motivates participation as students choose among differentiated tasks to earn points toward a grade for congress participation (see Handout 4.4: Your R.A.Y. Congress Grade on page 108). Students learn to present questions and arguments against ideas rather than against individuals. And they can make amendments to improve a project idea. Occasionally, the senators send a proposal back to committee for further revision before it can come to a vote.

The positive outcome of this activity is worth any risk you may feel is involved in giving control over to students. The parliamentary system provides boundaries to keep the activity focused. By investing time and thought in each project through the legislative debate, the entire class has greater interest in each group's success. The work teams generate their own high expectations for classmates to do well. The shared ownership with the class creates an unusual classroom culture in which the students feel accountable to their classmates as much as to me as their teacher and, in my opinion, produces higher-quality projects than we would achieve without the congress.

As with the two-person partnership activities, these group projects also accommodate different abilities and interests by naturally differentiating learning through group decisions. As students in a group begin to shape the project idea, they propose ways to involve each member at levels that meet individual needs.

One such situation involved a student who used a wheelchair and had limited use of his hands. The four-member team, whose goal was caring, wanted to prepare and serve a meal at a homeless shelter, but they recognized that only three of them could carry out that task. The student who couldn't help in the kitchen volunteered to move from table to table in the dining room to interact with the families who came to the meal.

By deliberately looking at ways to differentiate the roles, the group moved beyond using differences as a barrier toward finding a way to involve everyone as a contributor to the team's success. The experience was positive for everyone involved.

Reflective Writing for Project Assessment

The project paper follows guidelines similar to those for the Partnership Project, but I ask students to emphasize teamwork communication and leadership skills. Students focus their individual writings on the team processes and their particular roles as communicators and leaders, both within the team and in doing the work of the team outside of the team. They also analyze whether or not they succeeded in providing the asset their team aimed to achieve. I use a scoring rubric to assess their reflections (see Handout 4.5: Scoring Rubric for Work Team Project on page 109).

One female student's reflective writing gave her a chance to articulate her growing sense of the step-by-step planning process for a project's success. After listing the many ideas that the group brainstormed, she wrote, "Before we could say yes

Your R.A.Y. Congress Grade

This simple checklist motivates students to choose from among a number of differentiated tasks for the R.A.Y. (Raising Assets for Youth) Congress, as well as provides an opportunity to earn points toward a grade for participation. Using a legislative format helps students learn how they can refine decision making through opposition, as well as parliamentary procedure, preparing and delivering persuasive speeches, and the need for building a particular asset.

To qualify for 80 points, complete these tasks:

_____ Participate actively in discussion and decision making within your committee.

_____ Do *one* of the following as a representative of your committee:

- Keyboard the legislative bill and prepare a persuasive visual;
- Give an authorship speech emphasizing the need for your proposal;
- Give a supporting speech emphasizing the benefits of your proposal; or
- Give a supporting speech answering opponents' concerns.

_____ Keep a written record of the motions and amendments, the main reasons given for and against each motion, and the outcome of the votes taken.

To qualify for 90 points, complete these tasks:

_____ Do everything required for 80 points.

_____ Do at least *one* of the following:

- Call the previous question;
- Move to adjourn;
- Move to amend; or
- Make other motions appropriate to the situation.

_____ Do at least *one* of the following:

- Make a one-idea speech supporting another committee's bill; or
- Make a one-idea speech opposing another committee's bill.

To qualify for 100 points, do these tasks:

_____ Do everything required for 90 points.

_____ Make a supporting or opposing speech for another committee's motion that includes:

- An introduction to your position;
- Three or more points;
- Explanations / reasons for each point; and
- A persuasive concluding statement.

Scoring Rubric for Work Team Project

Level 4

The Level 4 Reflection contains all the basic requirements of the Level 3 Reflection (thoughtful analysis and a clear understanding and demonstration of leadership), but it also shows *insight* about your growth as a leader and team worker. You give support that your team's project provided the asset you targeted. You give convincing evidence that: **(1)** you observed your communication and leadership process as you and your work team planned and implemented the project; **(2)** you recognize the ways your involvement fits the definition and characteristics of a healthy group member and effective leader; and **(3)** you can specify how you grew as a communicator / team worker / leader through involvement in the project. Your material is well organized, well written, and presented neatly. Your artifacts are clear and convincing evidence of your involvement in the project as an effective team member, communicator, and leader.

Level 3

The Level 3 Reflection presents clear evidence of your leadership and teamwork skills as applied to your group project. You go beyond indicating what occurred in the narration and reflection to present *a thoughtful analysis* of your role as a leader and team member. You not only assert the use of teamwork and leadership skills and that your work with the project involved several characteristics of leaders and healthy team members, but your analysis and artifacts give clear evidence that you recognize the ways your involvement fits the definition and characteristics of leadership and effectiveness as a team communicator. You give support that your team's project provided the asset you targeted. Your material is well organized, well written, and presented neatly.

Level 2

The Level 2 Reflection shows limited evidence of your leadership and teamwork skills as applied to your group leadership project. Your narration and reflection indicate that you were involved in planning and implementing a project, and the artifacts support that the project occurred. You may assert the use of leadership and teamwork skills but *evidence is sketchy or support for your assertions is missing.* You either do not address or merely mention your goal of building an asset.

Level 1

The Level 1 Reflection gives *little or no evidence of your leadership and teamwork skills* as applied to a group leadership project. You are missing some commentary and / or artifacts shown about your role as a leader / team member.

or no to all of the nice ideas, we had to see if they were feasible, multi-dimensional, and also if they had a worthy goal."

The projects help some students shift from a self-centered to an other-centered view. A white male youth summarized:

> I listened effectively and spoke clearly so I could understand and share with others what needed to be done. I showed growth because before this experience I would not listen very well and tended to be boss. I used to make decisions based on what would be good for me, but to make the project a success, I had to make decisions that would be good for everyone.

The Whole Class Project: Marshaling Consensus

The third leadership project involves the entire class in one project. Students learn consensus-building skills that, in my estimation, demand the most complex communication and decision-making skills in our curriculum. And the project meets another core objective in developing effective communicators who *adapt to the needs of a particular audience and situation.*

Central to the project is the concept of respect for others' views and needs. I use an interactive lesson to teach students about natural differences in perception and the value of using communication to narrow perception gaps (see outlined lesson plan in Handouts 4.6A: Teaching Perception: An Interactive Lesson Plan and 4.6B: Perception and Communication: A Student Graphic Organizer on pages 111–112).

Once the students have an increased understanding of differing perceptions or points of view, we move into a short unit on negotiation skills using collective bargaining units to formulate proposals to solve a candy distribution problem. I also provide instruction about building consensus, using profiles of consensus-building and consensus-blocking behaviors and sample phrases to use when communicating for agreement. (For more on collective bargaining units and profiles of consensus building and blocking, see "Cooperating to Build Assets" on page 73.) We view the movie *Twelve Angry Men*[5] to observe consensus-building and consensus-blocking behaviors of jury members as they decide the fate of someone charged with murder. Students also write essays afterward describing their observations of consensus building and blocking in the movie.

We then move on to two more activities that help students talk about invisible skills with a tangible reference: using plastic building pieces similar to Lego blocks to create structures collaboratively (see again "Cooperating to Build Assets" in Chapter 3).

Community-Based Project Planning

For the final project of the leadership curriculum, the students must meet three specifications: the project must be multidimensional and feasible, and must target a worthy goal (defined as having a positive impact on our community).

Teaching Perception: An Interactive Lesson Plan

Central to a class project is the concept of respect for others' views and needs. This lesson plan helps teach students about natural differences in perception and the value of using communication to narrow perception gaps. Note: To implement this activity, give your students copies of Handout 4.6B: Perception and Communication: A Student Graphic Organizer.

1. Tell a personal story you experienced related to misperception. Or, use this scenario involving flying in the middle seat of a row on an airplane: The person in the window seat wants me to see the mountain or river or canyon below. I can't see what I'm asked to see (even though I lean over and try) because I have a different slant. *Our different physical slants cause us to see different views out of the same window.*

2. Define the term *perception*: perception, the process or act of perceiving, comes from the Old Latin word *perceptus*, the past participle *percipere*, meaning *to perceive*. One definition of perceive is *to achieve understanding of, to apprehend*. The concept of apprehend is related to the Latin combination of *per* and *capere* (meaning *to seize*), or *percipere*. Explain that the class will do an exercise that helps show how the brain "seizes" information.

3. Direct a perception exercise: Ask students to close their eyes and visualize every detail of a tree, then open their eyes and quickly draw the image they visualized (in the square on the graphic organizer). Lead students in a gallery walk to view all the drawings and to find trees that are identical. Although the drawings will generally look similar, they will be more unlike than alike. Explain that even though we all know what a tree looks like, our brains "seize" or pull images out of our individual memory and experience to give us differing perceptions. In this exercise, we have different views of a tree, and *no view is incorrect.*

4. Create a scenario for the class: Imagine being in a room overlooking the student parking lot. After hearing loud yelling outside, everyone runs to different windows to see what is happening below. Two students—one, who is well known, popular, and involved in a lot of school activities; the other, who is not as widely known and more disconnected during common events—are hurling insults at one another. As they are about to get into a fist fight, the school police liaison runs out of the building and intervenes by telling them to come along to the principal's office. Ask students: Do you think you would give identical accounts of what you saw? When students say "No," ask "Why not?" Have them list (in the slanted shape on the graphic organizer) the different "slants" that would affect what they saw: physical slant, emotional slant, experiential slant, previous knowledge, biases, gender, and so forth.

5. Discuss how understanding perception equals communication power. Explain that their role as effective communicators is to narrow perception gaps. While our brains will always "seize" impressions according to our biases or slants, review with students ways (to list in the plus shape on the organizer) they can work to help avoid misperceptions during consensus building:

- Make yourself clear.
- Listen and paraphrase to understand.
- Recognize differences with respect.
- Communicate to find similarities.
- Ask specific questions to clarify vague information.
- Move toward mutual understanding. (Students will list these five ways to narrow the perception gaps in the plus shape on the graphic organizer.)

Perception and Communication: A Student Graphic Organizer

Your role as a communicator and consensus builder is to narrow perception gaps.

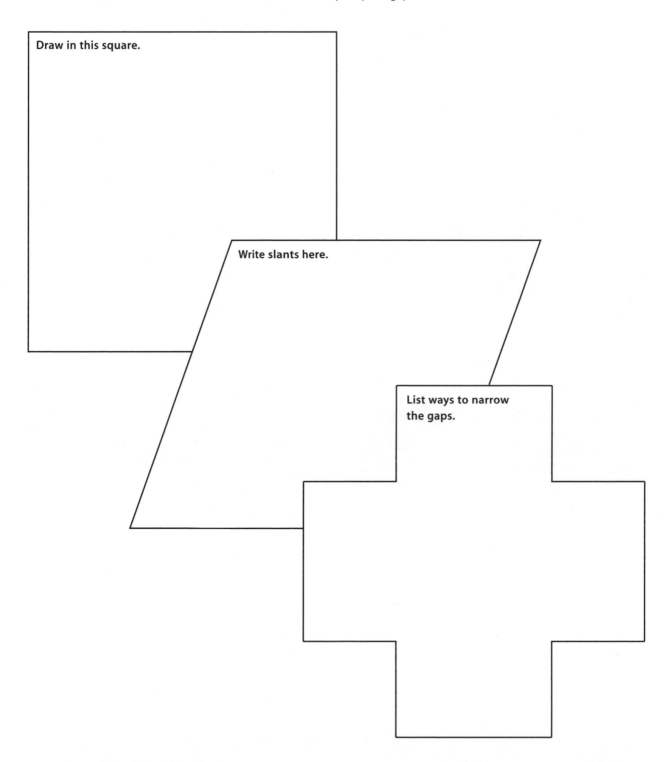

Draw in this square.

Write slants here.

List ways to narrow the gaps.

I guide the students through the beginning, structuring their discussion using De Bono's six thinking hats,[6] a problem-solving technique using the metaphor of different colored hats for different stages in a decision-making process. Once the class achieves consensus on a project idea, they clarify plans, develop timelines, and form committees in an interactive network requiring trust and responsibility.

These projects demand high involvement; every student assumes a role. Differing goals and diverse student needs shape the projects. As the students delegate tasks among themselves, they assign responsibilities to fit each individual's ability to perform in a context that is challenging to all but that also supports the group structure, if problems occur. Students who have social networks in the community usually volunteer to make the external contacts and serve as liaisons between their committees and the outside group. Those who prefer hands-on involvement find themselves making posters, puppets, or paper chains, or painting signs. Others use writing skills to compose brochures. Those who have stronger technology skills gravitate to those tasks that involve Web design, videotaping and editing, or charting survey results.

Some classes have created partnerships with children to improve literacy; others have worked to improve intergenerational communication through visits with elderly populations in care centers. One class worked with a community group to support a bond issue for an aquatic facility; another developed and performed skits to promote tolerance for middle school students. (For another teacher's experience promoting a class-based community project, see "Celebrating Folklore: Collecting and Publishing a Community's Stories" on page 114.)

Reflective Writing as Project Assessment

As with earlier projects, reflective writing helps the students process and analyze skills they've used and learned, and assess whether the project achieved the goal. Their responses vary according to their skill level and degree of insight they have developed. Collectively, however, their writings reveal patterns of self-discovery and achievement of complex skills. In addition, their reflections support Search Institute's research that service learning contributes to asset building, especially in enhancing aspects of personal identity.[7]

Students' responses after this project often show awareness that by doing something for others they benefit themselves. After working with 6th graders to increase involvement in after-school activities, one student wrote: "I felt really good about this project. Not only did I make a difference in their lives, but they also made an impact on mine."

Breaking down social, economic, and racial barriers and an increased understanding of differing perspectives are among the most powerful effects of the projects. "I never thought we were going to decide because a few people were keeping ideas alive just to be difficult," wrote a different student about consensus building. "But I realized later on my opinion wouldn't have changed if I hadn't heard people's feelings on the ideas. I wouldn't have been open to the nursing home visit and would have been less enthusiastic about it."

Celebrating Folklore: Collecting and Publishing a Community's Stories

H. WALLACE GODDARD, PH.D.
Extension Family Life Specialist
University of Arkansas Cooperative Extension
Little Rock, Arkansas

In rural eastern Utah in the mid-1970s, high school teacher H. Wallace Goddard was invited by a progressive language arts specialist in the school district office to develop a folklore magazine with his students. "I was young enough to undertake the task glibly," he recalls. "With today's technology, the tasks would be much easier." Most significantly, this classroom-based community project wholeheartedly supports numerous assets and content areas.

Most teens see the older members of their community as tired relics of days gone by. They rarely glimpse the full drama behind each lined face.

I sent students who signed up for my class out to interview old-timers in our community. Pairs of students collected stories from pioneer settlers, poems from a cowboy poet, knowledge about the art of paper cutting from a retired craftsperson, a collection of songs from a one-time entertainer, and a history of remote settlements from descendants of those settlers. Some of the students interviewed their grandparents and great-grandparents.

I provided the students basic training in journalism and layout. The students typed up their stories, designed the layouts, took pictures, and organized the first 52-page issue of *Tamarack: The Uintah Basin in the Making*.[1] We sold 1,000 copies in only a few weeks through local stores. The passing of the years has made those books even more valuable.

The project worked magic beyond our expectations. The students were delighted to see their work in print. The community was enriched by the commemoration of its elders. But, most important of all, the students came back from their interviews celebrating their aged neighbors as conquering heroes: "Did you know that Mr. Curtis was a football star?" "Can you believe Mrs. Smith's cutting?" "Have you seen Mr. Johnstun's woodworking?" "Have you seen the Bullock collection?" The students were regularly amazed.

In a second issue (84 pages) of *Tamarack*,[2] the students contrasted the stories of the high school's first student body president (more than 50 years previous) with the most recent president. They even included details from a decades-old teacher's contract. They unearthed pictures of some of the community's earliest schools. They continued the stories about local history, architecture, and lifestyle.

It is hard to imagine an activity that could cultivate a broader set of assets than involving students in collecting and publishing their community's stories. The students were connected to caring adults and neighborhoods. They had opportunities both to serve and to be appreciated by the community. They were connected with adult role models. They were involved in a valued, creative activity. Their care increased for previously neglected or scorned members of the community, as did their appreciation for people who have a different cultural and historical background. They felt a renewed purpose for their own lives embedded in a larger picture of generational humanity.

Today, with wide availability of computers, students can produce high-quality work more easily than ever. Copy machines can produce respectable volumes. Or students can publish Web material or articles in local papers.

Focusing on other subjects besides community folklore and local history is also of value for students: current culture, creative writing, family history, even investigative reporting on community issues. Yet hooking up students with generations before them provides a unique payoff: they come to appreciate the stories and gifts of older people.

One of the students' favorite subjects was Sue Watson, then in her 80s but still riding her bike around town. The students returned repeatedly to her home to hear her stories and admire her rock collection. They often took classmates—and their teacher—with them. Her spunk and energy amazed and fascinated all.

The students and I published two volumes of *Tamarack* before I was assigned to other projects. I miss that project. I would do it again.

Notes

1. Uintah School District. (1976). *Tamarack: The Uintah Basin in the Making.* Vernal, UT: Uintah School District.
2. Uintah School District. (1976). *Tamarack: The Uintah Basin in the Making,* Vol. 2. Vernal, UT: Uintah School District.

Another white female student wrote: "Even when people are not close friends and don't always see eye to eye, by listening and respecting each other's thoughts and opinions, they can come together to achieve a common goal." A Native American male student took the idea further: "At the beginning, we were different people coming from different backgrounds who might have looked at each other a little differently. Then, at the end of our project, we were able to relate to one another and even able to possibly call each other friends."

For some students, the projects even help them gain a positive view of their personal future. One reflected:

> Our team evolved greatly from this project. It made us more trusting because each of us had big responsibilities, and we had to trust others outside the group, not just ourselves. I also believe it made us stronger as people fighting to help others. After my mom died, I had little faith and didn't believe in happiness or miracles, and this project just showed me that little things like this go so far and give so much hope and inspiration.

The patterns that emerge in the students' reflections authenticate that their learning is about more than complex communication skills. The projects all also provide the added value of helping youth develop assets to succeed in school and beyond.

Notes

1. Maslow, Abraham, and Lowry, Richard (eds.). (1998). *Toward a Psychology of Being*, 3rd ed. New York: Wiley & Sons.
2. Benson, Peter L., Galbraith, Judy, and Espeland, Pamela. (1998). *What Teens Need to Succeed: Proven, Practical Ways to Shape Your Own Future*. Minneapolis: Free Spirit Publishing; Lutheran Brotherhood. (1999). *Building a Better Me: 40 Ways to Build Your Own Assets*. Minneapolis: Lutheran Brotherhood.
3. Kester, Kyra, et al. (July 1996). Five-Square Exercise. *Applied Communication Guidelines*. Washington State Department of Instruction. Kester and the Washington State Department of Education document their source as: Edited and adapted by Margaret M. Beilke, Ph.D., Central Washington University from *Communications and Human Relations Activities for Work Adjustment*, Utah State Board for Vocational Education, 1977; and *The Squares #, Human Relations Experiment Project*, by Dr. Donald O. Clifton, President. Selection Research Incorporated, University of Nebraska, citing Bavelas, Communication Patterns in Task Oriented Groups, *Journal of the Acoustical Society of America*, 1950, 22:725–730.
4. Zimmerman, Doris. (1997). *Robert's Rules in Plain English*. New York: HarperCollins.
5. *Twelve Angry Men*. (1997). Directed by William Friedkin. Performed by Jack Lemmon, George C. Scott, Tony Danza, and others. Videocassette. Orion Home Video.
6. De Bono, Edward. (1999). *Six Thinking Hats*. Boston: Back Bay Books.
7. Roehlkepartain, Eugene C., Bright, Thomas, and Margolis-Rupp, Beth. (2000). *An Asset Builder's Guide to Service-Learning*. Minneapolis: Search Institute.

Other Resources

Amodeo, John, and Wentworth, Kris. (1995). Self-Revealing Communication: A Vital Bridge between Two Worlds, in John Steward (ed.), *Bridges Not Walls*, 6th ed. New York: McGraw-Hill. This source includes information about "I" messages.

Mosaic Youth Center Board of Directors with Jennifer Griffin-Wiesner. (2001). *Step by Step! A Young Person's Guide to Positive Community Change*. Minneapolis: Search Institute and Mosaic Youth Center.

Search Institute. (1999). *An Asset Builder's Guide to Youth Leadership*. Minneapolis: Search Institute.

Creating Adaptations

You can adapt the leadership curriculum to any class in which you use collaborative learning strategies and student-driven projects. Design the activities to fit specific goals related to your class content—environmental projects for science, local and regional projects for history, design projects for art—or to any course in which you involve your students in community service or service learning. After-school programs, school clubs, young people's organizations, intergenerational service clubs, and church youth groups can also use parts of or all the curriculum. To support the process and aid student success, be sure to include time for skill building.

From Tragedy to Hope

ADDRESSING REAL-LIFE ISSUES IN *ROMEO AND JULIET*

AMY ALMENDINGER, M.ED.

English Teacher (grades 11–12)

New Richmond High School

New Richmond, Wisconsin

Like many sensitive issues that hit close to home, teen suicide is something students would like to believe—and perhaps also teachers and administrators—doesn't happen in their school. Sometimes students' outward reactions come off as less than serious, maybe as a defense mechanism to stay one step removed from the issue.

I had been teaching William Shakespeare's *Romeo and Juliet* in English 9 for about eight years when I first came up with the idea to address within that unit the contemporary issues of teen suicide, family communication, depression, and decision making. Applying the strategies of suicide intervention to literary characters—especially within the framework of the developmental assets—allows students to remove themselves one layer from reality *more productively*. It gives them a chance to experiment with options that they might be reluctant to face when dealing directly with their own lives or those of their friends.

Literature classes, really any language arts classroom at any level, are a natural fit for taking the assets "off the wall" and incorporating them directly into the curriculum. In the literature courses we teach at New Richmond High School, we commonly examine the assets of the characters in the books and short stories we read and discuss: How do the assets lend resiliency to the characters? Or how do the lack of assets affect their lives? We project "what if" scenarios and rewrite characters' lives as if they used their assets. We also talk about how each character could develop more assets to improve her or his situation. Students get a good understanding of the asset philosophy and see the powerful effects without first having to look at themselves, which can sometimes be too much to handle. Once students

SCHOOL DEMOGRAPHICS

New Richmond High School
New Richmond, Wisconsin

Students: 771

Grades: 9–12

Gender:

Male	48.00%
Female	52.00%

Race and Ethnicity:

Black / African American	0.13%
Hispanic / Latino	0.91%
Asian / Pacific Islander	1.81%
American Indian	0.26%
White / Caucasian	96.63%
Other	0.26%

Socioeconomics:

Free / Reduced Lunch	9.50%

are more comfortable with the issues at hand, we move discussion and writing on the topic to their own lives in a more meaningful and safe way.

The assets we emphasize in literature projects vary greatly and somewhat depend on the piece of literature. The assets a particular character already has and those strongly needed also vary from character to character. Similarly, student participation can vary with the personality of the class.

The sensitivity of the content in *Romeo and Juliet* merits particular consideration. Students who are reluctant to share, no matter what the subject, certainly won't choose this to be the topic to spill their guts on. Key to the lesson's success is partnering with the guidance department or counselor as well as timing when in the year you do this lesson.

How Do We Help Young People Get More Comfortable?

Although the majority of the projects in the entire unit address language arts curriculum, this specific *Romeo and Juliet* lesson covers important concepts in the guidance curriculum for which the counselors would otherwise have to find a place. In the case of the *Romeo and Juliet* project, key assets (or the lack thereof) that affect the life-and-death decisions Romeo and Juliet make include family support, positive family communication, adult role models, positive peer influence, restraint, planning and decision making, peaceful conflict resolution, personal power, and positive view of personal future. Fortunately, our very strong guidance department was most willing to address some of their curriculum in collaboration with ours. As a result, the *Romeo and Juliet* lesson is also a prime example of curriculum integration.

I collaborated directly with Marilyn Peplau, a guidance counselor who had worked in the district for a number of years; she has a strong background in literature herself and is a trainer for Search Institute. I approached her with the idea of developing a lesson together. Within a few days, she had reread the play, earmarked key passages, and come back to me with some preliminary ideas to get us started.

We agreed to team teach the lesson rather than just have a guidance counselor come in as a guest speaker. So much of high school students' days are pegged to particular subjects that they don't make connections from one class to the next. We wanted to make sure they understood that there were natural, real-life connections to literature.

Our major objectives were to:

- Show the relevance of issues within *Romeo and Juliet* to current youth society; and
- Help youth shift from engaging in at-risk behaviors to adopting "at-promise" behaviors.

Applying all areas of language arts (speaking, listening, reading, and writing), our language arts objectives included analyzing literature through a universal lens and relating literature to daily student life.

You can conduct the entire lesson in two traditional class periods or one block period. You can also expand it to incorporate more time for student investigation and performance.

Keep in mind, though, that in addition to approaching the topic with the collaborative professional knowledge of a guidance counselor, the point in the year at which you choose to do this particular lesson is also significant. Students' ability to share personal stories of suicidal feelings or instances they have faced with family and friends relates mostly to their comfort level with the people in the room rather than to other factors. If you do the unit far enough into the semester, then students are more likely to be comfortable with their classmates and student input can be intense.

The Lesson

Since we originally developed this idea eight years ago, at least eight faculty members have been involved in facilitating the lesson directly. In addition, several student teachers and interns have worked with us. The lesson works best when those facilitating it adapt it to their personal experience and use their own anecdotes and stories. It is important, too, that both parties involved with the instruction discuss the objectives to ensure that the intent of the lesson is consistent. The lesson is strongest if you truly team teach it, sharing responsibilities and engaging in natural discussion and handoffs.

Keep in mind that the immediate student response to the lesson is not always an accurate reflection of its effect on them. Because our school population is rather homogeneous, it is difficult to say if the race, culture, or ethnicity of students would affect its success. In terms of gender differences, girls seem to take the subject matter more seriously, but they tend to no matter what the subject. Current juniors and seniors often refer to their experience with this unit as freshmen. They remember doing the activities, learning the basics of warning signs, and reviewing what to do and not to do. Their comments one to two years later clearly reflect a level of effectiveness that is not apparent when the lesson is initially taught.

Instruction in the lesson includes cooperative learning and strategies that employ some of the latest brain research as well as attending to learning styles. For example, some aspects of the lesson involve small group work and changing the type of activity every 10 to 15 minutes, enabling students to physically move around the room with those activities. Making personal connections with material is also a brain-based instructional strategy that increases memory. In addition, the lesson addresses a number of learning styles since it incorporates reading, writing, listening, speaking, responding to others, functioning with a small group, collaborating with a partner, discussing as a class, and working alone. By incorporating walk-and-talk discussions or role playing, you can customize the lesson for students who are stronger kinesthetic learners.

Any time a student can find relevance in content, the chance of her or his understanding it and remembering it is greater. For this reason, this lesson has important academic implications beyond the academic skills and what the students produce (a writing piece, class discussion, literary analysis). By bringing to life a 500-year-old play and showing its universality to 21st-century teenagers, we open their eyes to other pieces of literature that they may read in the future and the relevance they bring to people's lives.

This lesson also bridges work with assets and character development to other pieces of literature and, in turn, to real-life situations. You can easily relate more than half of the 40 developmental assets to this project, or choose to focus on the ones your students need most and are least addressed elsewhere in the curriculum. By devoting an extensive lesson to the application of assets to a fictional character, we develop an effective framework that you can use in numerous ways in future lessons.

The following discussion outlines the basic lesson as Marilyn and I developed it over the course of about five years.

Share a True-Life Example

Marilyn Peplau begins the lesson with a true-life example from New Richmond High School:

> A student came to her and reported seeing a drawing of a tombstone on the wall in the women's bathroom. The birth date on the tombstone indicated that it could have been a current student, and the death date was one day in the future. After going through student records, Peplau was able to pinpoint the birth date to two specific high school girls. She questioned the girls, one of whom admitted not only that she had made the drawing but also that she had a plan to kill herself. Peplau addressed the situation further with the student and her parents, and the girl did not attempt the planned suicide. Fortunately, the student who had informed Peplau of seeing the tombstone drawing had been observant, insightful, and concerned enough to contact a guidance counselor. She may have saved a fellow student's life.

This anecdote confirms the very real issue of teen suicide in the halls of New Richmond High School. Since we first developed the lesson, two of our students have committed suicide. We now have to do less to convince students that teen suicide is a realistic contemporary issue. But we still have to do more to convince youth that teen suicide is not a wise planning and decision-making option.

Clues to Watch For

Once we have made the topic relevant to our students, we examine a continuum that lists clues indicating increasing levels of self-destructive behavior to watch for. Then we go directly to the text of *Romeo and Juliet*, finding examples of those clues and determining where on the continuum the characters Romeo and Juliet fall at different times in the play. At this point, we also discuss deficiencies that the main characters experience in asset 1, family support, and asset 2, positive family communication. We address the two assets as general topics, choosing to introduce the concept of 40 developmental assets later in the lesson. Because of the extensive work our district does with the assets, most students are somewhat familiar with the asset concept and the list.

You can do this step together as a class or divide the text between groups with each exploring a particular act and/or scene. Students share their findings and, as a class, determine that the play has many signs pointing to the double suicide that other characters missed or ignored.

How to Intervene

Once students determine that many warning signs flourish in the play, we introduce the idea of intervention. Our 9th graders have done work with Latin prefixes and roots, so I use this as an opportunity to have them define the word with that strategy: *inter = between* and *ven = come*.

We discuss how "coming between" a potential suicide situation can stop it from happening. Students then create individual acronyms using the word *stop* that will help them remember what they can do to intervene in a suicidal situation. They share their ideas with the class.

While we have established that suicides happen, warning signs are often prevalent, and interventions can save lives, we are also careful to emphasize that there *are* situations beyond our control. We do not want students to impose unnecessary guilt upon themselves because they were unable to prevent a suicide. With this in mind, we go through a list of "What to Do" and "What Not to Do." Students take turns reading the list items out loud, and instructors and students elaborate when appropriate.

We introduce the acronym SALT as a test for students to use when they face what they believe is suicidal intent:

- **S** stands for specificity of the plan;
- **A** for availability of the "weapon" (or method);
- **L** for lethality of the weapon; and
- **T** for time indicated.

We direct students who know of a youth who has a specific plan with an available lethal weapon to be very concerned. Asking the suicidal youth, "When *had* you thought of doing this?" reframes the planned act in the past—but discovers the fourth element of SALT—time! If the suicidal youth has selected a date, we instruct students attempting to intervene to get help for the youth immediately and *not* to leave her or him alone.

Connecting to the Characters

The next part of the lesson is the most important because it forces students themselves to come up with options that Romeo and Juliet could have taken to save their lives. It also gives students an opportunity to give the other characters a chance to "save" the main characters' lives—to change the asset richness of their experiences. At this point, we more formally introduce students to and distribute copies of the list of the 40 developmental assets.

We assign a character to pairs of students who are to find places in the play's text where their character has a "fatal missing asset." Student pairs change their character's behaviors (words and actions), speculating on different outcomes that could have occurred had the character possessed the missing asset. For example, if Romeo and Juliet had communicated positively with their family, they could have been honest with their parents about their marriage. Or, if Mercutio had been able to resolve his conflict peacefully with Tybalt, he would not have fought him. The pairs share their speculations orally with the class and then write them up using sound writing techniques.

You could choose to have your students role-play their speculations instead. Dramatic role playing provides a more kinesthetic approach, variety in the class period, and another learning mode.

We broaden the issues next to address some dangerous tendencies other than suicide. Together, the class labels different types of at-risk behavior found in high school students today as well as in the teenage characters of the play: impulsive behavior, aggressive male ego development, bonding too tightly with friends, extreme mood swings, inability to communicate with parents, seeing issues as wrong or right (not recognizing gray areas), and weak sense of morality are some of those tendencies. We encourage students to move from *at-risk* to *at-promise* behaviors by identifying the assets they currently have and the ones they would be able to develop. You can shorten or lengthen this discussion as time permits.

Finally, as homework, we ask students to complete the decision-making chart that lists different scenarios in the play (see Handout 4.7: Think Before You Act: A Decision-Making Chart for *Romeo and Juliet* on page 123). Students are to come up with the best option and the worst option each character has in a particular situation and then determine which assets he or she could draw on to deal with that situation.

By discussing the need for the characters to build additional assets, students learn that they can build assets as well. The characters' negative circumstances and relatedness to a lack of assets show students that all young people need assets. Relationships are key to the teenage characters' lives—and to our teenage students' lives. Relating character life to student life provides an opportunity for discussing consistent messages, and in the English classroom provides repetition of messages students have heard through the guidance department, as well as other classes. By determining which assets fictional characters would benefit from, we help our youth investigate the ongoing process of asset building.

Think Before You Act: A Decision-Making Chart for *Romeo and Juliet*

Throughout Romeo and Juliet, *many of the characters act before they think. This failure to examine options before deciding how to proceed often leads to undesirable consequences. Examine the following characters in the given situations. Complete the chart to show an option the character could have taken, the best-case result, the worst-case result, and the developmental asset he or she could have drawn on to produce a more positive outcome.*

Character	Act, Scene	Situation	Option	Best Case	Worst Case	Asset
Tybalt	I, 5	Wants to fight Romeo the "party crasher"				
Juliet	II, 2	Declares her love to Romeo				
Romeo and **Juliet**	II, 2	Agree to marry				
Friar	II, 4	Agrees to marry Romeo and Juliet				
Romeo and Juliet	II, 6	Marry				
Mercutio	III, 1	Fights Tybalt				
Romeo	III, 1	Fights and kills Tybalt				

Character	Act, Scene	Situation	Option	Best Case	Worst Case	Asset
Juliet	III, 5	Refuses to marry Paris				
Juliet	IV, 3	Takes potion				
Romeo	V, 1	Leaves for Verona with poison				
Romeo	V, 3	Kills Paris				
Romeo	V, 3	Kills self				
Friar	V, 3	Leaves Juliet in tomb				
Juliet	V, 3	Kills self				

Creating Adaptations

You could easily adapt this lesson for 9th graders to a different grade level of students who have read the same play or to students who have read any piece of literature dealing with teen suicide. With the exception of the specific examples from the play, you would have very little to change.

Similarly, in a social studies or science classroom, you can apply the asset lens to real-life historical figures or scientists. Investigating biographical information about nonfiction characters can also illuminate how assets each person had aided, or could have aided, her or his success. By comparing such individuals' assets with students' assets, you can identify true role models and heroes.

If you wish to focus further on the specific issues of teen suicide and dangerous tendencies of youth, consider pursuing the topics at a parent forum or evening seminar. For example, students could follow up their work with Romeo and Juliet to create evening roundtable discussions with parents. Students could serve as resources to teach their parents the signs to watch for, what to do and what not to do, as well as discuss issues concerning positive family communication in small groups of parents and students. If the students organize and facilitate the program, it may bring a higher level of credibility than if faculty put it together.

Compelling College Candidates

CREATING MEANING IN PREPARING APPLICATIONS

STEPHANIE KARNO, M.S.

English Teacher (grades 10, 12)

New Richmond High School

New Richmond, Wisconsin

Relating academics to students' real lives can be life-saving, not only for the here and now, as the preceding author points out, but also for the future. Connecting academics to real-life affairs that are life altering can also be opportunities for positive recognition. Helping students address their confusions and fears about their future, as well as the planning required for it, is no easy task. To assist seniors in getting admitted to colleges and obtaining scholarships, Stephanie Karno designed a college preparatory unit that infuses the developmental assets in a way that helps students gain a sense of personal power and purpose while they write a high-quality college entrance essay.

SCHOOL DEMOGRAPHICS
New Richmond High School
New Richmond, Wisconsin

Students: 771

Grades: 9–12

Gender:
Male	48.00%
Female	52.00%

Race and Ethnicity:
Black / African American	0.13%
Hispanic / Latino	0.91%
Asian / Pacific Islander	1.81%
American Indian	0.26%
White / Caucasian	96.63%
Other	0.26%

Socioeconomics:
Free / Reduced Lunch	9.50%

With the schedules our students keep, I felt they needed time and opportunity not just to reflect on their futures but also to learn something useful as they prepared. As a result of my school's work with the developmental assets model, I decided to create a unit that would develop students' assets—to gain valuable insights about themselves, about their relationships with others, and about the transitions through which they are about to move—as well as teach them skills to complete effective applications and get accepted into a college. The unit benefits the students (quite beyond my original expectations) in three particular areas by providing:

- Time *in school* to work on college applications;
- A positive turning point in relationships with their parents; and
- A therapeutic process for facing their fears and frustrations about the future.

The College / Scholarship Application Unit

The objectives of the unit, which is part of our College Prep English curriculum offered during fall semester of the senior year, include:

1. Develop assets of students.
2. Show students the value of the assets in their lives and the lives of others.

3. Develop writing skills: formal essay and writing process.
4. Create college applications and essays that will ensure acceptance into desired programs.
5. Create scholarship applications and essays that will earn students scholarships.
6. Prepare students for writing at the college level.

By the end of the unit, students must complete application forms and essays for a minimum of two colleges or universities and for two scholarships. If the college or university for which they apply does not have an essay requirement, students must still write an essay, choosing from a list of essay topics, to build the skills on which this unit focuses. Students also create a portfolio of their journey through College Prep, where they keep all their work (self-inventories, parent/adult surveys, journals, drafts/revisions, and other items).

The VIP Survey

As a part of the unit, students need to use family members to provide insight and support. Students ask their parents and other adult family members to complete the VIP (Very Important Person) survey at the beginning of the unit. This survey helps the students develop ideas for answering college and scholarship application questions.

The survey is the main vehicle—and my favorite part of the unit—through which students gather perspectives about themselves from others. (My favorite question asks parents to relate stories about their children that provide insight into their personalities.) The students weave into their essays the insights they acquire through the survey. We ask parents to support their children in meeting deadlines and choosing appropriate venues for their essays and scholarships. In addition, we invite parents to help in the revision and celebration stages of the project.

Students enjoy getting information and input from their parents. For some, the project even facilitates a positive turning point in relationships. When a number of students turned their VIP surveys in to me, they shared stories of how they had laughed and even cried with their parents as they completed this activity. Many of the students had tears in their eyes as they described their experience.

- Aaron's mom wrote a note to her son on the end of the survey expressing her pride in the man he has become. She let him know how she appreciated his decisions connected to home, church, school, and more—the type of note you wish every child could receive from his parents.
- Erika's mom wrote about how in elementary school Erika had gone to the store on her bike to get some groceries, but even after wiping out on her bike and breaking her arm, she still managed to deliver the groceries home. The message was clear: Erika has always been a responsible person who follows through on what she starts.

Stories such as these contribute to students feeling heightened personal power, and consequently also enhance their essays greatly. As one of the students, Meghan, put it:

> One of the most important people I got to know was myself! I was almost embarrassed with what my dad wrote in my VIP survey, not because it was anything bad, but because it was describing so many good things about me. One of the biggest stress relievers was the time we took for college applications, essays, and scholarship stuff. If I'd had to do that on my own time, I probably still wouldn't be done!

In learning to write quality essays, students discover how to write more than a basic piece that begins, "My name is. . . ." Students are pleased with the increased quality of their essays, as well. As another student, Lars, expressed:

> One of the most important things that I learned this year was how to write scholarship essays. Being able to write a thoughtful poem may be useful once I am in college or once I am trying to win over a girl's heart, but as for real life right now, I need to know how to write an effective scholarship essay. I always thought that when writing a scholarship essay a person was supposed to brag about himself the whole time, writing all about life's greatest accomplishments. Now, I have learned that a person should write an interesting story that will be remembered by the reader, not something that is the same as everyone else.

One of the unexpected extras that emerged from this project was the students using their parents' stories about them in other unit work. Many of these stories resurfaced in a later unit based on reading Sandra Cisneros's *House on Mango Street*. Students were required to write vignettes modeled after the ones in the novel. I was amazed how many of the students chose stories connected to those their parents told on the VIP survey.

More Asset Connections

In addition to emphasizing family support and other adult relationships, the unit incorporates other developmental assets in the very nature of the application process. To start with, recognizing well the stress college and scholarship applications and essays create for seniors, our department added this unit to facilitate our students' needs, especially time in school to work on their applications. Students' lives are so extremely busy, and incorporating their efforts into a class decreased their stress levels. Some students say it greatly decreases their parents' stress levels as well. The unit also inherently helps students engage with school during their senior year, a time they often struggle to stay focused.

Additionally, as part of promoting a caring school climate, we send an e-mail to all school personnel informing them of the project and inviting them to contribute support through written comments about any and all students in the class with whom they have a relationship. Following the unit, the seniors plan and present what they've learned to the 8th-grade English classes as a service to others.

We expect students to complete all assigned work, do a quality job on each piece, and meet all deadlines. To facilitate this, we create deadlines, checklists, and rubrics as part of the course. The students, though, also help develop their own timelines for requesting the college and scholarship applications they will use, letters of recommendation, financial aid information, and other items they need to help them meet the timeline. Requiring students to gather information from various colleges and universities imbues students with a sense of purpose in the assignment because of the way in which it relates to their own lives and futures.

Students need to complete particular pieces of the project, such as the VIP survey, outside of class. In addition, drafting, revising, and editing the essays all become part of homework responsibilities.

Self-discovery is an important result of their work, both using feedback from and to other students, as well as from a variety of self-inventories, such as the Myers-Briggs Type Indicator,[1] the list of 40 developmental assets, and a career inventory. As Meghan expressed:

> Perhaps one of the most important things I learned in college prep this semester
> was about myself and about life skills. I have gotten to respect my classmates for
> their opinions and beliefs, and I know I must accept people for who they are.

Learning Skills for Life

A remarkable aspect of the unit is its ability to allow students to see that they, individually, are not the only ones confused and frustrated about the future and the planning required for it. Some brave students share that they are flat-out scared, no matter what front they appear to put up, and this allows their classmates to admit their fears as well and deal with them as a group. Through evaluations required as a part of their semester final, students collectively indicate that they feel the unit is not only worthwhile but also "life saving," as one student put it.

The students helped me appreciate that what I felt in my gut about the incredible "extras" this unit did was truly a part of the students' realities. I know some relationships between parents and their sons or daughters are better. Although I work hard to get to know my students, I know these young people even better than others from the past because of what they shared and admitted and reflected upon. As Jessica voiced enthusiastically:

> The time that we spent on college essays, scholarships, and applications really
> helped me to feel like it was really going to happen. A lot of my life I felt like
> I was going to be nobody. I was going to end up with no education after high
> school and in a dead-end job with 16 kids. After talking to Mr. Whitwam and
> finding out what my options were, I found out that I may actually have a chance

at life. I got really psyched but I still couldn't pay for college. So, for College Prep [class], I looked through at least a million scholarships for the ones I could apply for.

A number of our students have not only been admitted to the schools to which they applied but they have received scholarships as well.

———

Notes

1. Briggs, Katharine C., and Myers, Isabel Briggs. (1998). *Myers-Briggs Type Indicator*. Palo Alto, CA: Consulting Psychologists Press.

Other Resources

We used the following resources to provide students with examples of essays to emulate:

Curry, Boykin, and Kasbar, Brian. (1990). *Essays That Worked: 50 Essays from Successful Applications to the Nation's Top Colleges*. New York: Ballantine Books.

For edits and critiques of sample college essays, see the Web site accessed November 11, 2002: www.essayedge.com/promo/samplework.shtml.

Creative Writing with an Asset Theme

PAMELA N. WIDMANN

Language Arts Teacher (grades K–7)

Cherry Creek School District

Aurora, Colorado

Teaching creative writing to 4th- and 5th-grade (or any grade) students provides an easy opportunity to infuse the asset approach. The eight asset categories themselves are ideal themes for any student, alone or with classmates, to develop characters and plot lines for an original story that has personal meaning.

Typically, I select one asset category as the theme for the story assignment. I encourage students to relate the theme to their life experiences and to literature they have read previously. We discuss the meaning of themes in literature as well as the personal meaning of the selected asset category before beginning to make up our own story, depending on the genre selected (e.g., folk tale, autobiography), through brainstorming and outlining activities, collaboration, and actual writing.

Creative writing allows for the spirit of play, in addition to helping students learn to think. Teachers, too, express delight in discovering their own creativity in the classroom and their surprise at finding student talents not previously revealed.

One of my goals as a teacher is to help students learn to think. To think is to take information presented and connect it to previous knowledge and personal experience and apply it in a new way, to turn an acquired skill into useful knowledge. Thinking involves subjective and objective reasoning, the ability to weigh opposing opinions and information, and piggyback on information presented, inventing original, creative ideas. In teaching creative writing and giving students an opportunity to strive for higher-level thinking, I use a variety of strategies, alongside asset building: whole class instruction and discussion, on-your-feet creative involvement, small cooperative learning groups, and independent work and presen-

SCHOOL DEMOGRAPHICS

Cherry Creek School District
Aurora, Colorado

Students: 44,228

Grades: K–12

Gender:

Male	51.0%
Female	49.0%

Race and Ethnicity:

Black / African American	10.0%
Hispanic / Latino	8.0%
Asian / Pacific Islander	6.0%
American Indian	0.5%
White / Caucasian	75.5%

Socioeconomics:

Free / Reduced Lunch	11.8%

tation. I use the asset framework and language explicitly in my instructions, responses, expectations, and classroom management.

Brainstorming in Multiple Learning Modes

The instructional strategies I use incorporate training I have received on Carol Ann Tomlinson's standards-based teaching and differentiation.[1] Her description of differentiation as a way of thinking about teaching and learning has influenced my every moment in the classroom. Tomlinson explains that teachers can encourage student success by "varying the ways in which students work; alone or collaboratively, in auditory or visual modes, or through practical or creative means." This unit incorporates all of those variables, and it is part of the asset mind-set and language.

After choosing one asset category as the theme for our story (for example, commitment to learning), students discuss what the theme means for them personally as well as in books they have read. I take notes on the board as they explain these connections, carefully responding to each student's ideas with equal acceptance. As we all know, responding without bias can be challenging at times, but it is crucial for students to feel that the classroom is a caring, encouraging, and equitable environment.

Actively involving yourself in the creative brainstorming allows you to model uncertainty and risk taking for your students, as well. Students can see when you are thinking creatively along with them, which helps them see teachers as the lifelong learners that we are.

Next, I ask students to think of their favorite books and to share the elements of those books that made them so much fun to read. Fourth- and 5th-grade students frequently cite adventures, surprises, and animals. Again, I list every example mentioned. Students who do not usually join in see that the teacher is valuing every idea and expecting every student to have thoughts and ideas worth sharing. If students don't volunteer, I invite them by name to participate.

We move into an open area where we stretch and warm up with creative improvisational games. Two of my favorite from my experience as an actress involve stretching and melting exercises. (Many wonderful resources for classroom movement and theater games that help incorporate a kinesthetic learning opportunity are available.)[2]

We stretch our bodies toward the ceiling as I invite students to call out the names of things that stretch. First, of course, you'll hear things such as "gum" and "rubber bands." Try to steer students' ideas toward more original, creative words by calling out of few words of your own, such as "highway" and "skin."

When you exhaust your students' stretching ideas, go into a "melt" and repeat the same activity. Students have more out-of-the-box ideas each time you do these exercises.

Primary-grade students often say the warm-ups are their favorite part of the lesson. At the middle level, students moan and groan at first, but eventually enjoy the time out of their chairs. Older students compete with each other to think of the most absurd things that stretch or melt.

For the next 20 to 30 minutes, the classroom is a little loud, but this is an important part of brainstorming. In schools with an open structure, I simply teach three classes at one time. We use the center space and do our best to keep the volume low.

If a doubting colleague or supervisor questions the validity of your loud work, you can explain that recent research on the human brain reports that using imagination as a source of content is one way that the brain learns.[3] Or, you can quote the nationally renowned storyteller Gail Herman: "Oral language skills learned in this way provide a springboard for the more abstract demands of nonverbal language skills associated with reading and writing literacy."[4]

Developing the Theme and the Outline

Before we begin to actually make up our own story, we review the lists on the board and the chosen theme. Then, I choose one element from the list, such as an animal character, and we begin brainstorming ideas: What kind of animal will be in our story? (In the story my 5th graders wrote, they chose a talking cat that wears sunglasses.) What kind of surprises will happen? (They decide he disappears and freezes time.) As the students give ideas, the whole group decides which ideas to keep. They create the characters and plot lines, and I organize those ideas by writing on the board. (For our example, they decide that a smart boy decides to slack off in school, hoping to be accepted by the "cool" kids.) When teaching this lesson to older students, you can select a couple of them to do the organizing.

I encourage piggybacking on ideas, and direct the discussion so that everyone has a chance to contribute. It is important to stop often to summarize, reflect, discuss, and organize ideas. Make sure the story is integrating the theme and genre guidelines you've selected.

When I think we have the beginning of a story that incorporates our original lists and theme, I ask myself these questions:

- Has everyone contributed?
- Are the students enthusiastic and attentive?
- Are the students ready to begin writing?

If so, I divide students into heterogeneous groups of about five and instruct them to specify some content details for beginning to write (see Handout 4.8: Outline for Writing a Story on page 134). As a small group, they must agree about the voice, verb tense, and elements they will use. Hopefully, each group will have ideas that are different from those of the other groups, but students within a group must agree. (In the story my 5th graders wrote, each group agreed that the voice should be third person and that they should write in the past tense. Each group made different choices about the additional elements within its story.) Each member of the

Outline for Writing a Story

Content Ideas

What is the theme of your story? _____

_____

Who tells the story? (Voice)_____

What one verb tense will you use? ☐ Past   ☐ Present   ☐ Future

Copy the class list of favorite story elements from the board here: _____

_____

_____

Organization of Ideas

Write a first draft of your GREAT, OPENING SENTENCE: _____

_____

What do you write in the first paragraphs to get readers to care about your main character? _____

_____

Where does your story take place? (Setting) _____

_____

_____

Choose some adjectives to use in your story to add color and detail to your writing. (Adjectives describe nouns

or pronouns.) _____

_____

_____

Select one new vocabulary word to use in your story: _____

Define the new vocabulary word: _____

What will be the conflict in your story? _____

_____

_____

How will that conflict be resolved? _____

_____

_____

Checklist

☐ All information above on this page completed

☐ First draft completed and includes:
  ☐ 1. Most of the favorite story elements listed above
  ☐ 2. Selected adjectives
  ☐ 3. New vocabulary word

☐ Draft checked for:
  ☐ 1. Spelling
  ☐ 2. Punctuation
  ☐ 3. Grammar
  ☐ 4. Verb tense

☐ Rewrite/second draft completed

☐ Another person proofed second draft

☐ Rewrite/third draft completed, incorporating edits

☐ Read aloud

☐ Visual presentation polished (margins, neatness, spacing)

☐ Final draft turned in

☐ Enthusiastic and proud of work

group is responsible for contributing ideas and also for helping classmates contribute and work together.

For each group of five students, I assign an organizational part of the outline that the whole class will later incorporate. For example, one group creates the setting (my 5th graders select a school), another group chooses some descriptive adjectives (the cat has an oversized tail, and the boy is clumsy), and another group selects a new vocabulary word (*time-space continuum*) from a vocabulary or spelling list. When all groups are finished, they share their decisions with the rest of the class. Everyone takes notes on her or his own handout.

Writing Unique Stories

Following this cooperative group work, older students independently complete the rest of the handout. Usually, it is the following day when we begin the actual writing.

With younger primary students, we create the whole story as a class. I invite very young children to draw pictures for the book. I type the story, include all of the illustrations, and place it with the other classroom books for independent reading. In doing so, students believe their story is "real" and refer to it often as we begin another similar lesson.

I also encourage students in grades 2 and 3 to imitate good writing—to read a sentence and notice its structure and components, and then write a new sentence copying that structure. Second graders enjoy creating elements of the story by taking turns, adding a sentence or two to the previous ideas. This learning experience is especially great for those students who are working on listening skills.

For students in grades 6 and 7, I focus on multiple drafts and self-editing. Depending upon the quality of their stories, consider extending the lesson to compare and contrast two original stories based upon the same outline.

Before we begin the independent writing, I read examples of first lines in books available in the classroom. As a group, we discuss why the opening line is well written or poorly composed. I encourage students to support their opinions whenever possible. "I just like it" can be a dead end for these kinds of discussions, and I suggest using *An Introduction to Shared Inquiry*[5] from the Great Books Foundation for ideas on follow-up questioning.

Depending upon the age and ability of your students, you may want to spread time for the independent writing over several days. When a majority of the students complete their first draft (some work at home, others do not), I teach the elements of good writing. My preferred lesson plan uses the *Original Student-Friendly Guide to Writing with Traits*[6] published by the Northwest Regional Education Laboratory. This model for writing defines key analytic traits, including ideas and organization, word choice, sentence fluency, voice, conventions, and presentations. Use these writing traits for teaching as well as for assessing various drafts.

Analyzing fiction allows for more spirit of play, and I like to use a particularly fun teaching technique with writing conventions. For example, I like to personalize punctuation: How does the comma feel about being overused? How about the semicolon that everyone forgets?

After students edit their first draft considering the writing traits, I group students in pairs (ability grouping works well here) to read their stories aloud to one another and make suggestions for improvement. Usually, I choose an element of focus. If we are working on punctuation, we look for specific errors in this area. I may ask 6th and 7th graders to vary the beginning of each sentence; I may ask younger students to circle the agreed-upon story elements, and so on. For advanced classes, you can accelerate or compact the pace and depth of this part of the lesson accordingly.

When students complete and turn in third drafts, they volunteer to read their stories to the class or elect me to read them. We always read the stories anonymously, unless the student decides to declare authorship, which is usually based on the class's response.

I then edit the stories and return them to the students for final polishing and presentation. Some include illustrations with their final draft, which they hand in for a grade. (I also like to use Benjamin Bloom's *Taxonomy of Educational Objectives*[7] to measure a student's level of competence in a subject area.) I keep the collection of stories with the classroom reading materials whenever possible.

I particularly like students to read aloud in pairs to ensure attending to all learning styles. Students who are *musical/rhythmic learners* relate to the way the language sounds and are best at improving sentence structure and rhythm. It is also why I read aloud again after the final drafts. This group of learners most appreciates the sounds of words and sentences. Students with diverse learning styles respond to each type of instruction according to their strengths, as David Lazear explains in *Seven Ways of Teaching: The Artistry of Teaching with Multiple Intelligences*.[8]

In this creative writing unit, the *verbal/linguistic learners* are usually exceptional contributors during the brainstorming sessions. The *logical/mathematical learners*, eager to expose errors or inconsistencies within a story, find their strengths in story structure. They are quick to see that an author may have mentioned something at the beginning of the story but altered or forgotten it near the end, contradicting the original information. Logical/mathematical learners are also good at sequencing the events in a story.

Students who are *visual/spatial learners* are most adept at selecting adjectives to express detailed mental images and create vivid pictures with words. Writing on the board throughout the creative process and using the handout help these students.

For the on-your-feet creative brainstorming, *body/kinesthetic learners* better assimilate the lessons begun at their desks. Reviewing the brainstormed lists and selected themes again at this time also particularly helps these students.

Interpersonally intelligent students have the ability to work cooperatively with others, which is why I start the unit with larger group activities and then move to smaller cooperative learning groups. These students lead small group situations well and have an innate ability to direct discussion toward common goals and agreement.

One of the reasons I end the unit with independent work, as much as why I relate the asset theme to personal experience, is to especially connect to those who are *intrapersonally intelligent learners* and have a greater knowledge of self. It is important to connect these learners to the lesson on a personal basis.

When you incorporate the asset framework into your curriculum, understanding multiple intelligences and creativity as an educational objective for all students, diverse learners of all abilities have an equal chance for school engagement and success.

Students respond overwhelmingly to the creative writing lessons, and their enthusiasm to begin another unit is exciting. Many students express a special enjoyment incorporating their friends' ideas into their story.

Notes

1. Tomlinson, Carol Ann. (September 2000). Reconcilable Differences?: Standards-Based Teaching and Differentiation. *Educational Leadership*, (58)1:6–11. Alexandria, VA: Association for Supervision and Curriculum Development.
2. Newton, Brad. (1999). *Improvisation: Use What You Know, Make Up What You Don't*. Scottsdale, AZ: Great Potential Press. See also Spolin, Viola. (1986). *Theater Games for the Classroom: A Teacher's Handbook*. Evanston, IL: Northwestern University Press.
3. Sousa, David A. (2000). *How The Brain Learns: A Classroom Teacher's Guide*, 2nd ed. Chapter 6, The Brain and the Arts. Thousand Oaks, CA: Corwin Press.
4. Herman, Gail N. (1999). Storytelling: The Art of Imagination. *Parenting for High Potential*, December, 8–11.
5. Great Books Foundation. (1992). *An Introduction to Shared Inquiry*, 3rd ed. Chicago: author.
6. Spandel, Vicki, and Culham, Ruth. (1993). *The Original Student-Friendly Guide to Writing with Traits*. Portland, OR: Northwest Regional Educational Laboratory.
7. Bloom, Benjamin S. (1969). *Taxonomy of Educational Objectives: The Classification of Educational Goals*. Harlow, Essex: Longman Group.
8. Lazear, David. (1991). *Seven Ways of Teaching: The Artistry of Teaching with Multiple Intelligences*. Arlington Heights, IL: IRI/Skylight Training and Publishing.

Other Resources

Ackerman, Karen, et al. (1999). *Differentiated Lessons and Units*. Englewood, CO: Cherry Creek School District.

Cashion, Kay, Everly, Jane, Hammond, Gail, and Weaver, Connie. (1999). *Teachers to Teachers Creatively*. Handout presented at National Association for Gifted Children Convention. Albuquerque, NM.

Craig, Susan, Hull, Karla, Haggart, Ann G., and Crowder, Elaine. (2000). Storytelling: Addressing the Literacy Needs of Diverse Learners. *Teaching Exceptional Children*, 33(5):46–51.

Cray-Andrews, Martha, and Baum, Susan. (1996). *Creativity 1, 2, 3*. Unionville, NY: Royal Fireworks Press.

Flack, Jerry. (1997). When Artists Speak: Translating Gifts into Action. *Understanding Our Gifted*, winter, 26–30.

Kingore, Bertie. (2001). Biographies and Autobiographies: Life Models in the Classroom. *Understanding Our Gifted*, spring, 13–15.

Renzulli, Joseph S., and Reis, Sally M. (1997). *The Schoolwide Enrichment Model: A How-To Guide for Educational Excellence*, 2nd ed. Mansfield Center, CT: Creative Learning Press.

Safe and Drug Free Schools Program. (1998). *Creative Partnerships for Prevention: Using the Arts and Humanities to Build Resiliency in Youth*. Washington, D.C.: Government Printing Office.

Sternberg, Robert J. (1996). *Successful Intelligence: How Practical and Creative Intelligence Determine Success in Life*. New York: Simon and Schuster.

Ready, Set, *Assets in Action*

PRODUCING A VIDEO FOR YOUTH

JOYCE ARNASON, M.A. AND CHERI SCHANEY, M.A.

Special Education Teachers (grades 9–12)

Smoky Hill High School

Aurora, Colorado

For students who have disabilities involving reading and writing, Joyce Arnason and Cheri Schaney have crafted an authentic class using multimedia technologies that improves students' writing skills, as well as enables them to produce much more sophisticated work than, say, a typical book summary. The exciting video production project highly engages students in school and motivates their achievement, as well as communicates asset-building messages to other students.

SCHOOL DEMOGRAPHICS
Smoky Hill High School
Aurora, Colorado

Students: 2,697

Grades: 9–12

Gender:
Male	49.0%
Female	51.0%

Race and Ethnicity:
Black/African American	8.0%
Hispanic/Latino	6.1%
Asian/Pacific Islander	8.9%
American Indian	0.6%
White/Caucasian	76.4%

Socioeconomics:
Free/Reduced Lunch	7.5%

To help students who struggle with their reading and writing, we created a unique, asset-rich class within the Learning Disabilities (LD) program that accesses a variety of exciting and fun technologies, including iMovie software to make a video. While the sophomores through seniors (maturity matters!) selected for the LD Technology Through Language Arts class have verbal skills and IQs ranging from average to high average, their writing shows immature expression, poor sequencing, and illegibility, with minimal content and errors in spelling and grammar.

Computers that have sophisticated word processing, word prediction, speech, and Internet access are among the various technologies students can use daily. Some students whose verbal skills well exceed their writing abilities have success with speech-to-text software. When given writing assignments that involve multimedia software, the students in this class produce exceptional and highly creative work.

Approaching this unit in the spirit of reality-based learning not only makes it more meaningful but also produces a greater impact on students. The final exam for the unit is authentic—knowledge and skills demonstrated in creating a finished video product.

In this extensive unit, students learn what the 40 developmental assets are, how to use iMovie,[1] how to write miniplays, edit, use digital video equipment, act, memorize parts, edit again, and follow through on a topic to its completion. As a result of completing this class, many students have, in fact, reached the goal of being able to function in regular language arts classes.

Producing the Video

In accessing technology for enhancing written language, using iMovie software was an exciting endeavor for producing a video, and taking the 40 developmental assets as a topic also was something fresh. Students were curious how they could show other students that assets were already part of their lives and that they could build additional assets, which would improve their ability to succeed in life.

First, we needed to learn what the assets were all about. Following an introduction of the assets from the district assets assistant, we participated in group activities to explore examples of the eight asset categories and talk about how the assets related to our everyday lives. We also watched Search Institute's video *Assets Happening Here*.[2] Students were fired up and ready to begin!

We decided our target audience for the video would be other students rather than adults. We brainstormed topics to hook the audience based on the recent popularity of the TV *Survivor* series. We began writing scripts in groups. Each group was to create a different contest, with the contestants' goal being to attain one or two of the eight asset categories.

As students wrote, they also chose parts for each script. They wrote and rewrote without even knowing that they were editing their own scripts. They chose actors and actresses, a videographer, and editors. Students who were musicians volunteered to compose original music and submitted a CD for class approval; others made props and created cue cards to assist the actors.

Each group drew storyboards to show other groups its contest. The students explored Internet sites that pertained to writing storyboards and making movies. We began to rehearse parts, collect props, and determine locations—and then we started filming.

Most of the students who had acting roles had never taken an acting class and were timid in front of the camera. Many of the students in the class, who have memory deficits, had to take extra time to learn scripts.

After initial film takes, we viewed and critiqued segments, then reshot scenes. Students were using all their language arts skills without realizing it and had a sense of purpose that kept their motivation and attention high.

Although the process of making the iMovie was more involved than we had anticipated, student gains were obvious. Students clearly appreciated others' differences as they observed their strengths throughout the project. The process enhanced their confidence, and students began taking more risks by speaking out and offering suggestions. Those with attention deficit disorder were thrilled by the unstructured and active learning style, and contributed creative ideas and energy. The quiet students liked the behind-the-scenes responsibilities. As a group, the students became more cohesive and respected others' suggestions and views. Rewrites for scripts came more readily as creativity flowed.

The *Assets in Action*

The students begin their video, *Assets in Action*, with three students discussing an assignment in a popular, local frozen juice drink shop—the story is not too unlike their real assignment and real world: the students must complete a film for class and want to use assets as the topic. They set the stage for the competition and introduce the actors, naming assets that each actor already possesses. They have chosen individuals from various school groups students frequently describe as "jock," "prep," "brain," and "druggie." The contestants work together competitively to gain certain assets they do not already have.

Support and Social Competencies

The video goes on to show that the purpose of the asset contest is to work together to build a cardboard house. Everyone needs to collaborate or their group will lose the competition. Their strategy involves team building, planning and decision making, interpersonal competence, positive family communication, and caring school climate.

The students edit the action into fast-forward to add humor. At the end of the contest, as the contestants admire their work, the videomakers pan the camera to a large mansion, indicating to each contestant the truly magnificent structure they've built together.

Boundaries and Expectations and Positive Values

In one scene, freshly baked cookies placed before a poster stating "No Food in the Academic Area" entice the contestants. One contestant follows the rules, while the others give in to temptation. In this scene, the students address school boundaries, positive peer influence, and high expectations, along with equality and social justice, integrity, honesty, and restraint.

Commitment to Learning

This miniplay depicts achievement motivation for a pop quiz. While one student completes the quiz effortlessly, the others are mentally involved in something else.

Empowerment and Social Competencies

In another short scene, students are working in the student store when a contestant enters and tries to buy candy without enough money. The scene demonstrates resistance skills, peaceful conflict resolution, and interpersonal competence, as well as youth as resources and service to others.

Constructive Use of Time and Positive Identity

The final script involves a track-and-field event. Students trying to run the track are confronted with compliments and put-downs. Those who receive praise continue to run, but those who get put down lose steam, much like what happens in life.

Next, the actors kick a football down the "field of life," which represents the difficulties life presents and the time and effort involved to overcome those difficulties. For some the task is easy, but for others, it takes longer.

In the following scene, each contestant runs and jumps the "hurdles of life," wearing signs such as "Drugs," "Peer Pressure," "Alcohol," and "Ditching School." Certain contestants struggle over some of the hurdles.

Finally comes the scene in which kicks are intercepted by a goalie, who represents the need to keep trying to reach personal goals despite interference.

Asset Awareness

To conclude the video, students informally comment on what they learned from this iMovie experience. For example, one actor, whose mother had recently passed away, described how work on this video and her new awareness of assets in her life have offered her the support she needed to get through difficult times. Another actor, a "druggie," was ready to drop out of school because of his real-life drug problem; he decided not only to stay but also to clean up his act. His attendance improved, and he remained in school.

Throughout the movie project, students began to incorporate an awareness of the importance of assets in their lives. They gained in maturity, self-awareness, and an increased ability to express themselves and cooperate with others. The project proved highly meaningful—and *Assets in Action* found a home in numerous lives!

Notes

1. Apple Computer, Inc. (2002). *Bring Learning to Life: Tips for Making Your Movie*. Apple Computer website. Web site accessed November 11, 2002: http://www.apple.com/education/dv/tips/index.html.
2. Noodlehead Network. (1999). *Assets Happening Here*. Minneapolis: Search Institute.

Other Resources

Benson, Peter L., Galbraith, Judith, and Espeland, Pamela. (1998). *What Teens Need To Succeed: Proven, Practical Ways to Raise Good Kids*. Minneapolis: Free Spirit Publishing.

Cherry Creek School District. (1999). *Wrap Your Arms around Cherry Creek Kids, Cherry Creek Schools*. A Cherry Creek School District video production. Greenwood Village, CO: Author.

Roehlkepartain, Jolene L. (1997). *Building Assets Together: 135 Group Activities for Helping Youth Succeed*. Minneapolis: Search Institute.

Search Institute. (2002). *The Asset Approach*. Minneapolis: Author.

Chapter 5

Infusing Assets into Social Studies

Liberty and Justice for All?

EXAMINING PERCEPTIONS, ASSUMPTIONS, AND INVOLVEMENT IN CIVIC LIFE

JONATHAN MILLER-LANE, M.ED.

Social Studies Teacher (grades 9–12)

Bainbridge High School

Bainbridge Island, Washington

When students come into our classrooms, what they really want to know, first and foremost, is whether or not they can trust us. As educators we may sometimes feel overwhelmed by the breadth of diversity in our classrooms, but to be an educator in the United States is to be committed to ensuring that all students have equal access—that in our classroom, there is no fear, there is no favoritism.

One way to address the overwhelming feeling is to welcome it rather than fight it. Ask yourself: do I care enough to be honest about my own development as a conscientious and engaged educator and to deepen my awareness of what it means to live in a genuinely pluralistic republic? The model social studies lessons I provide here challenge students—and teachers—to reflect more carefully on their own daily behavior and the diversity of classroom experience, as well as on their priorities in relation to those of the school.

In social studies education, our fundamental purpose is to provide students the opportunity to develop the knowledge, skills, and attitudes necessary for life in a diverse, democratic republic. Social studies must foster citizenship if democracy is to survive. The developmental assets are an important part of that process.

Placing a high value on equality and social justice, demonstrating a willingness to engage the school community, a commitment to resolve conflict peacefully, and a belief in the power of the individual to make a difference are just some of the key internal assets *and* citizenship skills we must address. The documents we select and require our students to read and analyze, the methods we employ, the ideas we bring to our classrooms for scrutiny, and the values we foster through our classroom

SCHOOL DEMOGRAPHICS

Bainbridge High School
Bainbridge Island, Washington

Students: 1,257

Grades: 9–12

Gender:
Male	48.0%
Female	52.0%

Race and Ethnicity:
Black/African American	0.7%
Hispanic/Latino	1.2%
Asian/Pacific Islander	5.3%
American Indian	0.6%
White/Caucasian	92.2%

Socioeconomics:
Free/Reduced Lunch	2.0%

environment are essential in creating a citizenry who cares about the well-being of the community.

The three model lessons presented here help build your students' assets for civic life. Two of the lessons include time-tested methods used in social studies: the Socratic seminar method to understand the Pledge of Allegiance, and concept formation strategy to address building asset 34, cultural competence. The third lesson offers a unique use of mental mapping skills and self-reflection: students draw both an exact map of the school grounds and a mental map of the school that represents their actual movement patterns through the school during the average day; then they evaluate how that mental map reflects their school priorities—and whether they are proud of those priorities.

Understanding the Pledge of Allegiance

Lesson Objective: At the conclusion of the lesson, students will have reached an enlarged understanding of the Pledge of Allegiance.
Method: Socratic seminar

> I pledge allegiance to the flag of the United States of America, and to the Republic for which it stands, one nation, under God, indivisible, with liberty and justice for all.

In many schools in the United States, students say the Pledge of Allegiance every day, yet few students actually ever discuss what it means or what our notions of liberty and justice are. (For learning more about the history of the pledge, see the work of June Swanson.[1])

Since everyone is familiar with the pledge, it is an easy text to use to introduce what is a deceptively difficult but powerful teaching method: the Socratic seminar. The Socratic seminar is an ancient method of teaching that has been refined by the National Paideia Center at the School of Education at the University of North Carolina[2] and the Great Books Foundation.[3]

A Socratic seminar has one fundamental learning objective: an enlarged understanding of a text. It emphasizes examining the ideas, issues, and values in the text as a group. No content objective is specified. Content learning occurs through the analysis of the text. But, the lesson objective is not that every student learns precisely the same content after 50 minutes. Rather, the objective is for each student to enlarge her or his respective understanding.

It is important to note that a Socratic seminar is not a teacher-led discussion, nor is it a lecture. In the classroom, we often call any interaction when two students (or more) talk and the teacher responds, *discussions*. Usually, students direct their comments or questions to you, and you remain the switchboard for the discussion, the expert; the students do not direct questions or comments toward each other.

Similarly, in a lecture, you also remain the expert. Of course, there are times when lectures are needed and important.

A Socratic seminar simply offers another option in your instructional repertoire—an option wherein you, the teacher, are an equal participant (see "Rules of Discussion in a Socratic Seminar" on page 148). A Socratic seminar at the end of the week can culminate a week of lectures and other activities.

The Lesson

■ **Begin with an opening question.**

For a Socratic seminar on the Pledge of Allegiance, start with this commonly used question after forming your circle: "To whom or to what are we pledging allegiance when we say the pledge every morning?"

■ **Allow for discussion to follow.**

The initial question may result in a discussion that lasts the entire 50 minutes of class time. It may seem odd to plan a whole lesson around the analysis of one sentence. However, the Pledge of Allegiance is rich with profound and meaningful words that you could, in fact, spend a whole school year exploring: *pledge*, *allegiance*, *republic*, *nation*, *God*, *indivisible*, *liberty*, *justice*. Follow-up questions can include:

- What does *indivisible* mean in this pledge? What exactly is indivisible?
- What is *liberty* and what does the pledge say about who should have it?
- What is *justice* and what does the pledge say about who should have it?
- Why are we "under God"? What does that mean here?

■ **Keep the class focused on the text.**

Keeping focused on the text is a challenge. It is a different question to ask, "Have we lived up to the pledge?" Or, "How do we ensure justice is achieved 'for all'?" Both are important questions, and you should discuss them. But, both lead *away* from the text, *not into* the text. As tempting as such a line of inquiry is, encourage students to really explore every word in the text and the relationships of the words to one another. Save the other questions for a follow-up discussion or a class research project. Meanwhile, clearly distinguish questions that are about enlarging understanding of the text itself from those that are inspired by the text but lead into an analysis of larger society.

■ **End the seminar approximately five minutes before the bell rings.**

Go around the circle and ask each student for one sentence that summarizes whether she or he has an enlarged understanding of the Pledge of Allegiance (beyond saying simply "yes" or "no"). Students may pass, should they prefer not to speak. Concluding the seminar this way helps affirm that it was a group process and reiterates the lesson's objective.

Do not summarize the lesson—there is no need to come to a common understanding. Allow the students to make their own meaning. Ideally, the bell rings just as the last student has spoken.

Assessing the Lesson

After the seminar, I generally give students a writing assignment to individually explore and reflect on these issues further. Allow students to choose one of the following options. The variety of choices makes for a better variety of papers for you to read.

Rules of Discussion in a Socratic Seminar

Review these rules[1] with your students before conducting a Socratic seminar. The information following each rule provides recommendations for the seminar facilitator.

1. Students must read the text before they are allowed to participate.

A good tool is to require students to turn in a "ticket" for the seminar. The ticket is a written response to a set of questions about the reading. If students have not read the text, they must sit outside the group and read it. Once they are finished, they may join the group.

2. Sit in a circle so that everyone can see each other.

Move the tables and desks. Do whatever you need to do to make a circle. Join the circle as an equal partner.

3. Contribute when ready, rather than raise hands.

Do not direct the conversation toward any particular objective; yet be sure that everyone who wants to has a chance to speak. Beware of gender balance. Is one gender dominating the conversation? Are the wealthy students doing all the talking? What about race? Be extremely sensitive to the group dynamics.

At most, ask for clarifications, using these phrases: "Could you say more?" "What did you mean when you said _____?"
"Anyone else want to speak to _____'s comments before we let her or him speak again?" Write these phrases on the board at the start of the seminar so that students also have formal phrases to use with one another. Asking for clarification can be difficult among peers. By providing students with formal seminar language, you help them learn the language of civil and civic discourse.

4. Talk to one another, not to the teacher.

Do not affirm every comment; rather allow for pauses in between students' comments. Follow up for clarification if needed, but if not, *wait!* Allow for silence to be a member of the circle. Sometimes, it helps to give participants a heads up at the outset, so they know that thoughtful silences are a normal part of seminars. Seven to ten seconds of silence can seem like a lifetime; be patient. Studies show that students whose teachers wait even three or more seconds for a response learn more and think more deeply.[2] Wait-time also encourages students of diverse backgrounds who may be learning English as a second language to think, participate, and formulate an answer.[3] Acknowledge that silence can be awkward, but ultimately enriching. Allow students to get used to the power of silence to deepen thought in a discussion.

5. Refer to the text.

Remember that the key objective is an enlarged understanding of the *text*. The purpose is not to hear discussants' personal stories. Encourage all comments and questions throughout the seminar toward deepening understanding: "What is unclear?" "Why?" "Who can offer some thoughts about that?"

6. Help each other—do not compete against one another.

A seminar is a chance to help each other better understand the text under discussion. Listen to one another. Ask for clarification. Offer your own insights. There is no test after a seminar.

Notes

1. I am indebted to Rebecca J. Downey of the Timberline and North Thurston School districts in Washington for helping me to clarify the role of rules in a Socratic seminar.
2. Rowe, Mary B. (1987). Wait-Time: Slowing Down May Be a Way of Speeding Up. *American Educator*, 11(1): 38–47.
3. Carin, Arthur A., and Bass, Joel E. (2001). *Methods for Teaching Science as Inquiry*. Upper Saddle River, NJ: Prentice-Hall, 171.

1. Summarize in 200–400 words your understanding of what the Pledge of Allegiance means—or of one word in the pledge—and why. Reference the comments of at least three other students from the seminar.

2. In 200–400 words, argue for or against requiring students to stand during the reciting of the Pledge of Allegiance. Draw upon the text of the pledge in your argument. Does *liberty* allow students the right not to stand? Or, does *allegiance* require them to stand?

3. Critique the seminar itself in 200–400 words. Is your understanding of the Pledge of Allegiance enlarged? How? How did the discussion, as opposed to a lecture or film about the pledge, help? Be precise.

This lesson supports many of the developmental assets. A good, honest question-and-answer discussion in which students are encouraged to offer their own thoughts engages them in ways that a lecture or teacher-filtered discussion doesn't. Emphasizing helping one another in the seminar promotes caring as well as interpersonal and cultural competence. Learning how to disagree in a more formal seminar format helps students learn important resistance skills, as well. A Socratic seminar, particularly about the Pledge of Allegiance, both builds assets and challenges students to think critically about key issues, ideas, and values that are part of being a citizen in the United States (see also "Learning Citizenship: Making a Positive Difference Every Day" on page 157).

Promoting Cultural Competence

Lesson Objective: At the conclusion of the lesson, students will be able to:

1. Write their own definition of asset 34, cultural competence;
2. Identify specific activities they wish the class or school, or both, to engage in to promote cultural competence; and
3. Present an action plan for how to implement those activities.

Method: Modified Concept Formation

Too often adults do the planning for and talking about young people, but do not bring young people into the process. We wring our hands about "those kids," but keep them fully removed from any meaningful decision-making responsibilities. We also rarely explain to students why we've planned the lesson the way it is, how it fits into this school year's plan, or even how this year's plan fits into the curriculum they're required to learn. We do our daily lessons and multiweek units—and the students are supposed to just "get" it.

This lesson offers an alternative approach by tackling one of the most complex social competencies head-on: cultural competence. The lesson challenges students and teachers alike to truly examine their own assumptions regarding what they think they know (see also "Labeling and Stereotyping: Do You Really Know What It Feels Like?" on page 159).

To address this issue, I use the time-honored method called *concept formation*, originally developed by Hilda Taba.[4] Concept formation requires students to collect, analyze, evaluate, and classify data. In this lesson, students form the concept (of cultural competence) by developing examples they feel best illustrate the concept, rather than forming a concept by analyzing data you have prepared and presented.

Concepts are ideas. Social studies teachers work with ideas all the time: justice, peace, war, revolution, civil war, citizenship, democracy, capitalism, socialism, inquiry, public good. In geography, we work with movement, region, human-environment interaction, location, and place. Each of these words is a concept label; each word is a label for an idea that has a unique set of critical attributes.

Cultural competence is both an idea and a concept label. It represents certain attitudes or behaviors that, when combined, form the concept of cultural competence. Those attitudes and behaviors are the critical attributes of the concept.

Any definition of a concept must include the critical attributes all examples share. Consider the concept label *democracy*. If you give students the examples of the United States, Canada, and Mexico, and ask them to compare their forms of government, they'll tell you the common critical attributes include the majority rules (laws are made by all citizens or their representatives), minority rights are protected, and laws are written down.[5] (The level of sophistication of the definition should match the grade level of the students.)

You can use the plan below to unpack the meaning of any of the 40 developmental assets. Follow the model for how to make the assets an explicit part of your curriculum and increase the potential for your students to understand their importance. The higher-order thinking skills required to complete the lesson are transferable to any content area. For social studies, they form the backbone of citizenship skills.

The Lesson

To cover the lesson in its entirety will take two or three days for a 50-minute period each day.

Day One

■ **Define cultural competence.**

Before class begins, write on the board Search Institute's definition of cultural competence: "Young person has knowledge of and comfort with people of different cultural/racial/ethnic backgrounds."

■ **Explain the purpose of this lesson: to carefully examine what cultural competence means and how the class can develop it.**

Convey to students that cultural competence is an idea you are very interested in working on throughout the year. However, you also believe people can interpret what this means differently. Clearly, Search Institute has a definition, but the goal of the lesson is for students to rewrite the attributes in their own words. To make the term meaningful for the class, explain how the class will develop a definition everyone understands. What you want to emphasize in spreading the lesson over several days is to encourage students to own the definition.

■ **Clarify the terms** *culture, race,* **and** *ethnicity.*

Each of these terms is, of course, a concept label in its own right and could comprise an entirely separate concept formation lesson. However, for the purposes of exploring cultural competence with your students, use the following definitions, developed by the Human Relations Program at the University of Minnesota in Minneapolis, to review these three concepts. (20 MINUTES)

Culture: Culture is the values, tradition, social and political relations, and worldview shared by a group of people bound together by a combination of factors that can include a common history, language, social class, religion, and geographic location.[6]

Race: Although cultural anthropologists do not accept the word *race* as a meaningful descriptor of human beings, the term generally refers to a group of people who are distinguished by hereditary traits. "Race is the perception of an individual or a group that is defined as different from the elite and other minorities on the basis of perceived physical criteria. Race is not truly a physical group, but one that is perceived and defined as different on the basis of physical criteria (i.e., skin color, hair type, etc.)."[7]

Ethnicity: An ethnic group is one "whose members are bound together by common cultural characteristics (e.g., values, ideas, food, habits, family patterns, sexual behavior, modes of dress, standards of beauty, political conceptions, economic forms, and recreational patterns)."[8] The group also usually claims or enjoys official recognition of its group identity.

■ **Use a "think-pair-share" cooperative learning strategy to identify what it means to:**

1. *Have knowledge* about people of different cultural, racial, or ethnic backgrounds; and
2. *Be comfortable with* people of different cultural, racial, or ethnic backgrounds.

First ask each student to *think* on her or his own and write a quick response. (5 MINUTES) Next ask students to *pair* with another student and compare notes (5 MINUTES), and then report to the whole class two examples of knowledge and two examples of comfort. (15 MINUTES) One pair can write the two lists of examples on the board as others *share.* If student comments are unclear, ask for clarification. Review the lists and focus class attention on what the lists indicate it means to have knowledge about and comfort with different people. (5 MINUTES) For homework, ask students to write a 100- to 200-word summary addressing the issues specified above and using at least five attributes listed on the board from each category. (This requires that students take notes during class.)

It is essential that students practice classification. Otherwise, it is unlikely that they will have a usable understanding of the term.

Day Two

■ **Students read aloud their written summaries.**

Divide the class into diverse groups of six. As the teacher, you can designate these groups best because you know your class better than anyone else. (Remember that socioeconomic status is a form of diversity also.) Three students in each group read their knowledge summary, and three others read their comfort summary. (10 MINUTES)

Then ask one student from each group to report to the class the common characteristics of the knowledge summaries and one student to report the common characteristics of the comfort summaries. Write these on the board as the students list them. (5 MINUTES)

■ **Pull a class summary together.**

Has a consensus emerged regarding what asset 34 means? Can the class agree on an acceptable definition? Challenge students to identify the boundaries of their definitions. How much knowledge is enough to meet the criteria? How comfortable with others do you have to be? What is a realistic expectation?

The process here is critical to concept formation. You must be able to write a single sentence that says: "Cultural competence is a combination of attitudes and behaviors characterized by **(a)**_____, **(b)**_____, **(c)**_____, and **(d)**_____." You must be able to determine the critical attributes of the concept. (30 MINUTES . . . OR A LITTLE BIT OF EVERY OTHER CLASS FOR THE REST OF THE YEAR!)

Display the sentence in a prominent place in the classroom for continued reflection.

■ **Devise a plan for implementing one component of developing asset 34.**

Explain that this homework assignment is to include two statements in response to:

1. What will I do?
2. What can the class or school do to make cultural competence a more normal part of daily life in the classroom, hallways, or school building?

In detailing the plan as precisely as possible, students should choose realistic actions and actions they're sincerely interested in pursuing.

Tackling the meaning of cultural competence head-on engages students in honest dialogue within the class about the comfort and knowledge level that exists regarding relating to people of other cultures: Who is really knowledgeable and comfortable with every person? What are you able to handle as the teacher?

Examining Assumptions about Schooling

Lesson Objective: At the conclusion of the lesson, students will be able to:

1. Define the purpose of a mental map;
2. Analyze how their own mental map reflects their school priorities; and
3. Evaluate whether they want to change those priorities.

Method: Mental Map, Museum Walk

The method for this lesson employs the popular mental map activity provided by the National Geographic Society.[9] However, rather than solely teach what a mental map is and how it reflects people's perceptions of school, this lesson uses the mental map to challenge students to carefully examine their own assumptions about the *purpose* of schooling and their involvement in that purpose.

According to the National Council for Education, which establishes national geography standards, mental maps are "personal and idiosyncratic and are usually a mixture of objective knowledge and subjective perceptions."[10] In other words, a mental map has information about the actual geographic features of a place and also includes impressions of that place that reflect the unique priorities of the mapmaker. A mental map of your city may include only those places you visit regularly, and show a location that is very important to you more prominently than locations that are not as important. Relative distance may be more important than absolute or accurate distance. Mental mapping is a strategy to evaluate your own thinking and values—to represent *your* unique understanding of your city.

The Lesson

Day One

PART ONE (25–30 MINUTES)

■ **Students draw and review the actual layout of the school.**

Begin the lesson by explaining to students that they will be examining the structure of their school day by using a tool that is well known to geographers: a mental map. Provide students with an 11-by-14-inch piece of paper. Ask students to draw in pencil a reasonably accurate map of the school that reflects the relative distance and location of buildings and playgrounds/fields on the school grounds. Students should label the various buildings. (10–15 MINUTES)

Ask students to compare their maps with those of at least four other people. Are there major items they forgot to include? Did every student know where the major buildings were? (5 MINUTES)

■ **Students delineate their daily patterns.**

Ask students to draw a continuous line, using a different color pencil, to represent the path or pattern they follow daily as they move through the school campus/

buildings: Do they begin in the bus parking lot or do they drive? Do they go to the cafeteria first or do they meet with friends in a hallway? Do they arrive late and rush immediately to class? Is lunch on campus or off? Do they avoid certain areas?

Then, ask students *to list on the back of the map* the areas of the school grounds they go to most often and areas of the school grounds where they go least. For example, do they go to the gym once a week or every day? Have they been to the library/media center this week? This year? (5 MINUTES)

Again, ask students to compare maps with those of four other people. Observe how students naturally start to draw conclusions about what the differences mean regarding priorities, but at this point do not start formal analysis as a class. (2–3 MINUTES)

PART TWO (20–25 MINUTES)

■ **Show students your map.**

Now it is your turn as the teacher. On the overhead projector, draw your map of the school showing your daily patterns. Do this by hand using colored markers on a transparency or, to save time, make a transparency of the map of the school grounds from your emergency folder and simply mark your own pattern line on that map.

Talk to students about the areas of the school you regularly go to and what areas you do not. Did the process of mapping your daily patterns reveal something of which you were not aware? What do you think your own map says about your focus at school? How often do you visit the library? gym? cafeteria? How does this map reflect your priorities? Describe your findings without judging yourself—omit references regarding whether you think your patterns are good or bad. (5–10 MINUTES)

■ **Describe to students your visual mental map.**

Now share the visual mental map that you have drawn that reveals what is important to you—the places you regularly visit, with the most significant pictured larger. (At this point, you are modeling what you will be asking the students to do for homework.) To highlight the features of a mental map, talk with your students about these questions:

- How does your mental map differ from the actual map of the school grounds?
- Did you include any abstract representations to represent your priorities? In other words, if lunch is a really important part of the day for you, did you draw a big sandwich where the staff lounge is? If the gym is important, did you draw a large basketball or volleyball?
- If you spend the entire day in your classroom, eat lunch in your room, and go to the office only once a day, how could you draw that in a symbolic way?
- Where are you happiest during the day? How could you represent that?
- If you have been at your school for a long time, how do you think your mental map has changed over the years? (5 MINUTES)

Allow time for students to ask you questions to ensure that they understand what you have represented in your mental map. Remember that objective 3 for this lesson asks students to consider whether the priorities they reveal in their mental map are ones they like. What about you? Does your map suggest to you things you would like to improve? Are you willing to share those with students to model what you are asking them to do? (5 MINUTES)

■ **Students complete a mental map of the school.**

Ask students to think about how they will draw their mental map. (LAST 5 MINUTES OF CLASS) Encourage them to begin jotting down ideas and to review the list they wrote on the back of their maps that indicates what buildings are most important to them:

- What symbols could they use to represent areas that are or are not important to them? Is there a part of the school grounds that represents something they like very much, or do not like? How will they reflect that preference in a manner that their grandmothers would find acceptable (the best censor check I have come across!)?
- To what extent does their daily movement pattern (and yours as a teacher!) reflect avoidance as opposed to active engagement? Do they walk the route they do every day through the building to avoid people and places or to engage people and places?

Hand students a second 11-by-14-inch piece of paper for completing the mental map of the school as homework. Have them write their names on the back instead of the front. Encourage them to be creative and thoughtful.

DAY TWO (50 MINUTES)

■ **Take a museum walk of the maps (students walk by the maps as if they were looking at paintings in a museum).**

As students come in (do not wait until the bell announces the start of class), have them tape their maps to the chalkboard, the metal strip along the white board, or someplace where everyone can see. Number each map as it is taped. (5 MINUTES)

Next, have students (in groups of five to seven) take a museum walk single file past the drawings. As the first group is halfway along, ask another group to start. Once they return to their seats, have students write down which maps they found most interesting and why. (10 MINUTES)

■ **Discuss how the maps reflect priorities.**

Begin by asking a student to comment on a map that he or she found interesting, particularly addressing how the map reflects school priorities. Then, ask the artist-geographer to explain what he or she had in mind. Challenge students to speak clearly and analytically about how their mental maps reflect their priorities. Save judgments for later.

Discuss each student's drawing for approximately one minute. Keep the process moving to ensure that everyone is allowed to comment. If conversations are rich, extend the lesson to another day.

In some cases, students may feel angry or resentful about school. Others may feel embarrassed about aspects of what they are revealing. If students are speaking honestly and appropriately, allow them to speak their minds—or not. The purpose of this group discussion is to explore both what a mental map is generally and how unique each person's mental map can be. The process encourages students to empathize with one another's experiences. (30 MINUTES)

■ **Goal writing.**

To conclude the lesson, ask students to write the following two essays as homework assignments:

1. A 70- to 100-word summary of their school priorities as reflected in the mental map; and
2. A 150- to 300-word analysis of whether their priorities reflect the priorities they believe the school has for them.

The second essay requires students to think about the school not as a physical institution but as a set of goals. What do they think the school's goals are? Do they consciously resist those goals? Are they aware of them? Do they see the school as a repressive prison or as a place of learning? Are there things they would like to change? Why? How might that occur?

Notes
1. Swanson, June. (1990). *I Pledge Allegiance*. Minneapolis: Carolrhoda Books.
2. Bender, Amy C. (1994). Paideia Seminar Teaching Guide: An Assessment Instrument to Identify Skills for Effective Seminar Teachers. Ph.D. diss., University of North Carolina at Chapel Hill; Microfiche, (1995). Ann Arbor, MI: University Microfilms International.
3. See Temes, Peter. (December 15, 2000). *Learning to Love Life Outside Academe*; Web site accessed November 18, 2002: www.greatbooks.org/news/archive/chronicleed.html.
4. Taba, Hilda. (1962). *Curriculum Development: Theory and Practice*. NY: Harcourt, Brace & World.
5. Parker, Walter C. (2001). *Social Studies in Elementary Education*, 11th ed. Saddle Hill, NJ: Prentice Hall, 259. As a high school teacher, I have found this text immensely useful for its clear presentation of time-tested social studies methods for students of *all* ages.
6. Puncochar, Judith. (Fall 2001). Educational Psychology 5135, Human relations workshop syllabus. Minneapolis: University of Minnesota, 209.
7. Ibid., p. 212.
8. Ibid., p. 209.
9. Buehl, Doug. (2001). *Classroom Strategies for Interactive Learning*, 2nd ed. Newark, DE: International Reading Association, 89.
10. Boehm, Richard G., Bednarz, Sarah W., and Downs, Roger M. (1994). *Geography for Life: National Geography Standards*. Washington, DC: National Council for Geographic Education.

Other Resources
Another source of assistance for the Socratic seminar is Oscar Graybill, director of Socratic Seminars Northwest, 514 South Division Street, Walla Walla, WA 99362, 509-522-2594.

Learning Citizenship

MAKING A POSITIVE DIFFERENCE EVERY DAY

DAVE GUILE, M.S.

Principal (grades K–5)

Forest Ridge Elementary School

Salem, Oregon

For focusing on the developmental assets in relation to being a good citizen, Dave Guile presents here a template his new school-within-a-school uses for a four-week unit. He and a team of teachers planned the opening of this new elementary school to include incorporating the assets throughout. (For more about the infusion of asset building into their new school, see his contribution "Designing a Naturescape: Cultivating Asset Growth" on page 181.)

Building Assets and Citizenship

Unit

Elementary Students as Asset Teachers

Grade Level(s)

4–5

Unit-Framing Questions

- What does it take to make a positive difference in every-day life?
- What is a developmental asset?
- How are developmental assets applied in everyday life?
- How does using assets provide a benefit to others?

Learning Objective

The student will explain, demonstrate, and give applications and benefits for one of the 40 developmental assets.

Overview

Students will review the 40 developmental assets. Each student will select one asset. Using PowerPoint presentation software, they will teach the asset selected, showing examples of how that asset is applied in today's society. Each student will develop an asset advertisement. Then the students, in groups of four or five, will design and publish a newsletter about their assets, including stories that show how using the assets benefits others.

Students demonstrate that they understand the personal rights and responsibilities of being a citizen or of history, by describing a key individual and her or his contribution to a significant event. Students are able to clearly convey in speech and in writing main ideas and supporting details to their peers.

Unit Design

A. Review and Development

During the first two weeks, students review the list of 40 developmental assets and select an internal asset to present to the class. Each student develops a two- to three-minute presentation that identifies and defines the asset, gives examples of its use in everyday life, and outlines the benefits of using that particular asset. The students also identify how the asset may relate to civic responsibility or a historical person or event. Students prepare a minimum of four PowerPoint slides to accompany their presentation.

B. Student Presentations

Week three consists of each student presenting their asset to the entire class. Presentations include a PowerPoint demonstration of the asset, from a perspective of history or civic responsibility. Using at least four slides, each student's presentation portrays the application of the asset in at least three everyday settings and at least two benefits to society with a tie to civic responsibility or a historical event.

C. Publishing Newsletters

Week four involves groups (four to five students each) publishing an assets newsletter. Each group writes at least one story that profiles an individual whose use of an asset represents being a productive citizen. The students create the newsletter title and headings, paste their edited stories, and add graphics. The newsletters go home as a classroom communication tool and allow you to assess what your students have learned about assets.

Resources Needed

1. The list of Search Institute's 40 developmental assets. For more information, see www.search-institute.org.
2. Childhood of Famous Americans Series (New York: Aladdin Books).
3. A dictionary, PowerPoint and Publisher software, index cards.

Labeling and Stereotyping

DO YOU REALLY KNOW WHAT IT FEELS LIKE?

JUDY TACCOGNA, ED.D.

Education Director

Search Institute

Minneapolis, Minnesota

Creating an asset-building environment depends not only upon what adults do with young people but also on how young people treat each other. In fact, results from Search Institute's Profiles of Student Life: Attitudes and Behaviors *survey about asset 5, caring school climate, show that students say it is how their peers act toward them that prompts them to report that their school's environment is not very positive. This interactive simulation, often referred to as the headband activity,[1] communicates powerfully the impact of labeling and stereotyping. It helps youth feel the effects of others' words and actions when they're based on assumptions and unfair generalizations about who people are.*

How often have you heard one student call another a name as they pass each other in the hallway? How often are those names derogatory or racially oriented? Or, how frequently does one student respond to another based on one particular aspect of that individual—that she or he is smart or a good athlete or runs with a different crowd? It happens more than we'd like to admit, most often represents a very generalized response, and usually involves labeling someone.

This activity is designed to help diverse groups of students become more aware that they are making such generalizations as well as directly experience what such generalizations sound and feel like, whether others whisper them under their breath or hurl them audibly across the room. The experience is most powerful when the leader takes the time to enlist the help of a variety of young people to role-model scenarios in the front of the room. Ensuring that peer opinion leaders—youth that other young people listen to, trust, and respect—from a variety of student groups represent the categories in the activity strengthens the message when those peer leaders return to their own groups.

Share with participants that creating an asset-building environment depends on what adults do with young people as well as on how young people treat each other. Ask participants if they know other students who are peer opinion leaders in their respective groups. Tell participants that if they want to change the environment of their school, they need to enlist other young people as their partners to do the necessary work most effectively, and that it is very important to involve a cross section of students who are those peer opinion leaders. This activity can effectively bring together diverse groups of students to make schools more asset friendly.

What You'll Need

- Eight to 10 student volunteers, preferably peer opinion leaders representing a variety of groups.
- Chairs arranged in a horseshoe in the front of the room.
- Large laminated headbands or cards (approximately 11 by 6 inches), each labeled with one of the following roles and the accompanying brief behavioral instruction:

Cute	*hit on me*
Gangster	*fear me*
Teacher's Pet	*resent me*
Class Clown	*laugh at me*
Minority	*exclude me*
Stoner	*disrespect me*
Slacker	*ignore me*
Nerd	*tease me*
Leader	*follow me*
Brain	*listen to me*
Airhead	*discount me*
Handicapped	*pity me*
Popular	*be like me*
Jock	*favor me*
Poor	*ridicule me*
Rich	*envy me*

What You'll Do

1. Ask for 8 to 10 volunteers to participate in a role play.

Enlist a mix of male and female, younger and older participants. Seat them in a horseshoe-shaped arrangement in the front of the room, and ask the rest of the participants to stand and move forward so that they can see and hear what will transpire.

2. Explain to the volunteers that in this role play you are the principal and they are high school students.

Tell the volunteers that you and they will discuss the problem of harassment of students in different social groups and the resulting violence at school dances and other events. Tell them that you have brought them together because they represent the various subgroups in this school and that you want to hear their ideas about how to reduce such harassment and prevent violence from erupting at future school-sponsored events.

3. Explain the one catch to this role play: They will each wear a headband that has a label and behavioral instruction that they cannot see, such as "Slacker—*ignore me*," and whenever they speak, people will treat them the way the headband instructs.

4. Let the entire group know that nobody is to reveal what the headbands say, and each role player is to keep her or his headband on and not look at it.

5. Place a labeled headband on each role player's head, taking care not to place a headband on anyone's head that could potentially stereotype that individual. (If headbands are not available, each student can simply hold a large card on her or his forehead.)

Assure participants that you have not distributed the labeled headbands with any malice intended.

6. Start the role play and ask the audience to observe body language such as facial expressions and positions as well as other subtleties that occur between the role players.

Begin by saying, "You all remember the dance last Friday night. And I'm sure you remember the fight that broke out during the evening." Go on to explain that several students got into a fight that erupted from harassment that had begun earlier in the week, and that it was the second time this year such an incident had occurred. Ask the volunteers, "What can we do to reduce such harassment between different groups in our school and to keep violence out of our school events?"

As the facilitator, call on the volunteers to share ideas for solutions, reminding them to respond as the headbands direct. To model that, make comments that may be encouraging to some volunteers and cutting to others, in accordance with the headband instructions.

7. Freeze the role play after about 10 minutes and reflect on responses.

Make sure when you first stop that volunteers keep their headbands on (or keep holding their cards on their foreheads) and don't look at the label. Ask participants to share what they think their headband says and how they felt when others responded to them the way they did. Ask the audience to share what they noticed about nonverbal and other behaviors. Then allow the volunteers to look at their headbands and applaud them.

8. Inform everyone that they are not to refer to any of the volunteers ever again by the label each wore.

9. As a group, discuss these questions:

   - How early in a child's educational experience do these stereotypes begin to develop?
   - How do these stereotypes affect relationships between groups at school?
   - What could be done to discourage labeling and stereotyping?

Remind students that they have tremendous potential to help or to hurt one another, and that it is each of our jobs to provide opportunities, skills, and rewards for helping if we want to make school a better place for *all* students. And if asset building is already a part of your school's culture, help students make the connection that learning these skills of positive communication strengthens their interpersonal and cultural competence assets as well.

_____

Notes

1. Permission to include the headband activity from the *Here's Looking At You, 2000*® Teacher's Guide © 1986 Comprehensive Health Education Foundation (C.H.E.F.®) was granted from C.H.E.F., Seattle, Washington.

Trekking Cross-Country

CULTURAL EMPATHY AND QUALITY DECISIONS

BRENDA DUFFEY, M.S.W.

High School Teacher (grades 10–12)

Juvenille Correctional Facility

Oregon

In this original three-week thematic unit, students gain not only intercultural competence but significant planning and decision-making skills as well. Although Brenda Duffey initially developed the lesson to enhance school engagement for a large population of ESL (English as a second language) students, she has adapted it to meet the varied needs of another unique student population: incarcerated male teens in a transition facility. By integrating language arts, math, and science content with that of social studies, her innovative approach helps meet the gaps in these students' educational progress and build strengths in asset areas.

Adolescence is a time when young people start to "spread their wings" and become curious about the world that exists outside the boundaries of their homes and family circles. Peer groups become the center of their life. One of the biggest motivators for school attendance is the opportunity to expand this peer group. When youth do class work in peer groups, which promotes this socialization, school engagement is enhanced. The Cross-Country Trip, a three-week, integrated-thematic unit that I teach in the context of the westward movement in American history, emphasizes doing the lesson work in hands-on, cooperative groups. I have found this approach to be the most successful in motivating and hooking students to learn, particularly those students who often feel—and in reality are—less connected than usual: students for whom English is not their first language or students who are not learning in a typical school environment, as are the cases for the students I've taught and teach.

While this unit I've created emphasizes a cooperative learning approach using skills from multiple content areas and addressing cultural competence on a number of levels, my primary intent is to focus asset building on planning and decision-making skills. More specifically, the objective is to give students the opportunity to plan a successful trip across the United States, to investigate the costs of a trip and understand budgeting and prioritizing choices. The bigger idea is that by appreciating what it means to be a critical consumer of information and analyzing an event, issue, problem, or phenomenon from varied or opposing perspectives or points of view, young adults can increase their cultural competence. And students who are somewhat disengaged from mainstream learning can also acquire important assets toward becoming healthy, self-confident young adults.

Meeting the Challenges of Unique Student Populations

I originally developed the Cross-Country Trip unit for 8th-grade students at a school in New Mexico where I was teaching at the time. More than 70 percent of the school population was Hispanic, with a dropout rate approaching 30 percent. School attendance was very poor, and there was a large population of ESL (English as a second language) students. The school also qualified for a higher number of special education and reading services than other schools its size.

We found an integrated, hands-on, cooperative learning approach to be successful in motivating and engaging these students in learning. During this time, we also were introduced to asset building, and I began to incorporate this into classroom lessons as well.

After moving to Oregon, I adapted my lessons to meet the needs of incarcerated male teens, ages 15–18. I now teach in a 25-bed transition facility with an accredited high school that serves a mix of Caucasian, American Indian, African-American, and Hispanic youth. The school provides services to issue a diploma, GED (graduate equivalency degree), or help students transition back to their original schools. The program also has a work-study component. Many students in the correctional facility receive special education services, and most lag behind their peers in educational progress.

We teach units in themes designed specifically to help students fulfill credit requirements, prepare for the GED, or meet state performance standards. The "Cross-Country Trip" is just one example of thematic units I teach.

Using this integrated approach helps address multiple content areas and identify needs in certain skill areas so that individual students in the high school correctional facility can develop education plans to focus on these skills or to work with tutors. Although the students here have great need, the facility has the luxury of a very low (8-1) student-teacher ratio most of the time. We also have auxiliary services from volunteers in the community who work as mentors and tutors.

Peer group work also provides value in the facility, as it did in the New Mexico middle school. By doing intensive work in groups, our students learn many interpersonal skills. Giving them a group-based assignment in school provides an additional opportunity for them to practice these skills outside of a clinical setting, practice that also helps build assets.

The Cross-Country Trip

The Unit Plan

The objective of the three-week unit on the Cross-Country Trip is to have students perform specific tasks designed to increase their mastery of the content standards in social studies as well as in math, English, and science. Their work on those standards then becomes the vehicle for building strengths in asset areas, for becoming competent, caring, and responsible young adults.

In addition to developing skills related to being able to plan a cross-country trip—reading a map, researching and gathering information, using technology, and comparing costs by understanding concepts of ratio and proportion, miles per gallon, and distance and rate of travel—students also gain a historical perspective of different cultures. The lesson emphasizes three cultures: Western European immigration to the West in the 19th century, American Indians, and the plant and animal "culture" disrupted by American settlement. By including socioeconomic systems, students develop a broader sense of cultural empathy and greater ability to make quality decisions concerning the use of land and limited resources. (A point-of-view writing assignment also helps hone their individual knowledge and appreciation of these cultures.)

Handout 5.2: The Cross-Country Trip Unit Plan (on page 166) outlines the daily activities, topics, and processes used in teaching this unit. At the middle school in New Mexico, where the unit was originated, we used four periods a day for teaching the unit: English, history, math, and science classes. At the correctional high school facility where I teach now, only three periods are devoted to teaching theme units. Three periods are enough. The skills of these high school students are for the most part above 8th-grade level. Assignments on the chart reflect the three-period format for instruction.

In adapting the lesson for the correctional facility, I found it necessary to gather research materials ahead of time for these students. Although of high school age, the vast majority of these young men lack library and research skills, and the campus has no available library. Students do have access to materials through the Internet, and respond very well to instruction regarding locating information sources using this tool.

Standards and Skills

Content standards and skills development integrate in the unit in the following ways: of significance in social studies is the understanding of a cost-benefit analysis of economic choices. Learning the realities of the costs of a cross-country trip will benefit students as they become responsible adults making budget decisions and choices. This relates specifically to planning a family vacation, as well as to the broader realm of choices they make about consumer spending.

Planning and decision making also relate directly to math: estimating solutions to problems, determining if the solutions are accurate and reasonable, and applying the relationships among whole number, decimal, fraction, percentage, exponent, and integer operations to solve problems (including relationships of ratio and proportion). It is extremely important to be able to estimate reasonable amounts of water, food, and other necessary supplies to last the length of the trip. To plan ahead and make sound travel decisions, it is also necessary to be able to use ratio and proportion to determine precisely how long you will need the supplies to last before restocking.

The Cross-Country Trip Unit Plan

	Period One	Period Two	Period Three
Week I Day One	Divide into four groups (Oregon, California, Santa Fe, Mormon Trails). Read material aloud, discuss. Begin presentation.	Continue work on eight-minute presentation to include trail map, trip purpose, settlements along trail, resulting states.	Oral presentations. Teacher scores using scoring rubrics. Students take notes in research notebooks and ask questions.
Day Two	In groups, compute trail length using string, textbook scale. Draw on blank map. Lesson on ratio and proportion.	Compute total travel time for ox-drawn wagon traveling at a rate of five mph 10 hours/day.	Determine personal items, amount of food and water, for family of seven based on wagon capacity. Geometry assignments.
Day Three	Life science maps: blank maps with physical features and land formations of areas through which trail passes.	Research one plant or animal indigenous to the group's region for three-minute presentation.	Presentation: describe or draw plant or animal, habitat and climate for growth, impact of human settlement.
Day Four	Continue research for presentations.	Continue work on presentations.	Presentations. Teacher evaluates. Students continue to take notes in research notebooks for future essay assignment.
Day Five	Begin library research on one American Indian group living in region through which group trail passes.	Prepare bibliography to turn in after presentation: one reference book, one periodical article, Internet reference.	Work on group presentation. Location—map. Food, clothing, shelter. Culture—religion, social roles, impact of American settlement.
Week II Day One	Presentations: 10–15 minutes. Students take notes in research notebooks.	Continue presentations. Students evaluate using instructor's forms.	Finish presentations and go over evaluations.
Day Two	Prepare journal using writing process of rough draft, editing, and final copy.	One-week diary of adolescent traveling with family on trail. Describe landscape, how time spent, major event or crisis.	Continue journals. Finished copy will be scored using scoring guide rubrics for writing.
Day Three	Continue journals.	Continue journals.	Continue journals.
Day Four	Library research to gather demographic information on modern states through which original trail passed.	Use Internet, almanacs, AAA tour books for information on industries, attractions, average incomes.	Library research. Take notes in research notebooks and prepare a bibliography.
Day Five	Library research.	Library research.	Library research.
Week III Day One	Choose a major East and West Coast city. Prepare route across country in fossil-fueled vehicle of choice.	Follow major interstate routes and find accommodations based on traveling 500–600 miles/day, 10 hours at 55 mph.	Compute costs for trip based on gasoline miles/gallon and number of days' costs for accommodations and meals.
Day Two	Finish travel routes, costs. Fill in blank maps and Trip Planning Project for evaluation.	Prepare essay on one of two writing assignments to be scored using rubrics.	Compare modern-day trip with that of an ancestor who has left a journal.
Day Three	Second-choice writing assignment: compare lifestyle of one American Indian culture before/after American settlement.	Work on essay.	Work on essay.
Day Four	Finish all assignments with evaluations and scoring as students finish essays.	Finish all assignments with evaluations and scoring. Some students still working on essays.	Finish all assignments with evaluations and scoring. Students need extra time for essay.
Day Five	Extra time for essays if needed in all classes.		

Key to promoting critical thinking, a vital component of effective decision making, is writing assignments. Spelling out plans in writing encourages students to organize their ideas and break down broad concepts into individual components—to enhance deductive reasoning and knowledge of cause and effect. Vocabulary building and the ability to read instructions (especially road maps) create self-confidence; individual students believe they can actually plan and initiate such a trip. Effective writing also promotes communication skills, further building student confidence and competency in networking to investigate all the components of a complex assignment or problem.

As our global community struggles with the impact of humans on our limited resources, it is vital that students also consider the natural world in their decisions and choices. The work in the natural science area promotes their thinking about the impact of human settlement on the natural world and, more specifically, uses of limited resources and the decision making involved in managing them.

Another aspect of the science instruction is developing technologic skills vital to any planning and decision making in today's society. In researching state demographics, for example, students use the computer to visit Web sites and gather information. Computer knowledge and training is a strong motivator for students, thus promoting school engagement. Gaining insight into the varying demographics of different regions of the United States also encourages cultural competence.

In both settings in which I've taught the Cross-Country Trip unit, parents and students, as well as administrators and community members respond enthusiastically. The hardest part is getting other teachers to join in working as a team. Once the initial steps have been taken, however, many colleagues realize how much fun teaching is when students are sincerely engaged and excited about what they are doing. Students and parents have truly provided the exciting momentum to keep the programs going for this type of learning. This lesson, as with others, has extended beyond the classroom into the community and individual homes, and it has brought the excitement and learning back, in a very asset-building way to other classrooms and teachers.

Chapter 6

Infusing Assets into Math and Science

There Is No Such Thing as a Stupid Question

ROLE PLAYING TO SUCCEED IN MATH

HELENE LOUISE PERRY

Mathematics Teacher (grades 7–8)

Clara Barton Open School

Minneapolis, Minnesota

In my classroom, there are no "stupid" questions—I tell my math students that every question creates an opportunity for learning. I believe that *all students can learn*, even those who previously have failed; this belief is fundamental to my approach to teaching mathematics and to asset building. Further, I believe that each student needs the opportunity to learn to think *critically*, so I provide rich mathematics problems for all—problems that require every student to identify which information is important, assess what he or she already knows, organize the information, and use more than one operation.

To provide rich problems and encourage greater math achievement in my students—many of whom face past math failure and deal with the daily obstacles of language barriers, poverty and homelessness, literacy and behavioral issues, and special education labels—I use a simulation game I call the "Amusement Park Design Company." Because I also believe that teacher expectations strongly correlate with student achievement and asset development, I make it my goal to provide each of my students with access to higher-level learning strategies that foster achievement and bolster confidence in their mathematical abilities. And the way I do this is through role playing. Role playing is extremely useful in tackling the unique challenges of my classroom:

- Teaching students appropriate classroom behavior;
- Helping them overcome their fear of math—particularly math that requires them to read, think through a problem, and communicate the solution; and

SCHOOL DEMOGRAPHICS

Clara Barton Open School
Minneapolis, Minnesota

Students: 600

Grades: K–8

Gender:

Male	unknown
Female	unknown

Race and Ethnicity:

Black/African American	25.0%
Hispanic/Latino	7.0%
Asian/Pacific Islander	12.0%
American Indian	4.0%
White/Caucasian	52.0%

Socioeconomics:

Free/Reduced Lunch	17.0%

- Assisting them in developing systems that allow them to be prepared and organized.

We use the Connected Mathematics Project (CMP) curriculum at my school, which focuses on developing mathematical reasoning to solve problems, reflect on solutions, and make connections to broader mathematical concepts. To further our curriculum goals, I cast my students in the roles of employees of the Amusement Park Design Company, a name that suggested itself to me through one of the word problems in our first "investigation."

The Amusement Park Design Company Simulation

I created the Amusement Park Design Company simulation to motivate my 7th- and 8th-grade students with a real-life situation and draw them into the CMP "Covering and Surrounding" investigation unit. The first lesson focuses on the concepts of area and perimeter in the context of amusement park bumper car rides—that grabs students' attention and supports building a variety of assets.

Students love theme parks and are eager to enter into the role play suggested by the company name. To introduce the simulation, I set up my classroom to resemble a corporate seminar room by rearranging student tables into one large conference table. Then I set the scene: "You have been hired to work for CMP's Amusement Park Design Company in order to solve some problems. But first, you need training about company procedures."

I ask students, "What do you think the employee rules ought to be?" We choose seven employee guidelines, which remain posted at the front of the class. As "employees," students are to be on time for work, come prepared with appropriate tools, complete homework, care for tools and the work environment, work cooperatively as a team, speak to others respectfully, and contribute to the group work.

I remind students that the employee guidelines they have chosen are similar to the class rules we establish at the beginning of the year (listen to the speaker, work cooperatively, respect others, stay on task, and turn in homework on time). In this way, I hold students to reasonable boundaries and high expectations, cornerstones of developmental asset building in adolescents.

Students earn "income" (points) as individuals or for the team when they comply with the company guidelines. Each day, I check the criteria and assign points. Soon, however, students monitor their own behaviors and their teammates'. They even work jointly to earn team "bonuses" (positive points for the team).

Next, I outline the skills needed to solve the company's problems, which are similar to those required in the work force. For example, real employees must be able to solve math problems, work cooperatively with a team, and comply with company rules (including wearing an identification badge—a different color for each work team).

From the outset, I maintain the company role playing completely. I introduce math problems in the context of the Amusement Park Design Company environment and explain that "customers" need the solutions by a particular deadline.

To keep students motivated, I periodically change the company name to correspond to the content of each new math unit. I also show students a 1988 movie, *Stand and Deliver*, about a teacher who inspires his inner-city students to overcome various odds to take the Advanced Placement Calculus Exam. We discuss the film, and students write an essay describing what the movie tells them about their ability to learn mathematics and how they are affected by the true story.

Building Respect and Confidence

Critical to my students' math success is first spending time building a safe and supportive environment in class that does not focus on math per se. Such asset-rich discussion, however, lays the foundation for promoting math success in students who are lacking in some social skills and insecure in their mathematical abilities. It's time and involvement well spent.

Setting the Ground Rules

To tackle these behavioral challenges, I use group expectations in concrete ways in my math class. For example, one of our class rules, "Be respectful of others," fits perfectly with my expectation that there is no "stupid" question—that it is okay to say "I don't know"—and further, that I *expect* students to ask questions about what they do not understand. We establish that there are no put-downs allowed in class—only buildups.

I address behavioral concerns that come up in the simulation games much as they would be taken care of in the workplace. As the supervisor, I advise, "If this behavior continues, I'll be forced to write it up and place a report in your file." Students are often more responsive to efforts to reshape their behavior in the simulation setting than they would be in the regular classroom. Now I spend much less time on classroom management and focus more on teaching. While there are still days when it seems goals are forgotten, my math classes are quicker to get back on track. The simulation also reinforces the assets about school boundaries being important.

Developing Small-Group Problem-Solving Skills

One of my goals is to help students work more independently and develop their ability to think through problems for themselves—to build more developmental assets. Almost all my teaching makes use of cooperative learning groups to reach this goal. Students work in teams to solve math problems. Small groups allow students to get the support they need—and not always from me. Students start out looking for solutions as a class and then move into partner and small-group work so that I can teach the interpersonal skills necessary for cooperative group success.

I structure roles that students are to use within their groups, so that they feel supported and directed. Groups of four usually include a *reader*, a *task facilitator*, a *clarifier*, and an *encourager*. I mix the groups by ability levels, strengths, and gender, deliberately choosing members of each group. The teams change many times during the year, so students learn to work with a variety of personalities and abilities (For another example of a cooperative learning group activity involving interval tables, see "The Jumping Jack Experiment" on page 175).

Creating a Fearless Math Environment

The class I describe here offers many instructional challenges, in addition to behavioral challenges. My students span two grade levels, three ages, low math and reading levels, and a host of learning barriers. Our math classes were originally grouped by ability on the basis of a general test, previous teacher input, and a district-standardized test. As a result, my 7th- and 8th-grade class is not racially diverse, and the majority of students are special education students. Because I have always encouraged heterogeneous groupings—by ethnicity, ability, gender, and socioeconomic status—I was concerned. However, I decided to view this as an opportunity.

Addressing the Achievement Gap

A gap exists in our district between European American and African American school achievement, a gap I believe is due to economics rather than race. I believe that *all* students can learn mathematics if we present material in such a way that students can process and hold on to what they learn. The challenge is to find strategies that work. While it has been a long process, I see a great deal of progress.

Math achievement is increased when we help students build the confidence they need to hypothesize, estimate answers, and make reasoned guesses. Often, students are unwilling to answer math questions because they fear being wrong and ridiculed. I encourage them to answer, because often they are correct. When no questions are asked or answers are given, misinformation remains. I tell students that an incorrect answer is important, as it offers an opportunity for learning. By working together, we can find the solution.

I teach strategies that good learners always use—talking to yourself as you read to process information and reflect on the context—as well as provide them with study and organizational skills. And I model those strategies as I move through the lessons, giving students tools for later success in math and developing assets that they can use for a lifetime.

Assessing Skills

For each new class, I first find out what my students' skills are and what they are missing. I choose curricula that isolate the key concepts students need to progress. For example, I may choose fractions, because rational numbers are always hard for students. From there, I create many concrete examples of how fractions are used in daily life, and as many hands-on and manipulative experiences as I can pull together to help students learn. In a recent class of 7th graders who were struggling with fractions, I realized that students were missing some prior concepts, so I taught them a 6th-grade-level fractions unit.

I also pay attention to providing *scaffolding* for my math students. That's the process of breaking down a complex learning task into smaller chunks and teaching the elements that then support—or form the scaffolding—for mastering the

The Jumping Jack Experiment

Another example of my use of cooperative learning groups to promote problem solving occurs in a CMP (Connected Mathematics Project) curriculum investigation involving interval tables. Students gather data during the Jumping Jack Experiment, and learn to record the data in a table. This is exciting to the students, even though many complain about having to exert themselves so early in the morning. It gets them actively involved in their learning, and they learn best by *doing* and by using visuals. They also like the opportunity to talk to each other.

Students record the number of jumping jacks they can do every 10 seconds for a total of 120 seconds. Each team needs four participants: a jumper, timer, counter, and recorder. They rotate these roles throughout the activity, giving each person the opportunity to learn to accurately record data. At the end of the experiment, each student copies data gathered from others in the group. Although I was initially concerned about supervision of the groups, the students managed themselves well.

When I first ask students to identify and explain patterns in their jumping jack data, they can identify only two patterns: students do not do the same total number of jumping jacks, and the total number of jumping jacks increases as time passes. When I press them to see other patterns, particularly how many jumping jacks students do in every 10-second interval of the 120-second experiment, they discover they cannot identify that information, because their tables show only accumulated jumping jacks as time passes.

I ask each team to find a way to tell how many jumping jacks each student does during each 10-second interval. Students analyze the tables they make and soon realize that if they subtract the previous total of jumping jacks from the next total, the difference equals the total for each interval.

I then ask all the groups to make another table showing how many total jumping jacks each person on their team does in each 10-second interval. When we analyze our interval tables, all groups note that the jumpers do more jumping jacks in the 10-second interval at the beginning of the 120 seconds, and then slow down in the middle. Jumpers seem to get a boost of energy and do more jumping jacks in the final 10–20 seconds. It is their dependence on each other, use of good interpersonal skills, and motivated engagement in an active learning task that helps students arrive at the answer.

I expect everyone to contribute to the group so that the group does indeed come up with a joint solution, rather than depending on just one person. I encourage students to listen and communicate their problem-solving ideas to each other. I hold the whole team responsible for understanding the problem, and in the follow-up discussion, I call randomly upon one student to contribute the team's answer.

Students know it is important that everyone understands the concept and works together. I encourage them to ask for help as needed. However, to reinforce the team's need to coach its own members, I use the "Ask three, then me" rule—I don't answer math questions until students have first asked others and are still stuck. In this way, students begin to feel empowered by their abilities and more confident in helping others—two more ways to build assets.

bigger learning. I build activities and lessons to teach concepts from the point students do understand them, based on missing skills and gaps in knowledge I have identified. Some students, for example, may not know how to read well, much less how to read a math problem.

We do a lot of "messy math" problems in our classroom. These problems involve more than one skill or require students to use more than one strategy to solve them. I try to connect all of the problems we do to students' lives. I change the context of problems from our CMP book to include the streets on which students live, the places they go, the things they buy, and the activities in which they are interested. This helps to interest them in the solution as well.

I also purposefully do not initially teach an algorithm, so that my class has time to understand the process before they know the quick path for solving a problem. This allows students to have a greater chance to apply the same thinking to similar situations.

Designing learning experiences that use multiple intelligences is also important to me. For example, when we study coordinates, I use movement and rhythmic chants to help students get the idea of moving back and forth across one coordinate and up and down the other. Students make up songs to learn the elements of surface area.

Modeling Questions to Solve Problems

I always ask students to present what they know so far. Even when homework is a challenge and students think they can't do it, I expect them to turn in a "work in progress"—what they think they know and how they tried to solve the problem. Many times their answers are not wrong; students may simply think about the problem in a new way or find a new route to the solution.

I use "hip pocket" questions to probe what students do know. For instance, "Have you tried _____? Did you think about _____? How is this like _____? Where would you find information about _____ to help you solve that?" Modeling such questions helps students ask similar questions of themselves and their peers in their cooperative groups when they are in the midst of problem solving. Modeling useful questioning techniques can help students develop a form of self-talk they can use over a lifetime of problem solving. In this way, we as teachers can empower students with the ability to seek answers inside themselves and build developmental assets in the process.

I let my students know that I don't have all the answers and am not afraid to admit mistakes. When I don't know the answer, I promise students I will find out. In this manner, students learn valuable lessons in lifelong learning.

Team Teaching

Because many of my students have failed at mathematics in the past, and most have special needs that qualify them for special education or other targeted assistance, I enlist the collaboration of my special education colleague. She and I work together daily as a team, which is especially important for students who need a great deal of attention and are easily frustrated. She also sees some of our students in a small-group class or homeroom and is able to give students additional help with lessons. I know that these students make greater gains because of the consistency of their math instruction.

It takes teams of people working together to create successful learning environments. What I don't notice, my teammate does; we can jointly reflect on a lesson and see much more than either of us could in isolation. That collaboration is also useful outside the classroom in the form of a support system of other teachers with whom I can discuss classroom strategies and develop solutions.

Organizing Students for Success

The other major challenge in my math classroom, besides addressing appropriate behavior and helping students overcome their fear of math, is assisting them in developing systems that allow them to be prepared and organized daily. Each of our CMP units has five or six "investigations" involving concepts for a large mathematical theme. Each investigation asks the students to solve a multistep problem, which often takes days to complete. Initially, I asked students to keep all of their work in a math journal/notebook. Many found it difficult to organize their thoughts or record their investigations in a sequential manner. Others lost or misplaced their notebooks.

I decided to create an advance organizer called an *investigation sheet*, which maps out the steps and expectations for each math investigation at a time. Each student keeps her or his personal file in the classroom, which holds investigations in progress so that they are handy for the next class period. Students also store completed investigations in their file, which we keep for their student portfolios.

The advance organizer helps reduce frustration and provides a guide for students to arrange their work for each investigation. A process approach that I use a lot along with the investigation organizer, particularly when students are working with word problems, is the K-W-H-L[1] strategy sheet, a chart that helps students analyze what they already know and what they need to know (see Handout 6.1: The K-W-H-L Worksheet on page 178). I tell students that K-W-H-L represents the following: **K** = What do I **K**now? **W** = What do I **W**ant to know? **H** = **H**ow will I solve this? **L** = What did I **L**earn?

I encourage students to "write" their answers in any way they can. Although writing their thoughts in complete sentences is my goal, if that's not where they are in terms of skills, I ask them to write words or draw, diagram, or sketch what they know in some other way. Even the students who have difficulty with writing know that they can use pictures, diagrams, and short phrases to explain their thinking.

One of the great benefits of using the K-W-H-L process tool is that what students *do* know surfaces immediately—and it is usually more than they think they know. It helps students better organize and remember their own thinking. Students' K-W-H-L sheets also give me a better feel for their prior knowledge so that I can build appropriately on it.

Strategies for Promoting Math Achievement

To successfully help students learn, teachers must know and continually use many strategies and methods. You must also attend to the ways your students learn and constantly try new techniques. I usually use heterogeneous groupings and try to connect my lessons to students' prior knowledge. Part of the time, I differentiate instruction based on ability, but I also provide some of my math instruction in a whole group to ensure access for all, rather than prejudging who can do what.

Wait-time is hugely important.[2] We as teachers have a real tendency to move on too quickly, leaving behind the struggling student who needs more time to process an answer. We must be prepared to wait for students as they work out their answers.

From the outset, I communicate high standards to my students, which plays into my later efforts to get students to take responsibility for their own learning and

The K-W-H-L Worksheet

Name _____ Date _____

Using words and pictures, show what you **know** about the problem, what you **want** to know about the problem, **how** you will solve the problem, and what you **learned** about the problem.

Investigation _____

Problem Number _____ Problem Title _____

Question _____

What do I **know**:

What do I **want** to know:

How will I solve this:

What did I **learn** (answer to the problem):

develop confidence in their mathematical abilities. I believe that an effective—and developmentally asset-rich—mathematics classroom is one in which:

- You, the teacher, hold high expectations for students' achievement— you believe that all students can learn mathematics, expose them to all aspects of the math curriculum, and encourage them to take higher-level math classes.
- Students can learn that mastering mathematics is as necessary as learning to read and can understand the importance of using math as a tool to solve problems.
- Students are allowed to solve messy problems using critical thinking skills in a variety of ways.
- Students can communicate their thinking and reasoning processes as they solve problems.

Notes

1. The K-W-H-L is based on the original K-W-L approach cited in Ogle, Donna M. (1986). K-W-L: A Teaching Model That Develops Active Reading of Expository Text. *Reading Teacher*, (39): 564–570.
2. Teachers typically wait one second or less after asking a question and before moving on to the next student for a response. Students whose teachers wait three or more seconds for an answer learn more and think more deeply, according to Rowe, Mary B. (1987). Wait-Time: Slowing Down May Be a Way of Speeding Up. *American Educator*, 11(1): 38–47. Wait-time also encourages students of diverse backgrounds who may be learning English as a second language to think, participate, and formulate an answer, report Carin, Arthur A., and Bass, Joel E. (2001). *Methods for Teaching Science as Inquiry*. Upper Saddle River, NJ: Prentice-Hall, 171.

Creating Adaptations

You can adapt the mathematics simulation approach to a variety of problem types and ability levels. Students love to role-play and enjoy taking on small-group roles to solve problems. When teaching students about addition, subtraction, multiplication, and division, it would be great fun to set up a classroom bank, complete with checkbooks, deposit slips, loan officers, bank tellers, customers, and mortgage bankers. Depending upon students' sophistication, you could teach concepts involving negative numbers, interest calculations, amortization, and investment strategies, as well.

For integrating other content areas, consider setting up an architectural and landscape design firm to explore math concepts involving area, volume, angles, and basic trigonometry. Music always seems to motivate students; why not create a record production company and explore supply and demand, inventory skills, order processing, and the like? For an extra challenge, advanced students could analyze wavelength and vibration data produced by various instruments and look for connections to sound production.

For younger students or students who need extra math support, set up a toy company similar to the Amusement Park Design Company, allowing students to decide what games their toy company will produce, how many pieces each game will involve, and how many players each game might need. Then have students set prices and "sell" the games, recording sales data and forecasting sales.

Really, the possibilities are endless for role-playing in the mathematics classroom. And you will be gratified by the confidence students develop in their problem-solving abilities when they are motivated by the context.

Designing a Naturescape

CULTIVATING ASSET GROWTH

DAVE GUILE, M.S.

Principal (grades K–5)

Forest Ridge Elementary School

Salem, Oregon

The issues of "Why does it matter?", "What does it mean?", and "How does it relate to me?" are critical for students to think about in order for them to find meaning in their learning. When students are highly engaged in project learning that involves real-life planning and decision making and when they live daily in an asset-rich school environment, they're more likely to address these issues. At Forest Ridge Elementary, the environment and scientific inquiry matter—and so do the students.

Through a unique project on the school grounds involving a naturescape—which students actually design and implement—the asset-building aspects of our environmental science program are front and center; students are active, excited, and interested in learning, which in turn increases their school engagement.

Although the naturescape project is one cornerstone of asset building at our school, it is by no means the only one. Forest Ridge is a unique, new suburban school: it houses a traditional neighborhood (public) school and a charter school, both of which are based on the framework of 40 developmental assets.

Starting with the end in mind, a concept from *Understanding by Design*[1] of beginning with what you want to achieve, was exactly where five teachers and I began to plan a new school. Eager to address the needs of children moving into the 21st century, we created a charter school to focus on three areas of study—environmental science, technology, and civic responsibility. Additionally, we wanted a school based on a conceptual foundation that would foster a sense of responsibility and could be used within the curriculum focus areas to enhance student, parent, and community involvement.

SCHOOL DEMOGRAPHICS
Forest Ridge Elementary School
Salem, Oregon

Students: 325

Grades: K–5

Gender:

Male	47.0%
Female	53.0%

Race and Ethnicity:*

Black/African American	<1.0%
Hispanic/Latino	5.0%
Asian/Pacific Islander	2.0%
American Indian	<1.0%
White/Caucasian	84.0%

Socioeconomics:

Free/Reduced Lunch	23.0%

*May be skewed because of a high percentage of no response.

Planning a Unique School

Located just north of Salem, Oregon, Forest Ridge, with an opening enrollment in grades K–5 of 325 students, has a total capacity of 450. Both the traditional neighborhood school and the charter school share much of the same facility, with five classrooms devoted to the charter program. In a symbiotic relationship between the independent charter and the traditional school, the district provides the space for the charter, and all programs that the charter develops are provided without charge to the traditional school. It is a win-win proposition. I, as principal, and other resource staff provide service to both schools.

After researching various programs and approaches, staff selected Search Institute's developmental assets framework as the foundation for both the charter and traditional school programs. Once we made this decision, and in a continued collaborative planning effort, staff tackled the task of backward design, following these stages:

1. Identify desired results;
2. Determine acceptable evidence; and
3. Plan learning experiences and instruction.

Desired Results

In stage 1, staff identified four specific results to achieve:

- Developing students who are technologically literate and use technology as a tool to learn, experience, and demonstrate content knowledge;
- Raising students who understand civic responsibility and engage in community service;
- Fostering student knowledge about the environment by directly participating in environmental projects; and
- Developing students who have many developmental assets and are asset builders themselves.

The staff also adopted as our mission statement a poem by Gabriela Mistral, the Chilean Nobel laureate in literature (1945). Her poetry addresses especially children, or others in need of protection. This particular poem of hers reflects our staff commitment to be active asset builders for our students:

> *Many things we need can wait.*
> *The child cannot.*
> *Now is the time his bones are being formed,*
> *His blood is being made,*
> *His mind is being developed.*
> *To him we cannot say tomorrow,*
> *His name is today.*

Acceptable Evidence

From this results-oriented approach, and with clear goals in hand, staff moved on to stage 2 to determine acceptable products evidencing success. To guide our decision making, we answered this essential question: *What tasks, tests, or projects will be reliable in determining if students have met the goals?* As the staff engaged in discussions regarding the environmental portion of the state science standards, it became increasingly clear that the standards, the school's goals, and the 40 developmental assets would integrate well and provide students with the needed relevance to maintain highly engaged students.

For example, the environmental studies portion of our curriculum fit perfectly with the state standards (primary students need to be able to form a hypothesis; upper elementary students need to design an inquiry and develop a record-keeping system). And by having students actually design and implement a study involving the naturescape plant growth, they would be strengthening assets for school engagement and using youth as resources as well as for planning and decision making.

It also became clear, however, that relying on the state-mandated science test at grade 5 would not suffice as the only evidence of achievement. We wanted much more. Staff decided that, in addition, each grade level—not just grade 5— would create a project through which students could demonstrate an understanding of a particular aspect of environmental studies. Students would also actively participate in a community service project related to environmental studies. Additionally, we would use the district's annual school climate survey that is administered to students to help measure asset building.

Learning Experiences and Instruction

For the next step in the backward design process, staff developed grade-level curriculum maps. For each grade level, the curriculum map required the following:

- Cover the required state content standards in all academic areas;
- Provide for community service;
- Include project-based learning;
- Integrate the three focus areas of the school: environmental science, technology, and civic responsibility; and
- Include asset development.

In this collaborative planning effort, each staff member contributed ideas that would give students opportunities to be problem solvers and contributors within the school. The curriculum maps emphasize key developmental assets in each focus area, with links to other content areas (for excerpts illustrating science and environmental studies and asset links from each grade level's curriculum map, see Handouts 6.2–6.6 on pages 184–188). We also developed a schoolwide community service component, with the expectation that all students should be involved in service learning.

Forest Ridge Elementary—1st-Grade Curriculum Map

Month	Science/Health	Environmental Studies	Comments Asset Development
September	Life Science: Plants and Seeds Inquiry: Observe and Compare	Plants and Seeds Types of Plants Migration Who Cares—I Care Naturescape Construction Teach 4 R's (Reduce, Recycle, Reuse, Repair)	Green School Assembly Assets 3, 4, 5, 6, 8, 14, 22
October	Inquiry: Observe and Compare	Plants and Seeds Types of Plants Migration Who Cares—I Care Naturescape Planting	Assets 6, 8, 14, 22, 24, 30
November	Earth Space: The Sky The Arts: Painting and Drawing	Observe, Measure, and Record Plant Growth Naturescape Maintenance	Assets 8, 22, 30
December	Health Just Say No	Observe, Measure, and Record Plant Growth	Assets 8, 22, 30, 35
January	Health Body/Teeth	Link with Everyday Counts—Tempera- ture Effect on Plants	Assets 8, 22, 30, 31
February	Earth: Matter, Matter, Everywhere	Observe, Measure, and Record Plant Growth	Assets 8, 22

March	Inquiry: Be a Scientist—Observe
	  Changes in the Real World
		Analyze Growth Changes—Predict
		  Growth for June
			Assets 22, 32

April	Life Science—Organism Diversity and Interdependence	Trees and Rainforest Integrated Project	Beach Cleanup Assets 9, 22
May	Life Science—Organism Diversity and Interdependence	Trees and Rainforest Integrated Project	Asset 22
June	Presenting Data	Analyze Growth Project Sharing and Speeches	Rainforest Project Sharing Assets 22, 27

Forest Ridge Elementary—2nd-Grade Curriculum Map

Month	Science/Health	Environmental Studies	Comments Asset Development
September	Watering Earth's Plants Inquiry: Observe and Compare	Plants and Their Parts Plants and Soil Classification Who Cares—I Care Naturescape Construction Teach 4 R's (Reduce, Recycle, Reuse, Repair)	Green School Assembly Assets 3, 4, 5, 6, 8, 14, 22
October	Inquiry: Observe and Compare	Naturescape Planting Observe, Measure, and Record Plant Growth and Rainfall	Assets 6, 8, 14, 22, 24, 30
November	Earth Space: The Sky The Arts—Painting and Drawing	Observe, Measure, and Record Plant Growth and Rainfall Naturescape Maintenance	Assets 8, 22, 30
December	Health Just Say No	Observe, Measure, and Record Plant Growth and Rainfall	Assets 8, 22, 30, 35
January	Health Body Systems	Link with Everyday Counts Math: Measure in Inches Rainfall	Assets 8, 22, 30, 31
February	Earth: Matter and Force	Observe, Measure, and Record Plant Growth and Rainfall	Assets 8, 22

March	Inquiry: Be a Scientist—Observe
	  Changes in the Real World
		Observe, Measure, and Record
		  Plant Growth and Rainfall
			Assets 22, 32

April	Construct a Presentation Using
	  a Simple Chart and a Simple
	  Graph with a Narrative State-
	  ment of Fact
		Home and Garden
		Backyard Habitat
			Beach Cleanup
			Earth Day Presentation:
			Rainfall and Plant Growth
			Assets 9, 22

May	Life Science—Organism Diversity and Interdependence	Home and Garden Backyard Habitat	Assets 4, 5, 22
June	Health	Prepare Garden for Summer	Home and Garden Backyard Habitat Project Sharing Assets 2, 8, 9

Forest Ridge Elementary—3rd-Grade Curriculum Map

Month	Science/Health	Environmental Studies	Comments Asset Development
September	Life Science: Diversity and Interdependence Inquiry: Forming a Hypothesis—What Will the Growth Pattern Be for the Naturescape Plants?	Plant Life Cycle. Drawing Seeds Germination Who Cares—I Care Naturescape Teach 4 R's (Reduce, Recycle, Reuse, Repair)	Green School Assembly Assets 3, 4, 5, 6, 8, 14, 22
October	Weather—Seasonal Patterns	Observe, Measure, and Record Plant Growth and Temperature	Assets 6, 8, 14, 22, 24, 30
November	Earth Space: Constellation Project	Observe, Measure, and Record Plant Growth and Temperature	Assets 8, 22, 30
December	Health Refusal Skills	Observe, Measure, and Record Plant Growth and Temperature	Assets 8, 22, 30, 35
January	Earth Science: Weather Patterns	Using Metric Measures: Temperature Effect on Plants	Assets 8, 22, 30, 31
February	Physical Science: Matter	Plant Growth: Link with Everyday Counts Math: Millimeters and Liters	Assets 8, 22
March	Physical Science: Force and Energy	Plant Growth: Link with Everyday Counts Math: Fractions, Graphing	Assets 22, 32
April	Inquiry: Presenting Data	Needs of Plants and Animals Greenspace and Urban Space	Beach Cleanup Earth Day Presentation: Temperature and Plant Growth Assets 9, 22
May	Health Hygiene	Create a City Model	Asset 22
June	Inquiry: Predictions of Growth for Summer	Prepare Naturescape for Summer	Assets 9, 30

Forest Ridge Elementary—4th-Grade Curriculum Map

Month	Science/Health	Environmental Studies	Comments Asset Development
September	Inquiry: Form a Hypothesis and Design an Inquiry	Plant Cells Microscopic Study Classification Ecosystem Native Plants Naturescape	Green School Assembly Assets 3, 4, 5, 6, 8, 14, 22
October	Inquiry: Develop a Record-Keeping Instrument	Observe, Measure, and Record Plant Growth and Sunlight Ecosystem Native Plants Naturescape	Assets 6, 8, 14, 22, 24, 30
November	Earth Science: Seasonal Patterns	Observe, Measure, and Record Plant Growth and Sunlight	Assets 8, 22, 30
December	Physical Science: Water	Observe, Measure, and Record Plant Growth and Sunlight	Assets 8, 22, 30
January	Physical Science: Matter and Energy Transfer—Heat and Cold Effect on Matter and Growth	Observe, Measure, and Record Plant Growth and Sunlight	Assets 8, 22, 30, 31
February	Physical Science: Electricity and Magnetism	Observe, Measure, and Record Plant Growth and Sunlight	Assets 8, 22
March	Health Refusal Skills Disease Prevention and Risk Reduction	Observe, Measure, and Record Plant Growth and Sunlight	Assets 22, 32, 35
April	Inquiry: Presenting Data Using Charts and Graphs	Desert/Arctic Microorganisms Ecosystems	Beach Cleanup Earth Day Presentation: Sunlight and Plant Growth Assets 9, 22
May	Life Science: Organisms	Desert/Arctic Microorganisms Ecosystems	Asset 22
June	Role of Science in Local and Global Issues	Desert/Arctic Microorganisms Ecosystems	Asset 37

Forest Ridge Elementary—5th-Grade Curriculum Map

Month	Science/Health	Environmental Studies	Comments Asset Development
September	Inquiry: Forming a Hypothesis, Designing an Investigation, and Developing a Record-Keeping Instrument	Plants and Seeds Types of Plants Migration Who Cares—I Care Naturescape Construction Teach 4 R's (Reduce, Recycle, Reuse, Repair) Observe, Measure, and Record Plant Growth: Soil Acidity and Water Temperature	Green School Assembly Assets 3, 4, 5, 6, 8, 14, 22
October	Physical Science: Force and Energy	Observe, Measure, and Record Plant Growth: Soil Acidity and Water Temperature Naturescape Planting	Assets 6, 8, 14, 22, 24, 30
November	Earth/Space Science—Resources and Physical Properties	Observe, Measure, and Record Plant Growth: Soil Acidity and Water Temperature	Assets 8, 22, 30
December	Weather Patterns	Observe, Measure, and Record Plant Growth: Soil Acidity and Water Temperature	Assets 8, 22, 30
January	Physical Science: Structure of Matter Chemical and Physical Changes	Observe, Measure, and Record Plant Growth: Soil Acidity and Water Temperature	Assets 8, 22, 30, 31
February	Health Body Systems and Food Refusal Skills	Observe, Measure, and Record Plant Growth: Soil Acidity and Water Temperature	Assets 8, 22, 35
March	Be a Scientist: Design a Presentation	Observe, Measure, and Record Plant Growth: Soil Acidity and Water Temperature	Assets 22, 32

April	Inquiry: Presenting Data Using Charts and Graphs
	Life Science: Organisms
		Habitat Study: Oceans, Rivers, Riparian Areas, Watersheds
		Integrated Project #35
			Beach Cleanup
			Earth Day Presentation:
			Soil Acidity and Water
			  Temperature Effect
			  on Plant Growth
			Assets 9, 22

May	Life Science: Diversity and Inter-dependence	Habitat Study: Oceans, Rivers, Riparian Areas, Watersheds Integrated Project	Assets 22, 35
June	Science/Social Perspective: Describe the Effects on an Ecosystem	Project Sharing and Speeches	Asset 37

The Naturescape Project

The centerpiece of the entire science and environmental studies effort was the development of the naturescape on the school grounds. Working with the school district facility department and the construction contractors, we designated an area approximately 100 feet long and 40 feet wide to be set aside unfinished during the school construction phase. The district provided a water source for a recirculating stream. A 5th-grade teacher, Scott Torgeson, took primary responsibility for coordinating this project and developed a plan to involve the 5th graders in creating the design of the naturescape.

Scott met with the future 5th graders in March 2002 for the initial planning session, and they began to develop ideas for the construction effort. Among the concepts they discussed were a butterfly garden, a community vegetable garden, a bioswale, and several native Oregon plant viewing areas. Scott also worked with local resource people and agencies to begin developing a list of native plants appropriate for the naturescape and for other locations around the school.

In addition to designing the naturescape, the 5th graders became classroom leaders for the rest of the students when the school opened in the fall. Assigned teams of 5th graders assisted the other classes as they planted and began maintenance of one area within the naturescape. For example, 2nd graders were responsible for the butterfly garden section, and the 5th graders assigned to the 2nd-grade classes helped them design a planting pattern, plant the area, and develop a maintenance plan.

Meanwhile the 3rd-grade teachers incorporated inquiry-based science lessons related to plant growth and temperature. These lessons are part of a six-month, ongoing investigation culminating in an Earth Day presentation in April on the effect of temperature on plant growth.

Each class, from 1st to 5th grade, has a particular area of investigation (as indicated in Handouts 6.2–6.6). Their projects support assets related to children having useful roles, serving others, and connecting to school. Cross-grade partnerships between students also help foster a positive school climate, promote positive peer interactions, and develop a sense of responsibility both for the 5th-grade mentors and the other students as they care for their portion of the naturescape.

Other curriculum areas also have asset integration and are well blended in support of each other. For example, students write and do art projects related to their naturescape efforts and use math concepts (including measurement, calculation, and graphing) as they record and display their results from the plant growth experiments. The use of technology is included in the sensor probe recordings and computer graphing.

This integrated environmental studies-science-technology curriculum approach has additional asset benefits as well. For example, Portland General Electric, demonstrating its valuing of youth, provided a $500 community builders' grant to the school to purchase the necessary hand tools for students to work on the naturescape. Providing additional adult role modeling, many adults, including members of the nearby church, worked with the students in the naturescape construction.

Since technology is also a school focus area, 5th-grade students "take the show on the road." Using a PowerPoint software presentation that they designed, they describe the planning, development, construction, and maintenance of the naturescape. Students give these presentations during Earth Day activities and to parent, community, and other interested groups throughout the year.

The 5th graders also use PowerPoint presentations as part of their service-learning activities, another important program component at Forest Ridge. These activities include assisting with local watershed cleanup and making presentations on asset building to other local elementary schools. All students participate in the annual Oregon beach cleanup effort when we take busloads of Forest Ridge students, staff, and parents to the Oregon coast on a Saturday in April and help pick up litter along the beach, as an extension of our own school beautification project. This asset-building experience blends positive adult role modeling with giving children useful roles in the community. Other service-learning activities include a local school-based activity for the Week without Violence in October.

The students' sense of pride and accomplishment is highly evident during their presentations. It is this sense of pride—a clear indication of the asset category, positive identity—that may be among the most telling regarding our success in meeting the goals we established. It is our hope that through active engagement in environmental studies and the other focus areas at our school, students will continue to develop high self-esteem, have a sense of purpose, and have a positive view of the future.

The process of planning and designing an asset-rich school with strong curriculum links has been and continues to be a renewal experience for me as an educator with 30 years of experience. It has not been a time free of sweat and stress as we worked to integrate the 40 developmental assets within the curriculum in a way that made the approach "doable" from a workload perspective. However, working with teachers who share a vision of promoting happy, healthy, and caring kids who are actively engaged in their learning and becoming asset builders themselves allows me to look forward to each day at Forest Ridge Elementary School.

Notes

1. Wiggins, Grant, and McTighe, Jay. (1998). *Understanding by Design*. Alexandria, VA: Association for Supervision and Curriculum Development.

Chapter 7

Infusing Assets into Health Education

Capitalizing on Strengths and Creating Solutions

LEAPING THE HURDLES IN HEALTH EDUCATION

COLLEEN MAHONEY, PH.D.

Health Education Consultant

Mahoney Consulting Group

Wadsworth, Ohio

I believe that the environment we create, the relationships we nurture, and the opportunities we provide middle and high school youth impact them more than any specific content we teach. During the middle school years, young people begin to wonder about topics that are controversial, such as power, beauty, compassion, and faith. They are fascinated by discussions of sex, gender, and moral and ethical issues.[1] Part of being a promoter of developmental assets is advocating for opportunities for youth to explore such questions and concerns.

The many potential hurdles to leap, the challenges to address, in teaching health education at the middle and high school levels can be daunting. Because of the sensitive nature of the content, health educators often face parental and community concern or opposition, insufficient administrative support, and administrative restrictions. As a health education teacher, you have limited class time and are working with youth who are focused on short-term needs. Two approaches hold promise, however: emphasizing students' strengths and engaging them as advocates.[2]

Emphasizing the positive, capitalizing on students' strengths, and empowering them to meet challenges successfully—exactly what the developmental assets are about—make the developmental asset framework a natural guide for health education. In an effort to move toward such a paradigm shift in health education, I am excited to provide here several practical ideas that you can incorporate into the classroom, no matter what your topic of the day, week, or month is. You can adapt them for either middle or high school health education classes.

You can enhance standardized health curriculum by intentionally addressing the internal and external assets while you teach. This does not mean abandoning risk-reduction curriculum or programs. Rather, it means shifting your way of thinking to focus on strengths versus deficits and on preparation versus simply being problem free; to concentrate on changing your way of behaving to creating solutions versus identifying problems and to engaging students versus merely disseminating information.[3]

In addition to the usual risk-reduction and health-promotion goals for health education, my personal objectives for middle and high school health instruction include enhancing developmental assets and promoting thriving indicators in youth. Specifically, those goals include:

1. Providing a caring, supportive, engaging classroom environment;
2. Developing social competencies, positive values, and positive identity;
3. Empowering youth by providing opportunities for exploration and service learning; and
4. Encouraging positive parent-child communication.

Setting a Positive Tone

Although the focus of this book is on curriculum and instruction rather than school environment, a number of instructional strategies (see Chapter 3 on page 54) contribute to achieving my first objective of providing a caring, supportive, engaging classroom environment. Done with building assets in mind, these strategies not only further learning but also contribute to strengthening a young person's assets.

One specific type of activity that helps create a caring and engaging classroom environment for health education, or other content areas, is appropriate for the beginning of the school year. Using icebreakers so that students can become familiar and develop trust with one another and with you sets the stage for success in cooperative learning groups and future discussions about sensitive subject matter. Allowing time for students to get to know each other and you pays dividends later.

Actively involving students in their learning experience early in the year by having them help set learning objectives and classroom boundaries, expectations, and consequences is another effective strategy. It uses them as resources in the process, as well as builds engagement, responsibility, and respect for the outcomes of the activity. One approach to doing this begins with your identifying for them some basic elements of teamwork, followed by your involving them in discussion of the importance of expectations, rules, and consequences.

To engage students personally, ask them to respond in writing to a prompt such as "What rules would help everyone pay attention and do their work in class, feel comfortable and respected in class, and enjoy their day?" Encourage students to describe what would help in light of the fact that this is a health education class. Explain that you will be helping them learn about and deal with sensitive, real-life issues.

Have students discuss their responses in small groups, with each group deciding what rules it would like to see adopted for the class and why. Have groups phrase those rules in positive ways, write them on newsprint with reasons for each, and post them around the room. Since this is a health education class, have them include rules applicable to this unique situation, such as use of correct anatomical terminology and the honoring of confidentiality. After groups present their suggestions for rules, look for similarities on which to base the final set of expectations to post in the room and follow throughout the year.

Use the same group process to determine a system of rewards and consequences, as well as to identify student and teacher responsibilities and ways parents can support both. Based on these determinations, create a compact or agreement that students, teachers, and parents all sign.

Although these processes can take time, they are well worth it in the long run. They clarify everyone's responsibilities, while at the same time empowering students and providing them with an opportunity to learn about the democratic process, community, and self-discipline. Having set the stage for cooperation and respect, you have a foundation to which you can refer as needed during the year.

Setting and maintaining a positive tone in class also involves helping students think beyond problems and risk behaviors. Emphasizing creating solutions and developing assets and protective factors provides a major avenue to making your classroom asset-based. For an activity involving students in looking at strengths and developing solutions, try "Asset Think Tank" (see Handout 7.1 on page 196). You can use this activity to clarify perceptions of any of the assets (especially the external ones) and to find ways to strengthen those assets in peers. Handout 7.1 illustrates a focus on just one asset, caring school climate.

Developing Social Competencies, Positive Values, and Positive Identity

You can consistently nurture the social-competencies assets through health education curricula. The ability to make positive choices (planning and decision making, and resistance skills) and to develop healthy interpersonal relationships (interpersonal competence, cultural competence, and peaceful conflict resolution) are prerequisites to maintaining health-positive attitudes and behaviors. You can present many activities in health in ways that promote the social-competencies assets through modeling, opportunities for self-exploration, relationship building, and active involvement in class activities. Peer education and peer mediation are asset-based approaches to developing social competencies in student leaders and their peers, as well as in younger children.

A variety of health curricula teach life skills explicitly, while others address problem-solving and conflict-resolution skills. For example, one popular conflict-resolution curriculum for secondary students is "We Can Work It Out! Problem Solving through Mediation."[4] Its objectives are to analyze and solve problems; develop critical thinking, questions, and active listening skills; generate nonviolent options when faced with conflict; find common ground when two people disagree;

Asset Think Tank

Use this activity[1] to clarify perceptions of any of the assets (especially the external) and to find ways to strengthen developmental assets in youth. The example here addresses caring school climate. You can use traditional brainstorming and rating techniques,[2] or you can take an electronic approach using an electronic meeting system.[3]

Time Needed

One or more class periods, depending on strategies used and objectives of activity (e.g., determining a caring, positive school climate, mapping project, solution-based report, and presentation).

Health Education Standards[4]

- Standard 4: The student will analyze the influence of culture, media, technology, and other factors on health.
- Standard 7: The student will demonstrate the ability to advocate for personal, family, and community health.

Lesson/Unit Objectives

- To provide a caring, supportive, engaging classroom environment.
- To empower youth by providing opportunities for exploration and service learning.

Introduction

Introduce topic and activity. Explain the process. If using an electronic approach, be sure students know how to use the equipment and software.

Brainstorming

Challenge students to brainstorm about topics. Use prompts, such as "Imagine a school that is positive and caring. Please list characteristics that describe what such a school would look and be like." Encourage students to accept and record all ideas without concern for practicality, popularity, or other issues. Allow about 10 minutes for brainstorming.

Categorizing

To illustrate patterns that emerge in brainstorming, use a strategy to group ideas logically. Electronic software such as the SuperGrouper Tool[5] provides additional tools for categorization.

Ranking

After grouping ideas by category, have students rank each category from "very important" to "not important at all." Identify the top 10 to 20 categories; then vote to determine the top 3 to 5 categories important to a positive and caring school climate.

Expanding and Elaborating

To extend students' thinking about the top 3 to 5 categories, ask them to elaborate ways to further develop the category or to implement their ideas to strengthen asset building in their school environment.

Prioritizing

Have students rank each of the expanded categories. Combine their rankings to determine the best and most important category on which to focus.

Taking Action

To provide students the opportunity to respond to and present their concerns proactively or produce a tangible final product, consider these projects:

- Students report on what a caring, positive school climate looks like.
- Students create an action plan from their ideas.
- Students map how well their school addresses their perceptions of a caring, positive school climate.
- Students write a report outlining solutions to their concerns and present it to the school principal, staff, or school board.

_____

Notes

1. This activity incorporates ideas from Teen Think Tanks of America, Inc; see the Web site accessed November 15, 2002: www.teenthinktanks.org; and from GroupSystems.com; see the Web site accessed November 15, 2002: www.GroupSystems.com.
2. See Web site accessed November 15, 2002: www.youthlearn.org/learning/planning/brainstorm.asp.
3. See Web site accessed November 15, 2002: www.GroupSystems.com.
4. Joint Committee on National Health Education Standards. (1995). *National health education standards: Achieving health literacy*. Available from the American School Health Association (P.O. Box 708, 7263 State Route 43, Kent, OH 44240); the Association for the Advancement of Health Education (1900 Association Drive, Reston, VA 22901); or the American Cancer Society (800-ACS-2345).
5. For the SuperGrouper Tool, see the Web site accessed November 15, 2002: www.pulaskiacademy.org/technology/kidspir2sd.htm.

and manage conflicts. Built-in asset richness! The program also includes a special event known as Mediation Showcases, designed for students to demonstrate and celebrate their conflict-management skills.

Character education is another example of a program that promotes developing social competency assets as well as positive values and service to others by building key values and character traits that youth need as they develop into healthy adults. You can enhance the asset richness of character education, no matter which specific program you use, by involving students actively in partnerships between school, home, and the greater community. You can incorporate and emphasize elements of whatever character program you choose throughout the school day, by integrating those elements into curriculum discipline policies and enforcement as much as experiential learning. This includes the overall school environment, together with consistent and positive adult role modeling.

Look for and incorporate the following key elements when selecting curricula and instructional approaches to promote the social-competencies assets:

- An emphasis on building attitudes and values, versus focusing on acquiring knowledge only or jumping from learning information directly to practicing skills;
- A comprehensive approach that touches on a variety of issues rather than only one—curricula that apply skills, such as resisting peer pressure across many risk behaviors (substance abuse, early sexual involvement, and others);
- Active involvement of youth in planning and implementing lessons;
- Use of a variety of activities and strategies to communicate content and build skills, versus lecture-based delivery of information;
- Opportunities for students to practice skills beyond the lessons, such as in classroom and school discipline approaches; and
- A parent education and support component.

In addition, you as a teacher can play a significant role in helping adolescents build cultural competence. One simple way to do this is to build respect for different cultures and explore cultural beliefs. You can easily create class rituals around birthdays to encourage sharing of traditions, norms, and beliefs from a variety of cultures and families. Encourage students to be creative by bringing in a sample of food or presenting the birthday student with some small token representing the culture. The activity obviously also fosters the positive environment I advocate in my first objective.

Empowering Youth through Exploration and Service Learning

Service learning is rich with asset-building opportunities, as Search Institute's *An Asset Builder's Guide to Service-Learning* illustrates.[5] Students can be involved in selecting these opportunities and providing input into making sure they are meaningful, using health education standards to help guide choices. One good example is spending time with the elderly and gaining an understanding of changes that occur as we age.

Another is focusing on the advertising that routinely bombards us all but is aimed at young people in particular. The medium is fascinating to students, and having them develop marketing campaigns promoting assets and healthy behaviors addresses important elements of the health standards: understanding the effects of advertising strategies.

Engaging marketing projects can include developing radio or television public service announcements as service-learning projects,[6] including those about building assets. Start with inquiry-based learning in which students seek out information about the assets, healthy behavior, and marketing techniques. Find ways to showcase their work to parents, school, and the community, including submitting video clips to local media and Web sites to a resource, such as the ThinkQuest Internet Challenge.[7]

Providing inquiry-based opportunities to explore and challenge the perceived norms and pop culture is also engaging for students and supports instruction about environmental factors that affect health. Providing dilemmas to resolve, such as controversial or complex issues or policies, requires students to explore psychological, social, and economic points of view. Their interactions while solving the problems give them experience in understanding complexity, taking other perspectives, and creating solutions incorporating ideas from many people that meet a variety of needs. (See Chapter 3, page 70, for a description of the asset-rich instructional strategy called *academic controversy* that you could use here.) Such activities are rich in opportunities to build the positive-values, positive-identity, and social-competencies assets of my second objective, as well.

Involving teens in youth mapping[8] is an empowering way to address health standards related to gaining knowledge of health resources: youth search out and map resources and opportunities in their school or community to build awareness of current health resources for them as well as resources they may need access to after high school graduation. Mapping in health education may include locating healthy food venues, arenas for physical or recreational activity, or counseling support; describing elements of school climate; and identifying opportunities for constructive use of time in and out of school.

Have students outline community or school strengths and needs, and present their recommendations to the school or district administration or others. To extend the project, have students develop a Web site or school or community hotline of information, resources, and opportunities for teens.[9] Sharing a positive report about local supports—the resources available—along with helpful recommendations about unmet needs sends messages to the larger community that youth can have a productive role in identifying resources, connecting with adults, and working with them to improve the quality of life in an entire community. A powerful example of using youth as resources!

A number of other curricula, projects, and activities empower youth as they learn. One example is *Generation Fit* by the American Cancer Society.[10] *Genera-*

tion Fit is a set of enrichment activities that gives young people ages 11–18 the opportunity to act on an issue related to nutrition and physical activity in their schools and communities. For example, one activity is surveying the food preferences of peers, selecting healthy and tasty recipes based on these preferences, and working with the principal and food service personnel to include the new choices in the school lunch program. Such activities build personal and social skills, while addressing policy and environmental issues in the health curriculum standards. Students learn through participation in such meaningful community service and advocacy activities.

Encouraging Positive Parent-Child Communication

Welcoming parents into your classroom is a sound first step in encouraging a solid partnership. Getting to know parents' interests, skills, and professions, and finding opportunities to use them as resources in your classroom, recognizes their expertise and engages them in the learning. For example, parents who have educational and professional backgrounds related to specific health topics (such as nutritionists), or who have personal stories (such as their commitment to health), can share information and inspire as role models as well.

Inviting parents to observe student presentations and class discussions when appropriate also reinforces engaging them in school. Involving parents in classroom projects helps them build relationships and become informed themselves about health topics they often do not know a lot about. For example, in the case of an inquiry-based research project that includes a core team with various roles, parents who serve as part of the core team become co-learners with youth—a strong asset-building strategy for increasing the number of relationships with other adults and positive adult role models.

Assigning homework that requires students and parents to work together is also a strong way to generate better understandings of health concepts. The activity "Let's Talk It Over!" (see Handout 7.2 on page 200) provides an excellent model for helping students engage with their parents on a health topic. To prepare students, develop in class a fact sheet on media literacy, and create guidelines for positive parent-child communication to send home with the assignment. Then provide time after all students have completed the activity for students to share and synthesize what they have learned. Families play an important role in a student's understanding of health-related concepts, issues, and decision making; involving parents in the actual learning of health content can increase knowledge and understanding of both parents and children as well as enhance communication between them.

Leaping the Hurdles

Generating better understandings of health concepts means emphasizing young people's strengths and engaging them as advocates. Involving youth as catalysts for change is more likely to lead to solutions that are meaningful and enduring. Advo-

Let's Talk It Over!

Interactive Homework Assignment

Student: _____ Parent(s): _____

Date Assigned: _____ Date Due: _____

(Allow a minimum of one week.)

Dear Family Partner:

We are learning media literacy—how to interpret and evaluate health-related messages from the media (TV, magazines, movies, newspapers, the Internet) in health education class. This activity[1] will assist you in helping build analysis skills in your teen. The students have put together a fact sheet and guidelines for discussion to assist you with this activity. I hope you and your child enjoy this activity!

Please note the assigned due date above.

Sincerely, _____

Health Education Standards[2]

- Standard 4: The student will analyze the influence of culture, media, technology, and other factors on health.
- Standard 5: The student will demonstrate the ability to use interpersonal communication skills to enhance health.

Lesson/Unit Objectives

- To develop social competence, positive values, and positive identify.
- To encourage positive parent-child communication.

Look It Over

- Review the media literacy fact sheet.
- Review the parent-child communication guidelines.

Watch and Discuss the Videos

A. Parent and Youth INDIVIDUALLY

1. Record a music video of your choice (from MTV, VH-1, BETA, etc.).
2. Watch the video with the sound off. Write down images and messages you see.
3. Get the lyrics to the song from the Web site (accessed November 15, 2002): www.songlyricssource.com. Read the lyrics.
4. Watch the video with the sound on. Answer on paper: Does the video send the same images and messages with the lyrics as without sound? Why or why not?

B. Parent and Youth INDIVIDUALLY

1. Switch videos and lyrics. (Parent gives lyrics and video he or she taped to youth; youth gives lyrics and video he or she taped to parent.)
2. Follow numbered steps 2–4 in section A above.

C. Parent and Youth TOGETHER

1. Watch one of the videos together.
2. Share and discuss how each of you responded when you watched the video alone. Carefully listen to one another and consider both perspectives. What do you agree on (even if stated somewhat differently)? Disagree on?
3. Watch the second video together and do step 2 for this video.

Record Perspectives

Student: Fill in the name of the videos and key words describing perspectives.

Name of Video	Parent Perspective	Student Perspective
_____	_____	_____
_____	_____	_____
_____	_____	_____
_____	_____	_____

Conclusions

Student: Answer the following questions, using complete sentences, on a separate piece of paper.
1. What did you and your parent agree on?
2. What did you and your parent disagree on?
3. What did you learn from this activity?
4. What did your parent learn from this activity? (Ask.)
5. Did you find this activity useful? Why or why not?

Home to School Communication

Dear Family Partner:
Please give me your reactions to this activity.
Enter a 1, 2, 3, 4, or 5 for each statement to reflect your opinion.
1 = Strongly Disagree, 2 = Disagree, 3 = Unsure, 4 = Agree, 5 = Strongly Agree

_____ The assignment directions were clear.

_____ My son/daughter and I enjoyed this activity.

_____ This assignment helped me know what my son/daughter is learning in health education.

_____ This assignment helped me communicate with my son/daughter.

Other Comments:

_____

_____

_____

Parent's Signature: _____

_____

Notes

1. This activity incorporates ideas from media educator Mary Byrne Hoffman as referenced in the 2001 newsletter *Families Are Talking: SIECUS Report Supplement*, 1(2); see the Web site accessed November 15, 2002: www.siecus.org/pubs/pubs0004.html; and from TIPS (Teachers Involve Parents in Schoolwork) from the National Network of Partnership Schools; see the Web site accessed November 15, 2002: www.csos.jhu.edu/p2000/tips/TIPSmain.htm.
2. Joint Committee on National Health Education Standards. (1995). *National health education standards: Achieving health literacy.* Available from the American School Health Association (P.O. Box 708, 7263 State Route 43, Kent, OH 44240); the Association for the Advancement of Health Education (1900 Association Drive, Reston, VA 22901); or the American Cancer Society (800-ACS-2345).

cacy activities give youth an immediate goal to work toward, while addressing inter-personal needs. They help clarify values, as well as specific factors, such as environ-mental policies, that contribute to good health in both the short and long term. They also open opportunities for youth and adult partnerships and build greater cross-generational communication skills and understanding.

The asset framework challenges us to unleash the power of adolescents to be active learners and connected community citizens. Adolescents are potentially excited learners who have a strong sense of exploration and discovery, a capacity to see the needs of others, and a desire to make positive contributions to their com-munity. Young adolescents need to know that they are competent, normal, lovable, and loving.[11] Older adolescents need to discover their inner selves, strengths, and spirits, and be optimistic about their roles and future.

I believe the ideas I've presented here provide the environment and opportu-nities to increase the likelihood that adolescents are going to thrive in positive ways and succeed in school and life. The strategies are designed to maximize adolescents' energies and optimism. They challenge youth to be discoverers of knowledge and critical thinkers, to explore themselves and the world around them, and to develop social competencies. If implemented in a caring, supportive environment, these strategies help ensure that youth view themselves as competent, normal, loveable, loving, and connected.

And, as for you, the teacher, the experiences will be exhilarating, meaningful, and rewarding.

Notes
1. Scales, Peter C. (1996). *Boxed In and Bored: How Middle Schools Continue to Fail Young Adolescents—and What Good Middle Schools Do Right.* Minneapolis: Search Institute, 18–27, 29–30.
2. Good resources about youth advocacy development are Advocates for Youth; Web site accessed November 15, 2002: www.advocatesforyouth.org/teens; and the Academy for Educational Development; Web site accessed November 15, 2002: www.aed.org/youth_proj-ects.html.
3. Benson, Peter L., Scales, Peter C., Leffert, Nancy, and Roehlkepartain, Eugene C. (1999). *A Fragile Foundation: The State of Developmental Assets among American Youth.* Minne-apolis: Search Institute.
4. *We Can Work It Out! Problem-Solving through Mediation*; Web site accessed November 15, 2002: www.streelaw.org/wcw10.html.
5. Roehlkepartain, Eugene C., Bright, Thomas, and Margolis-Rupp, Beth. (2000). *An Asset Builder's Guide to Service-Learning.* Minneapolis: Search Institute.
6. See the Public Service Announcement Project Menu at the Web site accessed November 15, 20002: www.pecentral.org/lessonideas/health/psaprojectmenu.html; and the Center for Youth Development and Policy Research; Web site accessed November 15, 2002: www.aed.org/youth_empower.html. Other interactive activities on the Internet (all Web-site accessed November 15, 2002) include Healthfinder: www.healthfinder.gov; Awesome Library for Teens: www.awesomelibrary.org/students.html; Educational Web Adventures: www.eduweb.com; Interactive Food Finder: www.olen.com/food; the Food and Nutrition Information Center: www.nal.usda.gov/fnic; and the Federal Citizen Information Center: www.pueblo.gsa.gov.
7. See the Web site accessed November 15, 2002: www.thinkquest.org.

8. For information on youth mapping, see the Web site accessed November 15, 2002: www.aed.org/youth_development.html.

9. Youthlink is a good example of a youth-created resource site; see the Web site accessed November 15, 2002: www.yl-va.org/v2/aboutus.html.

10. For more information, contact the American Cancer Society at 800-ACS-2345 or see the Web site accessed November 15, 2002: www.cancer.org.

11. Scales, *Boxed In and Bored*.

Other Resources (Related to My Objectives)

PROVIDING A CARING AND SUPPORTIVE AND ENGAGING CLASSROOM ENVIRONMENT

Starkman, Neal, Scales, Peter C., and Roberts, Clay. (1999). *Great Places to Learn: How Asset-Building Schools Help Students Succeed*. Minneapolis: Search Institute.

DEVELOPING SOCIAL COMPETENCIES, POSITIVE VALUES AND POSITIVE IDENTITY

Freedom Writers with Gruwell, Erin. (1999). *The Freedom Writers Diary: How a Teacher and 150 Teens Used Writing to Change Themselves and the World Around Them*. New York: Broadway Books.

EMPOWERING YOUTH

Stuecker, Ric, with Rutherford, Suze. (2001). *Reviving the Wonder: 76 Activities That Touch the Inner Spirit of Youth*. Champaign, IL: Research Press.

ENCOURAGING POSITIVE PARENT-CHILD COMMUNICATION

National PTA. (2000). *Building Successful Partnerships: A Guide for Developing Parent and Family Involvement Programs*. Bloomington, IN: National Education Service.

Powerful Strategies for Bullying Prevention

DEE LINDENBERGER, M.A.

Education Consultant-Trainer

Marquette-Alger Regional Education Service Agency and

Michigan Strategic Alternatives in Prevention Education Association

Marquette, Michigan

Dee Lindenberger discusses how asset building is connected with violence prevention—one of the major contemporary thrusts of schools and districts. Her summary of the major arenas needing focus to reduce or prevent bullying in a school reflects recent research. She shows how you can use these arenas as a way to view the components of local antibullying efforts through the asset lens to increase the likelihood of their success.

Elementary children who push, shove, tease, and taunt other children are more likely, as adults, to be convicted of crimes; have alcohol/drug problems; abuse their spouses; lack significant educational, social, or professional achievements; and parent children who push, shove, tease, and taunt other children. Not only does bullying risk the well-being and success of those students who engage in aggressive behavior, it also creates a pervasive climate of anxiety and fear that the entire school community feels, touching the lives of those targeted by bullying as well as those bystanders who witness their peers being emotionally or physically harassed. To whatever degree a school tolerates such aggression and bullying, so, too, will students' feelings of safety decrease—and their learning.

Closely mirroring the 40 assets framework are several school-based strategies that effectively address bullying. Identified by Dan Olweus in longitudinal studies,[1] these asset-promoting strategies serve as "countervailing forces" to the "aggression-generating factors" that promote aggressive attitudes and behaviors in children. Olweus describes these countervailing forces as the daily "attitudes, routines, and behaviors" within a school that prevent and control bullying behavior. In showing how the assets align with these strategies, I categorize them in five major components.

Positive School Climate

Students who bully tend to come from family systems where there's a lack of warmth, positive time, and attention. Such an environment is the opposite of a positive school climate that is warm, supportive, and provides students with opportunities for involvement in a variety of enriching activities, including regular class meetings.

In line with many of the benefits the asset framework promotes, Olweus underscores the importance of class meetings. In such meetings, students engage in activities designed to build relationships and a sense of community (e.g., non-competitive games, service-learning projects, art and physical activities) and to prompt discussion of bullying prevention (characteristics of bullying, ways to help, the difference between telling and tattling, skill building, stories/drama projects with related themes).

Additional asset-building strategies that contribute to a caring school climate are adult role modeling of respectful communication skills and consistent use of positive feedback that is behaviorally specific. Not only will students who bully benefit from a positive school climate, all students will profit from increased feelings of caring and connection to their school.

Clear and Fair Limits and Consequences

Students who bully are likely to have grown up in families with confusing and often violent norms with regard to limits and consequences for misbehavior: a high level of aggression is tolerated, clear limits are lacking, and consequences are unpredictable and punitive. Disciplinary strategies are often power-based, relying upon physical punishment and violent emotional outbursts.

To counteract in school these aggression-generating norms learned at home, it is important to clearly communicate school rules and consequences that are fair, and consistently apply them without hostility, again a very asset-rich strategy. A discipline rubric that starts with mild consequences and gradually escalates can be a useful tool.

Prosocial/Coping Skills

Social skills and coping skills are key predictors of who will bully, who will be bullied, and who will be able to effectively prevent or intervene in bullying incidents. Both students who bully and students who are targets of bullying have inadequate social and coping skills, including a host of distorted perceptions and beliefs (e.g., "It's not my fault!" or "I'm stupid!").

To create a caring, bully-free school environment, all students need to have skills that enable them to work together and get along with each other, another emphasis in the asset framework. You can teach effective social skills through class curricula, small skill-building groups, and "teachable moments" that arise throughout the year.

Positive Bystander Involvement

Most students in a school are usually neither bullies nor targets—they are bystanders. Sometimes bystanders ignore a bullying incident; sometimes they act as cheerleaders, chanting or clapping on the sidelines; and sometimes they join in the bullying. All of these reactions give the message "It's okay to bully!" to the student who's harassing another student. In whatever form it is given, that message serves as a powerful aggression-generating factor.

To counteract bullying, we need to enlist the support and active involvement of bystanders by teaching them what bullying is, how to recognize it, and what they can do to help when they see it happening. Equally important and asset consistent, we need to teach bystanders that they can help prevent bullying by reaching out in friendship so that no one is alone and isolated, or an easy target.

Strong Parent Partnerships

Not only can parents benefit from schools helping them understand the causes of bullying and effective strategies to prevent it, but schools and students also have much to gain from closer parent-school partnerships, just as in asset building. We need the support of parents to have maximum impact in our efforts to prevent bullying, both when working with individual students and when needing financial or other support from the larger community.

Ultimately, it's the students who benefit most from a team approach, with both parents and educators providing a consistent message and ongoing support for behavioral change. Many strategies can help build strong partnerships: awareness sessions, parent groups, and conscious relationship-building efforts that include frequent communication regarding students' positive behavior as well as problem behaviors.

Just as there is no single asset to meet all our students' needs for positive youth development, there is no single strategy to prevent bullying. Bullying prevention involves your taking a comprehensive approach based upon relationships, consistent and redundant messages, and learning opportunities for all students. It's a systems change that, at its core, is an ongoing asset-building process.

———

Notes
1. Olweus, Dan. (1994). *Bullying at School: What We Know and What We Can Do*. Malden, MA: Blackwell Publishers.

Kids Are the Core

KARLA McCOMB, M.S.

Director, Diversity and Prevention Services (grades Pre-K–12)

Clark County School District

Las Vegas, Nevada

Clark County Schools, the sixth-largest school district in the United States, illustrates one way to infuse asset building into a comprehensive K–5 drug abuse and violence prevention curriculum. In correlation with its elementary curriculum guidelines, the Curriculum Essentials Framework (CEF), the district also integrates the prevention and asset messages into a variety of subject areas in addition to health (language arts, social studies, mathematics, science, art, music, and physical education). You see these CEF elements cross-referenced in the sample lesson here.

SCHOOL DEMOGRAPHICS
Clark County School District
Las Vegas, Nevada

Students: 244,684

Grades: Pre-K–12

Gender:
Male   51.4%
Female   48.6%

Race and Ethnicity:
Black/African American   13.8%
Hispanic/Latino   30.6%
Asian/Pacific Islander   7.1%
American Indian   0.8%
White/Caucasian   47.7%

Socioeconomics:
Free/Reduced Lunch
(grades 1–8)   40.0%

Included in our elementary "Kids Are the Core" prevention curriculum are three promising practices in the fields of substance abuse and violence prevention—asset development, along with mentoring and normative education[1]—that appear to prevent or reduce (or both) substance abuse, violence, and disruptive behavior among youth. We expect that our teachers and counselors using the teacher's guide, which includes background on all three practices, will incorporate these practices in their teaching of the core lessons—and in all of their work with students.

Over the past three decades, the substance abuse and violence prevention field has moved from the generally ineffective scare tactics of the 1970s, through risk and protective factor-focused models in the 1980s, to resiliency programs in the 1990s. As we enter the new century, the asset-building paradigm offers a new way to look at preventing problems through developing healthy, capable young people. We recommend that other communities join us in implementing a two-pronged approach to prevention: one that focuses on reducing risks for young people, while at the same time building assets or protective factors.

We provide for teachers and counselors Search Institute's list of 40 developmental assets tailored for use with elementary school children.[2] We also star the assets that our "Kids Are the Core" health curriculum specifically addresses:

- **5.** Caring School Climate;
- **12.** School Boundaries;
- **15.** Positive Peer Influence;
- **24.** Bonding to School;
- **35.** Resistance Skills; and
- **36.** Peaceful Conflict Resolution.

A group of experienced teachers who had been trained in using the assets did a page-by-page correlation to our CEF. While some lessons in the teacher's guide explicitly include asset language, others do not (for an example of a lesson on resistance and refusal skills for 4th graders, see Handout 7.3A: Resistance/Refusal Skills and Handout 7.3B: I Make a Difference Daily Log on pages 208–209). However, the guide flags all content that relates to building one or more assets with the corresponding asset or assets, making it easy for a teacher or counselor to use the asset language while teaching the lessons.

───────

Notes

1. By normative education, we mean a conscious effort to change the perceived group position on an issue. In some cases, the aim is to truly change what is acceptable behavior in an area such as violence or drug use. The goal may also be to bring what students think more in line with reality so that students know what is expected of them.
2. See Appendix A.2: 40 Developmental Assets for Elementary-Age Children (Ages 6–11, English).

Resistance/Refusal Skills

Grade 4 Resistance/Refusal Skills
Title: I Make a Difference!

Curriculum Essentials Framework Correlation: Language Arts 4.2/Social Studies 4.9–4.12

Outcome/Objective: Students will recognize their own power to influence others as positive peer role models.

Activity: *Note to the teacher—Before beginning this lesson, make student copies of "I Make a Difference Daily Log"(Handout 7.3B).*

- Ask students to think back to when they were in 1st grade and remember how they felt about 4th and 5th graders. Use these suggested questions for discussion:
  - ☐ Were you afraid of the 4th and 5th graders? Why or why not?
  - ☐ Did you have any 4th- or 5th-grade friends?
  - ☐ Did the 4th and 5th graders ever talk to you?
  - ☐ Do you remember thinking that the 4th and 5th graders were cool?
  - ☐ Was there an older student that you wanted to be like? What was he or she like?
  - ☐ Do you think the 4th and 5th graders knew that you were watching them?
  - ☐ Do you think 1st graders are watching you now?

- In small groups, have students brainstorm a list of ideas, actions, words, and/or projects that they could do to positively influence younger kids (e.g., say "Good morning" to a group of 1st graders every day, help a 1st grader in the cafeteria, read to a 1st grader).

- Have students share their ideas with the whole class. Record the ideas on chart paper and post it in the classroom.

- Ask the students to make a commitment to be a positive peer role model at school. Have them record their efforts and successes on the "I Make a Difference Daily Log."

- Help students to design a whole class peer role model program. Ideas include:
  - ☐ One-on-one reading with primary students;
  - ☐ Schoolwide recycling project;
  - ☐ Skits about healthy choices performed for younger students;

- ☐ Reading of "Quote of the Day" during morning announcements; or
- ☐ Assisting primary classes during hands-on science lessons.

Reinforcement/Follow-Up: _____

_____

_____

_____

_____

_____

_____

Resources:
Student copies of "I Make a Difference Daily Log"

Teaching Tips/Background Information: _____

_____

_____

_____

_____

_____

_____

Content-Related Vocabulary: _____

_____

_____

_____

_____

_____

_____

_____

I Make a Difference Daily Log

Name: _____

Date: _____

Today, I was a positive peer role model! This is what I did: _____

_____

_____

_____

_____

_____

Date: _____

Today, I was a positive peer role model! This is what I did: _____

_____

_____

_____

_____

_____

Date: _____

Today, I was a positive peer role model! This is what I did: _____

_____

_____

_____

_____

_____

Date: _____

Today, I was a positive peer role model! This is what I did: _____

_____

_____

_____

_____

_____

Leaders of Tomorrow

MAKING HEALTH-POSITIVE CHOICES

GEORGIA TEPPERT, M.ED.

Assistant Principal (grades 10–12)

Greater Latrobe Senior High School

Latrobe, Pennsylvania

Georgia Teppert and a number of students created a club to practice skills learned in their health classes. Although not originally organized around the asset framework, the Leaders of Tomorrow Club illustrates how locally developed student activities support curriculum in the classroom as well as promote the development of assets in youth, and how staff recognize and enhance the asset-building qualities of what they are already doing.

SCHOOL DEMOGRAPHICS
Greater Latrobe Senior High School
Latrobe, Pennsylvania

Students: 988

Grades: 10–12

Gender:
Male	53.0%
Female	47.0%

Race and Ethnicity:
Black/African American	0.3%
Hispanic/Latino	0.8%
Asian/Pacific Islander	0.9%
White/Caucasian	98.0%

Socioeconomics:
Free/Reduced Lunch	20.0%

To reinforce skills in the health curriculum—skills of making good decisions about a variety of pressures and issues, of refusing to participate in risky behaviors, and of resolving conflicts peacefully—a group of juniors and seniors helped form our Leaders of Tomorrow Club. The students were also interested in sharing the message about how to make good decisions and lead healthy lifestyles to enhance self-esteem, self-respect, and respect for others.

While our school formerly had a club that focused on drug education, the students in that club and I thought it was very important to maintain a school group that promoted drug- and alcohol-free lifestyles, along with positive decision making. To actively involve students in the decision-making processes throughout their community, we also decided to form a student advisory council.

During the first meetings with this group of 50 students, we developed together these objectives for the club:

1. To deliver messages to youth in the community regarding self-esteem, decision making, drugs, alcohol, tobacco, and peer relationships;
2. To create an awareness of drug use and abuse in society today and to strive to live an alcohol-, tobacco-, and other drug-free life;
3. To develop personal integrity and learn to make wise decisions that lead to success;
4. To practice self-respect and respect for others;
5. To create an awareness of the importance of home and family;
6. To emphasize acceptance of individual responsibility as the basis of personal success and community improvement; and
7. To help my fellow "leaders."

Meeting at least once each week, the club provides a great opportunity for students to practice a variety of skills as well as to model what is taught in our health curriculum. They plan presentations on decision making, refusal skills, self-esteem, conflict resolution, and drug and alcohol issues, incorporating lessons from health in using good communication skills. The students then perform those presentations for elementary children in the district.

Other club projects include fund-raisers, such as T-shirt sales, and anti-drinking and driving campaigns. These events raise money to help defray costs for materials and prizes needed during the presentations to elementary schools. The students also donate money raised to charities, as well as volunteer for a local children's cancer support network.

The Leaders of Tomorrow Club supports many of the external assets as well as provides a forum for students to develop them as they put content and skills they have learned in the classroom into action. The health teacher, in fact, encourages students to put the concepts into practice by participating in the club. Club activities also address the internal assets of being involved in a youth program and providing service to others. Members meet annually to review progress the club has made in promoting assets and to plan ways to improve asset-building opportunities.

Chapter 8

Infusing Assets into Visual Arts

A Masterpiece Show

VISUALIZING THE ASSETS IN ART

KRISTINE WILLETT, M.A.

Art Teacher (grades K–5)

Independence Elementary School

Aurora, Colorado

Because young students tend to express themselves more freely through art, integrating asset building into the art curriculum is a natural fit. After all, "a picture is worth a thousand words." At the beginning of each school year, I introduce my kindergarten through 5th-grade students to a specific asset category at each grade level.

Over time, each student who attends Independence Elementary all six years creates her or his own artistic representations of each asset. Displayed throughout the building and accompanied by an explanation of each asset category and a rationale for the artwork, the students' art projects become visual reminders of the strengths and assets they possess.

Building Assets Year by Year

The idea of integrating the assets into the art curriculum came from a coworker, Mary Jo Miyazawa, our school's family/school/community liaison. Mary Jo ensured that I knew the assets and described them properly to my students. Together, we simplified each asset category into a basic concept; I then chose a project to represent the concept aesthetically.

When deciding which asset each grade should focus on, Mary Jo and I focused on the external assets. We felt they would be easiest for primary-grade students to understand and work with visually, as they involve specific people, actions, and activities.

SCHOOL DEMOGRAPHICS

Independence Elementary School
Aurora, Colorado

Students: 548

Grades: K–5

Gender: no response

Race and Ethnicity:

Black/African American	11.7%
Hispanic/Latino	9.3%
Asian/Pacific Islander	6.0%
American Indian	0.4%
White/Caucasian	72.6%

Socioeconomics:

Free/Reduced Lunch	23.2%

Grade Level	Asset Category
Kindergarten	Empowerment
First Grade	Constructive Use of Time
Second Grade	Support
Third Grade	Positive Values
Fourth Grade	Boundaries and Expectations and Commitment to Learning
Fifth Grade	Positive Identity and Social Competencies

When I introduce an asset category to a grade level, my objectives are simple—to help students to:

1. Understand what an asset is and why it is important in their lives;
2. Personalize the asset with examples (Who provides them with support in their lives? How?);
3. Brainstorm ways they can strengthen the asset within themselves; and
4. Visualize the asset more concretely by introducing an area in art that can be likened to the asset, offering them a meaningful visual representation.

Providing examples of the external assets to the youngest members of our school makes the assets more tangible to them. Initially, when I began the Assets in Art program[1] in 1997, students did not retain the asset language or comprehend why we created a particular piece of art. Over the years, I have changed and developed the asset-building art projects and continue to incorporate new ideas.

Students now frequently remember a particular asset from a previous year and are able to explain what artwork we created to represent that asset. Not only do they enjoy discussing the assets in art class and creating the artwork, but they also internalize the message that lies behind the work. This has helped me explain art appreciation and interpretation. The following asset categories and projects are those that have worked best with my young students to promote the greatest meaning when reflecting on their work.

Grade-Level Projects

Kindergarten: Empowerment

With kindergarten classes, we begin by discussing the meaning of community and the importance of belonging to, and feeling valued by, our community. Starting small, we talk about the different members of our families. I tell them that their family is a small community. I ask kindergartners if they know of any other communities to which they may belong. I often need to provide them with a few hints so that someone can identify our classroom as a community. From there, we are able to expand our definition of community from grade level, school, and neighborhood, to city and, sometimes, the state of Colorado.

Next, we discuss how we feel when we are safe and others care about us. We also discuss playing comfortably outside and knowing that people watch out for our well-being. In addition, we list actions we can take to improve our community, such as picking up trash, keeping our work areas clean, helping our teachers, and adding pretty things to our school grounds by planting flowers.

To emphasize the importance of the children's contributions to their surroundings, I then introduce the flower paintings we will make to brighten our school community. The first step in creating the watercolor flowers is to use the side of the paintbrush to create the petal of the flowers. After each petal is made, the student slowly turns the paper to continue making the rest of the flower petals. Using an 8-by-10-inch piece of watercolor paper, the kindergarteners work hard to fill the entire page with a variety of colors. Once the paint is dry, students use crayons to add detail to the flowers, such as stems and leaves. To finish the pictures, we color in the grass and sky.

First Grade: Constructive Use of Time

With 1st graders, we begin with what it means to use our time well. We brainstorm the various ways we use our time positively when we are out of school. Students provide examples, such as playing organized sports, playing with their friends, helping their parents do the dishes, reading, doing homework, and cleaning their rooms. I remind them that using our time keeps our minds and bodies healthy, and also allows us to be safe.

From the examples the students share, I choose one to demonstrate how to turn the activity into a piece of artwork. As the students draw, I remind them that their artwork needs to have a background, middle ground, and foreground, and that the main focus should consist of the constructive activity they choose. The children add detail to make the picture more interesting.

Once they complete the drawings on 9-by-12-inch white paper, following the above requirements, the 1st graders trace over their drawings with a black pen. Next, using colored pencils, they color their pictures so that no white space shows. Students then write a descriptive caption of their picture at the bottom of the page, which identifies the constructive use of time they've depicted in the drawing.

Second Grade: Support

To introduce the support category to 2nd graders, I show them pictures of elements of architecture that provide support. I ask students if they have ever seen houses and buildings when they are first being built. The skeleton frames are examples of support structures for the buildings. Concrete examples for our students are the exposed rafters in our gym and media center. We identify this feature as support for the building.

Artistically, we look at the various Romanesque types of columns that were used in the past and are still in use today. I tell them that initially, columns were a primary source of support for buildings, unlike the ornamental columns found in homes today.

From here we discuss the people in our lives who provide us with support. Parents, grandparents, siblings, teachers, ministers, and coaches are a few of the individuals the students identify. In addition, we acknowledge that the more people in our support system, the more likely we are to feel supported. By comparing the support system in architecture to the support systems in our lives, young students are able to see the importance of each.

Using photocopies of a variety of architectural columns showing details of the base and capitals, the students begin to draw the parts of a column to make a whole, which represent the supports in their lives. On an 8-by-10-inch brown textured piece of paper, the 2nd graders draw at least two complete columns, which are attached to an awning or roof.

Once they finish their drawings, we discuss adding a light source and shadows. Using this information, we color the columns and awnings with white oil pastels. To complete the columns, we use black color pencils to trace the detail in the columns and in the background.

Third Grade: Positive Values

Of all the assets, the positive-values category is often the most difficult for students to understand. Many 3rd graders have a hard time identifying what a value is, other than the price of an object.

What I have learned to do is ask them what types of rules their parents have regarding various issues such as homework, chores, and behavior at home, in restaurants and other public places, and at school. After the students and I share our experiences, I am able to categorize their answers as possible values. We notice that many of us have the same rules. Although rules are not the same as values, rules reflect values in a tangible way for 3rd graders.

Together, we are able to identify a value as something that guides our behavior because we strongly believe in it. When the students have an understanding of a personal value, I introduce them to a variation of shading in art. Using a soft lead pencil, I shade an area on a paper from dark to light. I compare the pencil variation to the personal value: like shading, our values may change, stay the same, or intensify as we grow. Hence, a dark-to-light scale represents our intensity of belief.

To begin our composition, I use a group of chairs as a still life for the students to draw. Once 3rd graders have completed a drawing, they use L-shaped viewfinders to focus on a smaller area. This area should have overlapping lines and a balance of positive and negative space. The students then transfer the smaller section to a 9-by-12-inch piece of paper.

On the final paper, the students identify the chair legs or chair seat. In the other spaces, they draw patterns to be shaded. Students then use a "B" pencil or any other soft lead pencil to create shade variations in the patterns.

Once they have shaded all their patterns, we discuss positive and negative space in art, and that the variation in pencil shading is also called a *value*. Students' work not only becomes a representation of values, but also becomes positive space in which the values reside, hence *positive values*.

Fourth Grade: Boundaries and Expectations and Commitment to Learning

To help 4th grade students understand boundaries and expectations, we brainstorm what these two words mean to us. *Boundaries* are the rules to follow at home, at school, while playing organized sports, and in the community. Students reveal why these boundaries are important in the different environments. A common response is that if students step outside the boundaries set by parents, teachers, coaches, or the law, they will "get in trouble."

These *expectations* become the guidelines for students' behavior when they are in different classrooms, homes, sporting events, and in the community. For example, behavioral expectations in physical education are different from the behavior students are expected to demonstrate in the media center. Despite the differences, 4th graders quickly learn what are the appropriate boundaries and expectations for their behavior. I point out that as we continue along the journey of life, we learn from the books we read and the people we meet. Each new part of the journey provides us with a different set of boundaries and expectations.

With popular children's books in mind, I ask students to look at them with a different artistic purpose. For this project, I choose books that contain positive messages. Some students have their own books in mind and are free to use those. With a partner, the students read a book to discover a lesson they think the author is trying to convey.

Because the students use the techniques of the illustrators of these books in this project, I gather a variety of examples that also show the use of collage, color pencil, watercolor, mixed media, and oil and chalk pastels. Students begin to illustrate the lesson in their book using the technique of the book's illustrator. Since the students are using a variety of books, the size and type of paper vary for each project. After the students finish the illustration, they use their statement of the lesson as a caption for their work.

Fourth graders also focus on a commitment to learning. We start by talking about what it means to have a commitment to something. Students discuss what it means to work hard to get something done, and we identify where the commitment begins. It usually begins as an expectation from their parents or other adult until the student becomes intrinsically motivated and takes pride in her or his academic achievements.

From here, we focus on the commitment to learning as coming from within. We discuss the importance of lifelong learning in academics and other activities in which students participate. We talk about how, as we progress through school, the commitment to learn must become stronger within ourselves, how we each need to learn to internalize the commitment. As an example, I share with them that I, and other teachers in school, attend classes to continue learning to improve our teaching.

As a symbol of their dedication to learning, students learn how to create self-portraits. Before we begin drawing our portraits, we determine how the length of our face is in proportion to the length of our eyes. Drawing our eyes first, we use our eye length to measure where the rest of our features need to be. Throughout our portrait drawing, we refer back to the eye to ensure our portrait is in proportion.

The students work extremely hard to create their faces, so we use the "sloppy copy" as our template to transfer our final image onto a 9-by-12-inch piece of white drawing paper. When finished, the students use oil pastels to color their self-portraits and background. I encourage the students to use a variety of colors to make their portrait more vibrant.

Fifth Grade: Positive Identity and Social Competencies

Fifth-grade students also create self-portraits, this time based upon the positive-identity asset category. After discussing the importance of feeling positive about their future promise, we look at a variety of portraits from abstract artists.

Then, using a digital camera, the students manipulate their image in a photo program to distort their appearance and print it on standard paper. The distortion of their images allows us to discuss the importance of positive identity versus seeing only the outer appearance. Our outer appearance often can be deceiving, not representing accurately who we are on the inside. Feeling great and believing in ourselves are the starting points to all we do in life. Creating a masked image reminds us that we are more than our outward appearance.

Students then transfer the printed copy to a final 9-by-12-inch piece of white drawing paper. Depending upon the type of distortion created, the students use watercolor, crayon, color pencils, or pastels (or some combination) to color their images. A great benefit to this type of artwork is that every self-portrait is a success: the self-portraits (much like some of Pablo Picasso's portraits) are not supposed to look exactly like us.

Fifth-grade students also explore social competencies. Because we are a diverse community, I read Katie Couric's *The Brand New Kid*,[2] which tells the story of the new boy in class who doesn't look or speak like the other kids. Students respond to him by taunting and teasing. One girl reaches out to him, however. Besides making a new friend, she helps her classmates understand an important lesson about accepting people who are different.

Together, the class addresses how the characters interact, conflicts between characters, and the resolution. Learning to accept all students and people for their diversity is important to leading a productive life.

In each class, we talk about where our ancestors came from and the various nationalities that are present throughout the world. Using flags from around the world, we also look at similarities between the colors, shapes, designs, and symbols each country uses.

Then we're ready to create a collage that represents equality and peace. Each student starts by drawing six to eight flags that represent their nationality(s) and that they think are "cool." Next, we use a 12-by-18-inch piece of white paper and draw a border around the page. Students then divide the page into six sections that must provide an interesting visual balance. Using a black permanent marker, students trace the border and sections before they draw their flags in each space. I encourage the students to identify the most distinctive parts of the flags and draw those features in each space. They use colored pencils to finish the flags, covering all white space. Then they trace the names of each country in the borders with a fine-tip black pen and color in with colored pencil.

Asset Masterpieces

Regardless of the diverse needs within a classroom, each student can successfully create an asset masterpiece. Displayed throughout the school, the work the young students create and the message the artwork conveys awe many other teachers and visitors, as well as parents. When students share why they are creating a particular project, the depth of meaning combined with aesthetic values impresses teachers. As one student puts it, "They [the projects] teach us how to draw and paint, but we also learn about what is important in life." Parents say those pieces their children have created in the Assets in Art program are their favorite.

With each new year and each new class, I learn more about how to improve my delivery of the assets in art. I continue to look for new projects that may better represent each asset. The most effective programs are those teachers can embrace personally. Those programs allow teachers to be lifelong learners, to learn and grow alongside their students. As the art program grows and the school begins to incorporate the assets into other areas, students are able to take ownership of their choices and internalize each asset.

───────

Notes

1. Some of the asset-related resources I used in developing the Assets in Art program include Roehlkepartain, Jolene L., and Leffert, Nancy. (2000). *What Young Children Need to Succeed*. Minneapolis: Free Spirit Publishing; Roehlkepartain, Jolene L. (1997). *Ideas for Parents Newsletters*. Minneapolis: Search Institute; Benson, Peter L., Galbraith, Judy, and Espeland, Pamela. (1998). *What Kids Need to Succeed: Proven, Practical Ways to Raise Good Kids*. Minneapolis: Free Spirit Publishing.
2. Couric, Katie. (2000). *The Brand New Kid*. New York: Doubleday.

Creating Adaptations

Integrating the assets schoolwide in other content areas, with each grade level focusing on a specific asset category throughout the year, can strengthen student comprehension of the assets. When reading novels, writing biographies, studying historic figures, or discussing current events, language arts, social studies, history, and even math and science, students can illustrate their vision of a main character's or historical figure's asset traits, or compare and contrast the character with themselves. School psychologists and social workers also can adopt the asset framework as they work with each grade level.

Gaining Cultural Insights Through Art

JAIME L. SHAFER

Art Teacher (grades 10–12)

Greater Latrobe Senior High School

Latrobe, Pennsylvania

Art surrounds us everywhere: just examine where you are right now and what surrounds you. For example, as I sit at my dining room table, I observe glassware, fabric, a pattern, a telephone, and salt and pepper shakers. Each of these objects begins as a design. In almost any content area, you can introduce art by identifying elements of design and use art projects to enhance the curriculum and reinforce learning. And integrating art into the regular—that is, non-art—curriculum, along with fine arts instruction, provides myriad opportunities to develop asset building for and with youth.

Whether the art or an art form embodies a unique significance or origin, students can learn that art is not just an aesthetic experience but a tool. And whether that tool is used for education, pleasure, or another purpose, art communicates an important message about a culture and its beliefs. By looking at or creating their own art, students can learn to express themselves individually in a different style; to use knowledge from math, science, history, and other areas to produce their own designs; and to understand other cultures in relation to their own.

I design class art projects so that students can succeed and gain self-worth. The class atmosphere is structured but relaxed. I introduce projects, show students quality examples, and then give them time and freedom to work independently. As students work, I circulate around the room to build relationships with them, reinforce course concepts, and redirect. I include in my classes at least one assignment that introduces art from another culture: it is this cross-cultural project, the Kachina Sculpture Project, with which I have had particular success in integrating asset building and teaching cultural understanding. To help students reflect on their

SCHOOL DEMOGRAPHICS
Greater Latrobe Senior High School
Latrobe, Pennsylvania

Students: 969

Grades: 10–12

Gender:
Male	52.0%
Female	48.0%

Race and Ethnicity:
Black/African American	0.1%
Hispanic/Latino	0.6%
Asian/Pacific Islander	0.7%
White/Caucasian	98.6%

Socioeconomics:
Free/Reduced Lunch	25.0%

art experience, I also require them to complete a group project, working together as an entire class, and to provide an artifact to leave behind for future classes.

The Kachina Sculpture Project

To support building cultural understanding, I came up with the idea of having students create a ceramic sculpture project based on the carved wooden kachina dolls found in Hopi Indian culture. By prompting the students to consider how the art of one culture can provide inspiration to another, I get them to think about how that same art form might function in, or represent important aspects of, their own lives and culture.

I developed the project idea by first researching the meaning and role of the kachina in Hopi culture.[1] Next, I examined the kachina's appearance, particularly noting the spiritual importance of color in the creation, design, and identification of the kachina's origins.[2] In adapting this art form for the class project, I set the following objectives:

Photo by Jaime L. Shafer

- **Art production:** To construct a small clay kachina sculpture using additive, subtractive, and assemblage sculpture techniques.
- **Art history:** To identify the importance the kachina plays in Hopi culture, to learn what it represents, and to understand how it is used.
- **Art criticism:** To critique the kachina for quality, craftsmanship, and color usage.
- **Art aesthetics:** To determine student likes and dislikes about the kachina project and learn what the student would do differently if the project were done again.

Taken as a whole, the Kachina Sculpture Project helps me in building assets with students. From the start, I give students creative control over their projects. Given the opportunity to plan and design as they like, rather than using a "cookie cutter" approach, students can make the end result unique. By studying Hopi kachinas, the students strive to produce quality kachinas of their own, while expanding their knowledge of another culture. I also gain an opportunity to further my relationships with students by getting to know each one individually as I guide them on the project and as they reveal their personalities through their plans and designs for their project.

Developing Inspiration and Ideas

To start the project, it is important to teach aspects of the Hopi culture to the students. I caution my students that imitating or adapting the art form of another culture without understanding the culture is not what building cultural competence is about. I explain to them that the kachina is a sacred element found in Hopi culture, and begin the lesson with a short reading from Nancy Bonvillain's book *The Hopi*. From this reading, students learn that, for the Hopi, everything is spirit. They come to understand the significance of the kachinas to the Hopi and learn that kachinas are powerful manifestations of sacred spirits; particularly, that "they are all-powerful spirits and deities who make the Hopi feel that they are communing with a reality that lies behind and sustains the everyday, visible world."[3]

From other resources, I read students descriptions of sacred spirits represented by kachina dolls and show them photographs of the dolls.[4] I also give them a handout I created from these resources that includes a brief description of the kachina and its significance in the Hopi community. Students study additional reference books and various photographs of kachinas for inspiration and ideas as they begin to develop their own projects. In class, we also look together at the artwork of the Zuni, Iroquois, and Tewa for comparison. Students also examine a kachina doll I have made.

Students see that while some of the kachina examples shown in books are detailed and sophisticated, others are not all that elaborate. The wide variety of examples tends to reduce feelings of intimidation when students create their own dolls. Rather, they are excited to see that a simple kachina can be just as effective and valuable as an elaborate, detailed kachina.

Creating a Kachina

As part of my efforts to focus on developmental assets with students, I usually permit them personal power over the creative decisions that need to be made for projects. For example, in projects other than the kachina sculptures, such as supervising students painting dramatic scenery and sets, I offer guidance and feedback when necessary, but try, for the most part, to permit them to select colors, choose a specific technique, or sort out how to solve a design problem. By making their own decisions, students develop a sense of ownership and care more about the outcome of the project.

For the Kachina Sculpture Project, though, I require students to use authentic colors of Hopi kachinas on the faces of their dolls to signify the "origins" of their kachinas (specific colors are associated with north, south, east, and west). In this way, students show their understanding of one way that color functions in the art of the Hopi.

Each student designs her or his own kachina and completes three sketches. Each sketch must include detailed information and notes on colors, designs, materials, and assemblage. Students have time in class to work out their ideas and seek feedback from each other. They must turn in their sketches with a note indicating which design they feel is their strongest and why. I review all the sketches; I either approve them or return them and ask the students to elaborate on their designs.

During the next class, I demonstrate how to create a small-scale sculpture of a kachina doll. Using my own sketch and notes, I show the students how to use basic shapes to create the body. I remind them to use their sketches as blueprints for the sculpture and ask them to try to stick to their original design. Nearby, I have a second kachina already started and ready for carving and detail work. I show the students various carving tools and ribbon tools that work well when designing and adding detail to their clay sculptures.

Students have the opportunity to create a sample or practice model of their project designs while I rotate around the room to provide individual attention to each person. By practicing techniques first with one-on-one coaching, the students have a greater chance of success with a given project—and with asset building for both of us.

While our school student population is not diverse in terms of ethnicity, race, or culture, our students are, however, diverse in their learning styles. Students in my classes range in age and ability levels from having learning needs to advanced placement. To reach them all, I incorporate various teaching styles. For example, if I verbally describe what I am doing as I visually demonstrate a project, I reach more students. I also provide a written, step-by-step explanation of what students need to do for a particular project, along with tips and questions to spark their imaginations. The class itself requires a hands-on approach, which also addresses students who are kinesthetic learners.

Students work at different paces due to their individual skill levels. In order not to rush them, I have all students start the project at the same time, but give them some freedom to decide how much work time they need. Students learn to plan their time so that their projects meet the end-of-quarter deadline. I find student planning works well with ceramics projects because of the extended time involved in making the projects.

After the students complete their clay sculptures through the firing stage, I demonstrate how to mix colors and apply acrylic paint to them. I also give the students materials such as feathers, ribbon, and foliage to use in completing their dolls. When the students finishing painting and embellishing their dolls, I display them in the hall case and encourage students to enter them in contests.

Connecting to a Culture

The Kachina Sculpture Project is a remarkable experience for students. By introducing them to a culture and people they have not yet studied or been exposed to, I help them develop an appreciation for, and acceptance of, diverse cultures. And in the process, they also learn that people support their cultural beliefs with art, and with rituals and traditions that use that art. They see that art is both an aesthetic experience *and* a tool, and regardless of its purpose as a tool, it communicates an important message about a culture. Students learn that the message varies, based upon individual experience and perspective. In this instance, the message students receive is the importance of the Hopi kachina and its role in Hopi culture.

Students who take part in this project now look at art and other cultures a little differently. They can begin to see that art does not exist in isolation from culture. Most students say they have not thought about the art of other cultures before this project; they enjoy this project because it is different and they learn something new and interesting. This is, in part, exactly what asset building in youth is about—to have the opportunity to examine and gain an appreciation for another culture and begin to understand it in relation to your own.

Arts Integration

Integrating art into the regular curriculum is another way to build assets with and for youth. Often, students may not perform well in one area of study, but by integrating art into the lesson, you can offer students another way to succeed.

I find that many of the students in my classes who do not do well in traditional subjects, such as math, do well in my ceramics class. Many of these students are kinesthetic learners and gain confidence by taking my hands-on class and doing well in it. In addition, by collaborating with teachers in other content areas, I am able to build relationships that are conducive to developing assets that students need to succeed.

Recently, I worked with two colleagues to incorporate Renaissance art history into their European history and literature class. The lesson began with an introduction to the various discoveries made in art during the Renaissance and included an introduction to key artists, whose contributions to the art world I identified using slides and books. Students had an opportunity to create paintings based on a specific design element: depth. We then took the students to the Carnegie Museum of Art in Pittsburgh, Pennsylvania, to view Renaissance art and architecture.

Photo by Jaime L. Shafer

I have also worked with students who studied the art and life of Pablo Picasso in their French class. On a visit to the Cleveland Museum of Art in Cleveland, Ohio, students had an opportunity to see Picasso's two-dimensional work, much of which was produced while he lived in France. Since Picasso worked with clay as well as paint, I showed the students how to construct coil pots and paint Picasso-style portraits. Students were able to connect Picasso's art to their study of French culture and language.

With another colleague in family and consumer sciences, and supported by a grant we applied for and received, we embarked on an exciting project allowing students to make an oven from natural earth materials (clay, sand, and straw). Students planned and constructed the oven using art, math, and environmental science to create their design. They also studied the tradition and history of this type of oven. After constructing the earth oven, students tried their hand at baking in it. They invited 14 preschool students to learn about the oven and share bread they baked.

The students took charge of the project. They worked in teams on each aspect of the planning: site preparations, artistic design, foundation, floor, walls, and finishing. The students created special bonds with us, their teachers, as well as with each other. They developed self-esteem and a sense of purpose that came from the personal power they gained through their planning, decision making, and successful execution of the project. The students liked creating something unique and special that would remain at the school long after they were gone. It gave them an opportunity to bond to their school.

Working together as an entire class and bonding to school are important developmental assets I also emphasize in my own art classes. To help students reflect on their art experience, I require them to complete a group project (from

15 to 22 students). For example, the group might choose to create a class book that represents their time together. Each student brings completed artwork to class and photographs it. They also photograph each other throughout the semester as they work on projects. Finally, they assemble and present the book. Students must work well together to successfully complete this aspect of the course.

The success of all of these projects reaches beyond fine arts instruction and content integration, supporting asset building for the instructor as well as the students and other teachers. They provide inspiration to continue to design new projects for new subject areas. If we all continue to infuse an asset mind-set in our instruction, I believe that we will progressively see asset building proceed hand in hand with arts integration across all curricula.

Photo by Jaime L. Shafer

Notes

1. Bonvillain, Nancy. (1994). *The Hopi*. New York: Chelsea House; Billard, Jules B. (ed.). (1974). *The World of the American Indian*. Washington, DC: National Geographic.
2. Bonvillain, *The Hopi*.
3. Ibid., p. 65.
4. Campbell, David (ed.). (1993). *Native American Art and Folklore*. New York: Crescent; Cassidy, James J. Jr. (ed.). (1995). *Through Indian Eyes*. New York: Reader's Digest; Maxwell, James A. (ed.). (1978). *America's Fascinating Indian Heritage*. New York: Reader's Digest.

Creating Adaptations

You can easily adapt the Kachina Sculpture Project to other content areas, grade levels, and contexts. Consider these modifications for elementary-level students:

- Reduce the scale of the project: Introduce the Hopi and their culture, but alter the sculpture size to suit specific needs. (At the high school level, our kachinas are approximately five to seven inches tall.)
- Require students to create one design, rather than two or three.
- Use self-hardening clay, clay that you can bake in a conventional oven, or Egyptian paste instead of regular clay (what high school students use) that needs to be fired in a kiln. Self-hardening clay projects can dry overnight and be painted the next day. This reduces the amount of time spent on construction and eliminates the need for large equipment. The Egyptian paste is a self-glazing clay—the color is already mixed into the clay so that the students do not have to paint.
- Simplify the painting if it is an important aspect of the lesson and curriculum. By minimizing details, make the painting suitable to younger students' skills and developmental stages (manipulative, symbol making, and preadolescent).[1]
- Also simplify self-evaluation for elementary students. Use open-ended questions, but require a complete-sentence answer from each, or have them dictate to older partners their individual responses, which you can combine into an all-class summary.

You can adapt any of the projects I have introduced to my classes and to other teachers' classes to suit other content areas and grade levels. If you want to adapt the Kachina Sculpture Project to your social studies class or history class, have students study in depth many more aspects of the Hopi culture by examining geography, economic conditions, crafts, language, and so on.

Literature and music teachers can study the literature, art, and music of specific periods, such as the Romantic and Rococo eras, and plan art projects to reinforce learning. Whatever your content area, art offers a unique opportunity to reinforce learning and support asset building.

Notes
1. Hurwitz, Al, and Day, Michael. (2001). *Children and Their Art: Methods for the Elementary School,* 6th ed. Belmont, CA: Wadsworth.

Part III

*Advocate for Assets **beyond** the Classroom*

Chapter 9

*Creating Asset-Rich
Educational Systems*

■ *Individual teachers in single classrooms can work passionately to build relationships with and among students, to create environments conducive to both relating and learning, and to infuse asset building into what and how they teach. But the benefits young people gain during that one time of their school day spent with an asset-building teacher can be wiped out totally by one negative encounter with another staff member later in the day.*

The real key to supporting youth in a community involves, of course, the efforts of more than one teacher in a single classroom—or even of one school. It involves the collaboration of many individuals, organizations, and systems within a local area or region. The power of change comes through the coordination of many asset builders who move an entire system through the shifts in paradigm needed to work positively with youth based on their strengths instead of their deficits.

Although most of the focus in this book is on what happens within classrooms, some of the success of classroom work depends upon supports that we orchestrate outside of classrooms.

Taking the First Step

LINKING SUPPORTS FOR HIGH SCHOOL SUCCESS

STEVEN HENDERSON, M.A.

History Teacher (grades 9–12)

Aragon High School

San Mateo, California

In rising above the challenges of an environment of change in our classrooms, it is important for us teachers to remember that our students have always faced, and will always face, confusing changes throughout their school years, because of the very nature of growing up. Knowing from Search Institute's research that the number of assets students report in high school drops significantly compared to middle school,[1] we work to support building and maintaining the presence of the assets as our students transition from one level to the next.

Stories abound of youth who experience social as well as academic challenges in transitioning from elementary to middle and from middle to high schools—whether about harassment by older students or fear of being humiliated or lacking preparation for the particular structure of new class schedules and academic expectations.

To ease these kinds of transitions for youth already facing a myriad of confusing changes, our high school has developed a program to help 9th graders acclimate to high school, to help them be academically as well as emotionally successful as they move from middle school. The program represents a collaboration of staff in several academic disciplines in one school, a coordinated way of providing support so that no young person is without assistance and a significant adult on whom to depend. In other words, "First Step," as we call our program, is a solid infusion of asset building into an academic support system.

Based on the idea that a successful transition into high school will continue to contribute to students' success throughout the next four years, First Step's multidisciplinary approach involves building assets as well as teaching particular skills

SCHOOL DEMOGRAPHICS
Aragon High School
San Mateo, California

Students: 1,550

Grades: 9–12

Gender:

Male	52 .0%
Female	48 .0%

Race and Ethnicity:

Black/African American	2.0%
Hispanic/Latino	18.0%
Asian/Pacific Islander	30.0%
American Indian	0.5%
Middle Eastern	2.0%
White/Caucasian	47.0%
Multiracial	0.5%

Socioeconomics:

Free/Reduced Lunch	3.0%

to incoming 9th grade students who are likely to struggle with their social and academic adjustment to high school. In my experience, helping students realize their potential involves establishing relationships with them that help them move forward. The tools provided through asset building give educators a proactive approach for creating an educational environment in which all students can achieve.

Basement Grades: Our Dilemma and Our Objectives

Underachievement

In recent years, my school has struggled with a difficult phenomenon. For at least the past ten years, an average of 20 percent (approximately 72 students) of the incoming freshmen attending our upper-middle-class, suburban school of approximately 1,550 students have earned a grade point average (GPA) of under 2.0 by the end of their first semester of high school. Many of the students stay at the same level, achieving less than a 2.0 GPA during their entire high school experience. Further analysis of our district student performance statistics indicated that underachievement by incoming students was consistent in each of the six district high schools.

First Step Objectives

To increase the performance of underachieving students, I designed First Step as an intervention program. Operated by a coalition of students, teachers, community members, and businesspeople linked to the school, First Step maintains a mission to ensure the success of all high school students. The vision of the First Step Foundation, which was established mainly to fund the program, is that students entering Aragon High School never earn a GPA under 2.0 (no Ds or Fs) during their four years in school.

We intend to sustain the program by obtaining funds from the district and through securing grants. Our long-term goal is to amend the program so that other schools can replicate it. We would also like to establish an after-school tutoring network for students to support them toward consistent positive academic change throughout their high school experience. Managing the First Step Program as an extension of a school and district helps avoid the costs involved in establishing an independent nonprofit organization. Since public school districts are already classified as nonprofit organizations, donations made to the program are automatically tax-deductible.

In an example of asset building supported beyond the single classroom, or school for that matter, the San Mateo Union High School District, of which Aragon High School is a part, is committed to doing everything possible to be certain that every student has a genuine opportunity to be prepared for success in high school.[2] The First Step Program is aligned with the district in this effort.

In addition, the performance requirements promoted by the program reinforce the *Expected School Wide Learning Outcomes*[3] that the school requires students to strive toward achieving. The San Mateo Unified High School District Leadership

Team is developing new language across disciplines describing standards that students must achieve to succeed. These performance standards, which the school and district are adopting, are in concert with the language about student performance in the First Step Program.

First Step is also designed to help students develop the skills necessary to prepare for and pass the state-mandated California High School Exit Exam. This exam serves as the academic competency test for students in most California schools. Students who do not pass the exam will not receive a diploma at the end of high school.

In its pilot year beginning in August 2001, the foundation's two initial objectives for the First Step Program included:

1. To decrease by 5 percent the percentage of students at Aragon High School who earn less than a 2.0 GPA in their first semester of school, by providing educational services for students entering grade 9 that will enable them to merge into the rigorous academic demands of high school in an exemplary manner.
2. To promote participation in extracurricular, team-building, asset-rich activities, and help students make healthy lifestyle choices through organized activities introduced during the one-week institute, the first stage of the program.

Many of the events in which students participate during the weeklong institute mirror cocurricular choices we encourage students to make during the school year. In addition, the program supports peer and adult relationship building.

The Summer Institute

Fifteen incoming freshmen were part of our one-week, end-of-summer institute pilot. The counseling departments of the middle schools that send students to us identified at-risk students who were not meeting their school's academic and social demands. Many of the students in the program were selected because they performed at a level below average in middle school. The rest of the students were mixed in ability and were chosen as a result of consultation between middle school staff and the coordinator of First Step.

A team of teachers from math, social studies, English, and special education created the five-day institute, which operated half days in the morning. Each day, students participated in an academic-readiness session; listened to a speaker from the community talk about student preparedness, motivation, study skills, and career life; and participated in sports or team-building activities.

Creating connections to the school academically and socially in the summer institute helps create an asset-supportive partnership between at-risk students and the school and the community, which supports increased student performance. The relationships that are forged as a result of this partnership help to create an environment in which students develop and work a plan to succeed as the year progresses. Guest speakers suggest many positive and practical career paths, inspiring students to identify and take the steps necessary to achieve both socially and academically. Ultimately, we hope students are encouraged to express their dreams.

A Three-Pronged Plan: Cocurricular Activities, Academic Support, Healthy Lifestyle

Our methods for addressing our two objectives focus on a balance among cocurricular activities, academic tasks, and healthy lifestyle behaviors, promoting a holistic approach that is consistent with the developmental assets.

Cocurricular Activities

Our thinking about cocurricular activities derives from a study by Edward Klesse showing that students that devoted 7½ hours/week in cocurricular activities (the average amount of time spent) fared well academically, spent more time on homework, and expected to go further in school.[4] Klesse also indicates that participation in cocurricular activities relates to a number of desirable characteristics, including self-esteem, educational aspirations, increased feelings of control, and reduction in students' feelings of alienation.[5]

An inherent socializing element is associated with participating in cocurricular activities. Learning to work as part of a team while using principles of play anchored in fairness helps to shape one's individual and group identity positively. Building a culture of school success underscored by pride in one's efforts, as a part of a team or club, is essential to a student's success in school. To support this important element of success, fitness, theater, recreational, and health activities comprised approximately one-third of each student's half day during the institute.

Our intent with the end-of-summer institute is that the students' introduction to and involvement in extracurricular activities carries over into the school year. Research by Grenchik, O'Connor, and Postelli indicates that students' lack of personal responsibility and academic ownership, negative or indifferent attitude, and lack of initiative and general motivation are often of concern to teachers and parents.[6] This attitude of indifference is evident in low-achieving students in many cases. Providing motivation for students to excel in school through participation in school-related activities is a major focus of First Step.

Students in First Step are required to participate in an extracurricular activity of their choice during the school year, exposing them to the opportunity to experience success and build their confidence. Students, it is hoped, will more likely pursue academic challenges with less trepidation once they are connected to extracurricular school experiences.

Academic Support

Helping students attain standards-based skills is another major focus of First Step. The institute provides instruction that helps map out how students can succeed in specific subject areas. The instructional strategies the institute teachers embrace and the learning strategies they encourage the students to use are those geared specifically to motivate "at-risk" students to achieve a high level of academic performance. Institute teachers show students how to use tools such as active listening and analytical reading, participate in class discussion, and take notes effectively, among others. Further, they provide students short consistent messages throughout the school year to reinforce using these tools; students do get assessed on using these strategies, as well.

The success of the program in part lies with our teachers. They possess a high-energy, can-do attitude and attempt to instill that among program participants. Tutors proficient in core subject areas in which students have a demonstrated need (mathematics, English, and history) also provide services by appointment during the school year. Tutors are college and upper-division high school students as well as teachers. Research indicates that such tutoring is particularly effective when, in fact, teachers are used as tutors.[7] Patricia Gensemer also suggests that successful programs should help teachers to become facilitators who oversee their students' mastery of necessary concepts and skills, and guide them toward independent learning.[8]

Goal Setting

At the beginning of the weeklong institute, we also introduce students to goal-setting skills (see Handout 9.1: First Step Student Academic Goal-Setting Form on page 240).[9] Knowing expectations, identifying performance goals, and learning how to achieve them are fundamental components of First Step.

If expectations of students are like one-way streets—coming only from the adult, teacher, or parent to the student—the student is more likely to fail and be disillusioned. For at-risk students, experience with school-related failure and personal frustration due to overwhelming expectations is significant and often deeply embedded in their histories. Through active engagement in the program, we seek to turn a set of circumstances, perhaps previously seen only negatively, into situations that have created strengths for a particular individual. Developing students' planning and decision-making skills helps them to set expectations for themselves and meet the expectations of others.

After introducing the students to study skills and setting goals, the daily schedule for the week of the summer institute allows for academic instructors from different disciplines to describe their courses during a portion of each day (see "First Step Summer Institute Daily Schedule" on page 242). The instructors introduce overlapping expectations for students to demonstrate the similarities among expectations (see Handout 9.2: First Step Student Education Plan and Interdisciplinary Expectations on page 241).

During the institute, teachers role-play what it is to be an effective and an ineffective student in their classes. Modeling and role playing are useful tools that make learning concrete for the students. The program teachers seek to help the students reduce the list of skills and activities on which they will have to focus to succeed in school.

Supporting effective academic performance by students in core academic courses is a focal point of this multidisciplinary transition program throughout the

First Step Student Academic Goal-Setting Form

Your Focus Goals

Complete items 1 and 2 on binder paper, following the instructions and example.

1. Select four of the academic performance categories from the First Step Student Academic Performance Assessment Form (Handout 9.3), on which you intend to focus and improve during the next six-week grading period.

2. List two beginning steps for each of the four academic performance categories, which you will regularly do to progress toward maintaining or improving your ability (score) in that performance area.

Example

Goal 1: I will improve my reading score from a 3 to a 4.
   Beginning Step 1: I will read carefully, taking time to be certain that I know the meaning of key words and ideas.
   Beginning Step 2: I will read and examine charts and graphs that are a part of reading assignments.

Meet and discuss your plans with your assigned teacher mentor every other week.

Your Focus Expectations

3. Select one expectation from each group of interdisciplinary expectations for each six-week period from the First Step Student Education Plan and Interdisciplinary Expectations (Handout 9.2). You may use the same expectation for more than six weeks if you and your teacher mentor agree that your progress toward achieving the expectation is not yet satisfactory.

4. List each of the expectations on which you have decided to focus during this six-week grading period. Use the example below to guide you in talking to your teacher mentor.

5. For each expectation you list, explain activities (using concrete examples) that you have performed to move closer to achieving your goal. Write a two- to three-sentence explanation about what you did to achieve each goal.

6. Rank your performance level now and your expected future performance level for each:

   5 = excellent performance, 4 = above average, 3 = average, 2 = below average, 1= poor.

Example

Expectation: I will be an active listener.
Preassessment performance level: 2
Explanation: I have been avoiding distraction during class lectures and discussion. I ask questions when I am unsure about topics being discussed.
Postassessment performance level desired: 3

First Step Student Education Plan and Interdisciplinary Expectations

Education Plan

Students: Select one expectation from each group of interdisciplinary expectations listed in the second column. Meet with your teacher mentor at the beginning of each semester and at other recommended intervals to discuss your progress toward achieving the expectations (your goals).

Teachers: During the semester, all teachers of First Step Program students will know their students' Education Plan goals (the expectations on which they have chosen to work). Evaluate student progress in the selected areas using this five-point scale:

5 = Achieved goal(s);
4 = Above average progress toward achieving goal(s);
3 = Average progress toward goal(s);
2 = Below average progress toward achieving goal(s); and
1 = No progress toward goal(s).

At the end of each six-week grading period, discuss progress with students and decide with them whether they have met the expectation or need to continue working on the same goals. If the student has met the expectations, collaborate on selecting new goals.

Interdisciplinary Education Plan Expectations

Study, Communication Skills:

Maintain Posture.
Have a pleasant tone of voice.
Activate your thinking.
Inventory your strengths, and set goals.
Listen, respond, and ask questions.
Develop time-management skills.

English, Reading Development:

Be organized; follow the system that the teacher gives.
Do all work completely.
Complete work on time.

Math, Logic, Teamwork:

Be an attentive listener.
Be a contributor to a group, and use the ideas generated by its members without depending only on the efforts of others.
Be an active participant in class activities.
Avoid being disruptive.
Avoid being lazy.

History, Effective Decision Making:

Attend school—you have to be present to win.
Accept responsibility for your own learning experience; be honest.
Be organized; turn all materials in on time.
Participate in extracurricular activities to make school and life outside of school fun.

First Step Summer Institute Daily Schedule

8:00–9:30	Primary academic instruction in one of the key academic areas.
9:30–9:45	Break, healthy snacks.
9:50–10:55	Professionals from the community, working in careers linked to a specific academic area, will speak to students.
11:00–12:20	Team-building and sports activities.
12:20–12:40	Debriefing of the day's events.
12:45	Dismissal.

year. Because teachers from different subjects are central to the program, they can focus on helping students to understand the content of their respective courses during the school year. We schedule students in the First Step Program into regular courses with the same academic instructors who served in the summer institute.

Routing students from the summer institute into the participating instructor's courses is among the most important steps in supporting the students. Daily contact between First Step students and those instructors reduces the pressure on all to create timely solutions to challenging circumstances that arise. Such careful supervision allows positive changes to occur a little bit at a time. Instructors who know students well can also slowly allow them more freedom to make their own decisions.

Understanding Assessment

Early discussions about assessment are also designed to help students achieve. At our school, students are graded in three six-week periods. During the first two grading periods, students receive *progress report grades*. At the end of the third six-week period, the grade for the entire 18 weeks becomes the student's semester grade. Students in the program are required to set six-week Education Plan goals drawn from the list of expectations (see Handout 9.2). At the end of each six-week period, students themselves evaluate their progress toward their goals using a five-point scale.

In addition to assessing themselves on their goals, students also rate themselves on performance skills in each of the 10 areas on the First Step Student Academic Performance Assessment Form (see Handout 9.3 on page 243): reading, writing, note taking, listening, following instructions, participating in discussions, preparing for tests, managing time, attending school, and getting appropriate help. Teachers consistently also reinforce student productivity, making sure that students value taking responsibility. Students demonstrate evidence of possessing such values when they adopt the behaviors reflected on the performance assessment form.

Healthy Lifestyle

Teaching students the connection between academic performance and healthy lifestyle choices is another important part of our approach. During the week of the

First Step Student Academic Performance Assessment Form

This handout will help you evaluate your progress toward your performance goals. When you have filled it out, discuss your progress with your mentor and determine new goals for the next weeks.

1. Examine the following list of student performance categories.

2. Rank your performance level on each category, giving yourself a score of 1 to 5:

   5 = excellent performance, 4 = above average,
   3 = average, 2 = below average, 1 = poor.

3. Once you have given yourself a score for each category, add the numbers across all categories. Divide the total by 10. The result of your division is the average score, indicating your overall academic performance level at this time.

_____ Reading.

_____ Writing: Assignment completion, legibility.

_____ Note taking.

_____ Listening.

_____ Following written and oral instructions.

_____ Participating in class discussion.

_____ Spending appropriate time preparing for tests.

_____ Time management: The way I use my after-school time helps me to complete homework regularly.

_____ Attendance: I attend school regularly. I am rarely absent from school.

_____ Appropriate help: I seek help from the appropriate people—peer, teacher, counselor—when I'm facing challenges.

_____ **Total Score**

_____ Performance Average = Your Total Divided by 10

institute, we encourage students to prepare themselves to learn throughout the school year by eating well. We also address the importance of getting enough sleep.

Physical education teachers and recreation supervisors collaborate to plan, implement, and evaluate a comprehensive program focusing on healthy lifestyle behaviors. Activities and recreational sports emphasize team building, including basketball, volleyball, softball, role-plays, and a ropes challenge course. Healthy snacks are, of course, provided daily.

Helping students make healthy choices when dealing with adversity in school experiences is particularly useful. For example, after studying relentlessly but performing poorly on the exam, a student ideally would go to after-school sports practice, hit the gym, or run a mile to release frustration or disappointment. The physical activity alleviates the feeling of failure, and the positive feelings of belonging that come from being on a team diminish it. In essence, a healthy lifestyle behavior helps sustain a positive outlook during an academic setback.

Relationships Are the Key

The cornerstone of the First Step Program is building relationships. Supportive adult-teen and teen-peer relationships are fostered during program activities. Participants listen to each other and have the opportunity to affirm their independence and interdependence. As the regular school year progresses and program participants involve themselves in school athletics, music, theater or other clubs, and community activities, they further develop empathy, sensitivity, and friendship-making skills.

A significant component of the summer institute involves finding out what students are all about and advocating for their support. We come to know the students in ways that include their families and community. First Step does this in part by encouraging the development and maintenance of more than 20 of the developmental assets identified by Search Institute; and, in an effort to be teen friendly, we've modified the asset language to include *teenager* instead of *young person*.[10]

Learning about students' school-related or other concerns by modeling listening skills gives value to their ideas. For example, students identify that they want to be better test takers or learn how to plan and make good decisions. Linking their ideas with other specific, teacher-directed performance goals enables teachers to guide students in setting goals. Then teacher mentors can work with students in similar areas, such as spending appropriate time preparing for tests or managing time well.

Being supportive and establishing empathy among students allow an instructor to work *with* a student in setting goals, blending teacher and school expectations with the student's own expectations. While not equal, the student and the teacher can relate more on the same level than in the traditional student-teacher communication models. Setting up this dynamic creates buy-in from the student related to mutually accepted student performance goals. Students in the program are thereby supported toward successful academic and social performance in the school setting.

Tending more specifically to students' needs regarding social adjustment to high school is also critical. During the week of the summer institute, as well as during the school year, caring teachers and members of the community are available to listen to participants' stories and share their own by describing what striving to achieve the high expectations of adults meant to them as teenagers and what it means to them today. Students in the program share their views on the same theme. Other stories students and adults share involve resisting negative pressure from others. Mentor teachers in regular meetings throughout the school year continue to monitor closely how students are adapting to both the academic and social demands of high school.

So What Is Success?

We define success in the First Step Program as follows:

- Achieving a GPA of 2.0 or higher in each grading period;
- Earning semester grades in all courses that exclude Ds and Fs; and
- Participating in extracurricular activities, sports, clubs, theater, and/or music in at least one season during the school year.

The teachers in the First Step Program regularly assess the extent to which students are using our ideas. We assess student performance in the core academic courses to ensure ongoing support. During the first year of our pilot, 90 percent of the program students earned a GPA over 2.0, without earning any Ds or Fs. All participated in extracurricular activities. By our definition, students in the program are succeeding. The summer 2002 participants are performing similarly to the pilot group.

School and district administrators support the mission of our foundation and have encouraged growth of our program. Teachers who were not directly involved in the pilot but who teach First Step students during the regular school year express support for our efforts. Many positively acknowledge that the relationships forged during the summer extend into the school year, enabling teachers to more effectively support the academic performance of those students involved.

We ask students from our program who excel in the first year to share their success stories with incoming 9th graders during upcoming summer institutes and participate as student mentors. Creating a network of caring students, teachers, and parents for the participants in the program helps to support their achievement by giving them positive resources to access before a crisis develops. As Moses Pita, a member of the Aragon High School football team, whose first semester GPA was 2.6, says:

> I've turned in more homework, and completed it better than last year. I pay more attention in high school than I did in middle school. I understand more things when the teacher explains stuff than I did in 8th grade.

Notes

1. Benson, Peter L., Scales, Peter C., and Roehlkepartain, Eugene C. (1999). *A Fragile Foundation: The State of Developmental Assets among American Youth*. Minneapolis: Search Institute.
2. Academic Focus for All Students. San Mateo Union High School District, District Wide Goals and Standards, 2000.
3. Rarden, Ann, principal, and committee members. (1999). *Expected School Wide Learning Outcomes*. Burlingame, CA: Aragon High School. Prepared for the Western Association of Schools and Colleges.
4. Klesse, Edward J. (1994). *Student Activities: The Third Curriculum*. Reston, VA: National Association of Secondary School Principals.
5. Ibid.
6. Grenchik, Denise, O'Connor, Elaine, and Postelli. Gina. (1999). Effective Motivation through Meeting Student Needs. M.A. Action Research Project, Saint Xavier University and IRI/Skylight, Chicago.
7. Ainsworth, Robert, G. (1995). Turning Potential School Dropouts into Graduates: The Case for School-Based One-to-One Tutoring. Research Report 95-07. Washington, DC: U.S. Labor Department, National Commission for Employment Policy.
8. Gensemer, Patricia. (2000). Effectiveness of Cross-Age and Peer Mentoring Programs. Educational Resources Information Center, U.S. Department of Education, ED438267.
9. All of the forms used in the First Step Program are published in a packet: Henderson, Steven. (2002). *Assessment and Goal Setting Handouts: First Step Institute Student Materials*. Burlingame, CA: San Mateo Union High School District.
10. Aragon High School. (2001). *Assets That Teenagers Need to Succeed*. Adapted from Search Institute. (1997). *The Asset Approach: Giving Kids What They Need to Succeed*. Minneapolis: Search Institute.

Other Resources

O'Brien, Eileen, and Rollefson, Mary. (1995). Extracurricular Participation and Student Engagement. Washington, DC: National Center for Education Statistics. Report # NCES-95-741. ED384097

Search Institute. (1999). *Pass It On! Ready-to-Use Handouts for Asset Builders*. Minneapolis: Author.

For more information about First Step, see the Web site accessed February 14, 2003: http://costello.smuhsd.k12.ca.us/ahs/school/firststep/firststep.htm.

The Graduation Project

AN ASSET-RICH JOURNEY

DENNIS J. TULLI, ED.D.

Superintendent (grades K–12)

Lebanon School District

Lebanon, Pennsylvania

Another whole set of school changes in the past few decades has occurred in measuring student success. What used to involve perhaps only objective tests and rather standard essay exams in classes and schools has now broadened to include a range of strategies that assesses much more inclusively how students are learning and growing. This example captures one way a district has incorporated asset building into a newer approach to assess its students as they leave high school.

Nationally, high school graduation requirements vary, but the successful completion of a cumulative project is becoming the norm rather than the exception. During the 1999–2000 school year, the successful completion of a graduation project became a mandated requirement for students in Pennsylvania.

The Lebanon School District's requirement for a graduation project is designed as a schoolwide asset-building opportunity for students, faculty, administrators, parents, and community members. Search Institute's asset-building strategies are embedded in the project process, enabling our students to become stronger, healthier adults, better prepared to meet the challenges of their postsecondary options.

As freshmen, approximately 18 students are designated to each homeroom. An assigned faculty member serves as an adviser-mentor to these students through their senior year. During the freshman and sophomore years, each faculty member spends time getting to know her or his students—their likes and dislikes, strengths and weaknesses, challenges and plans. As a team, faculty members and students spend time discussing goal planning, career options, hobbies, and extracurricular and cocurricular opportunities. Through these learning opportunities, students become more engaged in school and more bonded to our programs, two of many developmental assets that are strengthened in the process.

At the end of their sophomore year, students define more clearly their graduation project topic. They submit topics for approval to their advisers and then to a member of the high school administrative team.

At the same time, students register for their junior year coursework, which includes a required humanities course. This class is an integral part of the graduation project. It provides students with a framework for presenting their projects, as

SCHOOL DEMOGRAPHICS
Lebanon School District
Lebanon, Pennsylvania

Students: 4,200

Grades: K–12

Gender:
Male	50.0%
Female	50.0%

Race and Ethnicity:
Black/African American	5.00%
Hispanic/Latino	30.0%
Middle Eastern	1.0%
American Indian	0.2%
White/Caucasian	63.8%

Socioeconomics:
Free/Reduced Lunch	52.0%

well as promotes and encourages their participation in community volunteerism, an impressive component of our humanities curriculum. Students may elect to perform 32 hours of community service in lieu of taking the course final. At the end of their junior year, students have the tools they need to successfully complete their graduation projects.

Dates for seniors presenting their projects are assigned during November, December, and March. Each senior's project is evaluated on a set of rubrics designed by administrators, teachers, and students. Each rubric is designed to fit the type of project—career research, community service, creative work, interdisciplinary study, or cultural study. Each project is evaluated on three components:

1. Oral presentation;
2. Written content (which may include a research paper, a journal, or a log); and
3. Visual or other supplementary information (e.g., charts, display boards, a PowerPoint presentation, or a video).

Every student must successfully complete all three components of her or his presentation to pass the graduation project requirement. The evaluation committee consists of the student's adviser and at least two other staff members. Other adults who have served as topic experts or resource people are also invited to attend the graduating senior's project presentation, but do not serve as part of the evaluation committee.

During the first year of the graduation project requirement, a male student, under the tutelage of his grandfather, rebuilt an old car. The student's grandfather and other relatives, along with an assistant principal, who is an old-car buff, attended his presentation. Last year, a female student demonstrated the art of floral arrangement and design. To develop her skills, she worked with a local florist, who was part of her committee.

When we first required the graduation project, some students and parents resisted. Neighboring school districts were not requiring their students to complete a formal four-year, three-dimensional graduation project. Our high school staff, however, is committed to quality education and integrating asset-building strategies. The staff believe the graduation project impacts students' lives and is broader in scope—a lifelong learning experience that contributes to growth in assets as well.

Most of our seniors have succeeded. During the 1999–2000 school year, only 13 students out of 187 were not adequately prepared for their original presentations. We do give students who do not successfully complete their requirement additional opportunities to succeed. For example, if a student does not pass the written component, he or she may resubmit the written section only at a later time.

Although we did not award three students diplomas in our first year of implementing the project, one of the students completed the requirement during the summer and received a diploma. The following year, only one senior chose not to complete the project.

We have found, as expected, that while the project is a learning process in itself, much, much more is involved than the final product alone. The process is what makes our graduation project requirement a special program—a program that involves adults and students working together toward student success.

We have come to appreciate the wisdom of Pulitzer Prize-winning newspaper columnist and novelist Anna Quindlen: "Love the journey, not the destination." And an asset-rich journey it is.

Keeping Youth Engaged

JUDY TACCOGNA, ED.D.

Education Director

Search Institute

Minneapolis, Minnesota

The classroom is only one system through which a paradigm shift toward working with youth based on their strengths can occur. It can happen at the school, district, county, regional, or state level as well. Asset-building educators within any one of these levels can be powerful forces in modeling, encouraging, and facilitating the infusion of assets in schools and classrooms. Educators can provide supports, coordinate expectations, involve students as viable resources, ensure their safety, provide opportunities for constructive use of their time, enhance their school learning, reinforce core values, help them learn social competence, and reflect with them on their own identities.

You, as an individual educator, need not act alone in looking differently at what you teach and how you deliver it. As part of a critical mass of many educators who look through a developmental assets lens to enhance both instructional practices and the benefits for students, we can all increase satisfaction with teaching because of the energy that using the asset model breathes back into our days with children and adolescents in the classroom. Whether you are a specialist, staff developer or administrator, or in a service or leadership role, you, too, can work to infuse assets intentionally and explicitly in the content and practice of your work.

At the School Leadership Level

Moving beyond the classroom teacher, the school principal has often been the catalyst for change through use of the asset framework lens. The opportunity to create and open a new school provides one venue for a principal to set the stage for incorporating the asset model into the practices that are new to an entire staff.

Sarah Boly, incoming principal of Southridge High School in Beaverton, Oregon (suburban Portland), did just this several years ago when she invited a Search Institute trainer to present the asset model to her entire staff. Her expectation: that the school's mission reflect the asset approach and that the school environment, indeed, be different for young people than in their prior high schools. And it was! The same trainer dropped in unannounced a year later and randomly asked students what they were experiencing. They reported a positive difference. Numerous other schools and students report the same.

But, as critical to the asset-building process as nurturing relationships and creating positive environments are, this book, as we have shown you in the many authors' examples, is about going further—about connecting asset building to the very content and process of teaching itself. Another Oregon school models this level of infusion. For his new elementary school in Salem, Oregon, Principal Dave Guile charged the team of teachers who were planning the school with him to build the assets into the content of the three curriculum focus areas of the school: environmental studies, civic responsibility, and technology (for more about the school's science program, see "Designing a Naturescape: Cultivating Asset Growth" on page 181). Their work illustrates the centrality of the asset model to their early thinking about developing a new school and provides an organizer for doing such planning.

At the District Level

At the district level, Hopkins School District in Hopkins, Minnesota, has merged the asset approach with its districtwide prevention activities as well as with its implementation of the research-based and validated components of teaching from the Educational Testing Service (ETS): Charlotte Danielson's book *Enhancing Professional Practice: A Framework for Teaching* describes the complex set of practices ETS identifies as producing effective teaching.[1] Across the four domains in this work (Planning and Preparation, Classroom Environment, Instruction, and Professional Responsibilities) are 22 components and a number of discrete elements within each, most of which are obviously consistent with asset building.

For example, the Instruction domain includes the component of "Using Questioning and Discussion Techniques," and enumerates three elements that promote such teaching. One of these elements involves discussion techniques. Danielson describes particular teacher behaviors that represent unsatisfactory, basic, proficient, and distinguished levels of teaching: Whereas the unsatisfactory performance is described as "predominately recitation style, with teacher mediating all questions and answers," the proficient level states "classroom interaction represents true discussion, with teacher stepping, when appropriate, to the side."[2] Distinguished teaching is described as "Students assume considerable responsibility for success of the discussion, initiating topics and making unsolicited contributions." Asset-building possibilities abound when you engage students, give them responsibility, and honor them as significant resources.

As you can see throughout this book, asset-building teachers demonstrate many behaviors at the proficient and distinguished levels identified by Danielson, illustrating that outstanding teaching is, indeed, asset building in itself. When you as a teacher are asked to focus on improving instruction by using research-based practices, you are often also opening a variety of asset-rich opportunities for learning to students in your classrooms.

School districts also incorporate the asset approach into other initiatives that affect multiple schools. For example, the 30,000-student Beaverton School District in Oregon, used the asset approach as the overarching concept for implementing revisions to the K–10 health education program several years ago. Before introducing any of the health program revisions or new materials, the district provided systematically, through half- and full-day workshops, staff development in developmental assets to all elementary-level teachers and administrators and to all middle and high school teachers of health.

With that philosophical foundation and initial engagement in asset building in place, the district later introduced in subsequent workshops the curricular changes, new books, and other support materials addressing discrete health topics. Depending on their degree of engagement with the asset model and its linkage with priorities on local agendas, individual district schools then often pursued additional staff development and created planning teams to further asset-building work within the school, the school community, and classrooms.

Another example is in Colorado. In the Jefferson County Public Schools, a consolidated district of 80,000 students, a document created for the schools that connects the asset framework to academic content standards has promoted far-reaching success. Two principals from the district, Muriel Brainard and Georgia Peterson, were influential in producing the document, *Linking Assets to Action,*[3] though it grew out of three different initiatives working together—the Jeffco Schools' Accountability Planning Process, the Jefferson County Safe and Drug-Free Schools Prevention Program, and the Jefferson County Master Planning group's Caring for Children Campaign (out of the Human Services Division).

Highlighting each of the 40 assets as well as specific projects that schools can do to promote student success, *Linking Assets to Action* became an outstanding tool for educators and others interested in students' achieving academic success in district schools. In 1999, the document contained three distinct features:

1. A listing of Search Institute's 40 developmental assets;
2. A listing of the percentages of:
   - Youth nationally who report they have a particular asset;
   - Jefferson County Public School students, grades 6, 8, and 10, who took Search Institute's *Profiles of Student Life: Attitudes and Behaviors* survey and report they have a particular asset;
   - Adult residents of the area surveyed using a locally developed tool who perceive that youth in their district have a particular asset; and
3. School-based ideas and strategies to integrate developmental assets into specific content standards in Jefferson County district schools.

The developers planned to look next at adding a fourth feature: linking the assets to strategic planning (see Handout 9.4: Linking Assets to Action on page 255 for an excerpt from the plan of Jefferson County Public Schools' Safe and Drug-Free Schools Initiative publication).

At the State Level

At the state level, two examples illustrate approaches to connecting asset building to academic standards. In Michigan, a network of professionals created some years ago by the Michigan legislature, now called Strategic Alternatives in Prevention Education (SAPE), has worked to promote asset building in the schools by creating and offering training and technical support around assets. SAPE has developed research and, more recently, asset-based prevention programs. Several intermediate school districts involved (Eaton, Calhoun, Kent, Macomb, Marquette-Alger, and the Regional Educational Service Agency of Wayne County) have collaborated to produce a three-ring guidebook called *Asset-Building in Schools and Communities*.[4] Its purpose is to help teams of educators and community members infuse assets into their schools and communities.

Emphasizing academic achievement, the guidebook strives to help move youth to points in their lives where such success is possible. The work of Michael Fullan, a leading consultant in the area of school change, helps inform the guidebook's segment on understanding and implementing change and helps districts connect asset-building efforts with pressing school reform and change agendas.[5] In addition, training outlines the emphasized progression from problem- or risk-focused prevention to resiliency, positive youth development and assets. The training also focuses on Eric Jensen's work regarding brain-based instructional models,[6] the work of Bonnie Benard and Karen Pittman in resiliency and positive youth development,[7] the effective schools research of Ron Edmunds and David Berliner,[8] and Peter Senge's systems change thinking and the characteristics of high-powered, successful organizations.[9] These connections to educational thinking that is already familiar to school and district leaders make this training guidebook particularly useful in helping teachers see how the assets align with their work as well as in crafting advocacy messages about including asset building in the school work plan.

At the state level, a number of groups also have reframed their standards or reshaped their staff development emphases around the asset model. Michigan, in particular, for the past several years has advocated for infusing the assets into its work in health education. Working in collaboration with Central Michigan University and the state's Department of Education, Sharon Zajac from the Ottawa Area Independent School District in Holland, Michigan, authored a project designed to "analyze the Michigan Model for Comprehensive School Health Education to identify which lessons provided 'asset' building content or activities."[10]

In 1997, the Educational Materials Center at Central Michigan University in Mt. Pleasant published *A Correlation of the Michigan Model for Comprehensive School Health Education with the Search Institute's Developmental Assets*, a note-

Linking Assets to Action

This excerpt from the plan Linking Assets to Action, *of the Safe and Drug-Free Schools Initiative in Jefferson County Public Schools, Colorado, shows how it links Search Institute's developmental assets to the county's academic standards.*

Asset Type	Asset Name and Definition	School-Based	Jeffco Content Standards *(revised 10/99)*
EXTERNAL ASSETS **Boundaries and Expectations**	**16.** High Expectations Parents and teachers encourage young people to do well. 41%— Youth Nationally 39%— Jeffco Youth 86%— Jeffco Adults	■ Tell students what you expect from them. ■ Talk to parents about school expectations. ■ Hold high expectations for *all* students. ■ Encourage students to take positive risks and act on their dreams and ideas. Teach the difference between positive risks and foolish risks. ■ Give students the tools they need to develop their talents and abilities. ■ Provide learning opportunities that challenge students who have all types of learning styles and abilities. ■ Notice when students do well. Let them know that you admire their skills. ■ Encourage independence. ■ Ask students what they expect of themselves. ■ Help students set goals. ■ Find and share inspiring stories about people who have overcome obstacles and adversity. These could be stories that students share about their families and/or ancestors. Newspapers and magazines can serve as additional resources. ■ As a teacher, share with students how you are challenging yourself through classes or skill growth.	*This asset needs to be integrated across the curriculum and throughout the school day.* **English Language Arts** ■ Standard 1: Students read and understand a variety of materials. **Students will:** *Identify and relate events and conditions in texts to their own lives and the lives of others.* ■ Standard 2: Students read and recognize literature as an expression of human experience. **Students will:** *Read to understand their own experiences and the experiences of others.* ■ Standard 8: Students evaluate and improve the quality of their own reading, writing, speaking, listening, and viewing. *Evaluation of one's own work is a key step in the learning process and is necessary for improvement. Evaluation builds independence, self-confidence, ownership, and engagement. Learning to take personal responsibility for such improvement is a lifelong learning skill.* **Civics** ■ Standard 1: Students understand the concept of government. **Students will:** *Recognize that civic life is people working together to accomplish goals they could not achieve alone; and Be involved in the formation, evaluation, and amending of rules and laws for their classroom and school.* ■ Standard 2: Students understand the fundamental principles and the democratic values basic to the United States constitutional republic. ■ Standard 3: Students understand the structure and function of local, state, and national governments in the United States. ■ Standard 5: Students understand the roles of citizens. **Physical Education** ■ Standard 5: Students demonstrate responsible personal and social behaviors during physical activity. **Students will:** *Develop positive self-concept by assessing skills, setting individual goals, accepting feedback; Develop appropriate social and emotional behavior through communication, problem solving, and critical thinking; Make safe and responsible choices about using time, applying rules, and following through with decisions; Develop behaviors that promote personal and group success; Demonstrate cooperation, teamwork, and ethical behavior; Demonstrate a willingness to participate in learning new or different information with students of varying abilities; and Develop respect for different cultures through participation in integrated activities.*

book resource for state teachers and administrators as they work to infuse assets throughout their health programs. The resources goals are to:

- Provide additional justification for the time spent teaching the Michigan Model Health Program;
- Assist teachers in seeing that they can become asset builders without taking additional classroom time; and
- Provide documentation of the asset-building activities with the Michigan Model Curriculum.

The resource developers reviewed each lesson in grades K–6 of the Michigan Model and established grade-level tables to show how the health education program contributes to asset development. Team members devised a code to describe just how a lesson supports an asset:

- **"S"** for those lessons that either support an asset or provide an opportunity for the asset to develop;
- **"P"** for those lessons that actually teach a skill providing the asset; and
- **"A"** for those lessons that help students become aware of assets they already have.

The notebook also includes in an appendix a key showing topics or themes (e.g., problem solving, anger management) that thread through all grade levels, and identifying the specific assets each lesson addresses. It also organizes, by grade level, the lesson names and numbers as well as the codes (S, P, or A) for how an asset is addressed (for an excerpt from the 6th-grade level, see Handout 9.5: A Correlation of the Michigan Model for Comprehensive School Health Education with Search Institute's 40 Developmental Assets on page 257). Another chart in the notebook presents *all* of the assets so that no matter what grade level you teach, you can quickly see how the asset support is infused throughout the health curriculum as a whole.

Some years ago at the Vermont Department of Education in Montpelier, Lynda Van Kleeck created a framework for connecting developmental assets to the state standards and relevant resiliency factors (for an excerpt, see Handout 9.6: Relationship between the Developmental Assets, Resiliency, and *Vermont's Framework of Standards and Learning Opportunities* on page 258). This framework serves as a model for bridging those three agendas in any district, as well as at the state or programmatic level.

More recently in Maine, Portland School District's Safe and Drug Free Schools Coordinator Michael Clifford worked with the Portland Partnership, the Portland Schools' vehicle for connecting the schools to businesses, to demonstrate how asset-building efforts fit into the state standards. The *Learning Results*,[11] the published standards, specifies six "Learner Expectations": collaborative worker, knowledgeable person, quality producer, versatile thinker, involved citizen, and self-directed learner. As a result of the work of this team, you can now identify the assets that either support or are built through work in these six areas of expecta-

A Correlation of the Michigan Model for Comprehensive School Health Education with Search Institute's 40 Developmental Assets

Michigan's model addresses all of the assets across grades K–6; highlighted here is only a sample showing how the model connects elements of health education curriculum for 6th graders to the social-competencies asset category.

Sixth Grade
Asset Category: Social Competencies

32. Planning and Decision Making—Young person knows how to plan ahead and make choices.

Phase I: Resolving Conflicts and Having Friends
- Lesson 6: Gaining POWER in Positive Problem Solving—Part I (P)
- Lesson 7: Gaining POWER in Positive Problem Solving—Part II (P)
- Lesson 8: Using Positive POWER Between Two People (P)

Phase II: Having Fun and Staying Safe
- Lesson 1: Remembering Safety around Wheels, Sun, and Water (S)
- Lesson 2: Safety in Public Places (S)
- Lesson 5: Avoiding Fights and Resisting Gangs (P)
- Lesson 8: Helping Others Stay Safe (S)

Phase III: Drugs Make the News—Bad News
- Lesson 4: Advertising Tactics (S)
- Lesson 5: Advertising for Healthy, Drug-Free Activities and Products (S)

Phase VI: Important Considerations: Nutrition, Exercise, and Stress
- Lesson 2: The Basic Facts (S)
- Lesson 3: What's In the Food? (S)
- Lesson 8: Setting Goals (S)

33. Interpersonal Competence—Young person has empathy, sensitivity, and friendship skills.

Phase I: Resolving Conflicts and Having Friends
- Lesson 1: Health and Risks (S)
- Lesson 2: The Challenges and Hazards of Friendship (P)
- Lesson 3: Checking Out Emotions (P)
- Lesson 4: Expressing Emotions in a Positive Way (P)

Phase IV: Becoming You
- Lesson 4: Living with Disabilities (S)

34. Cultural Competence—Young person has knowledge of and comfort with people of different cultural/racial/ethnic backgrounds.

Phase IV: Becoming You
- Lesson 4: Living with Disabilities (S)

35. Resistance Skills—Young person can resist negative peer pressure and dangerous situations.

Phase II: Having Fun and Staying Safe
- Lesson 3: Getting Out of a Tight Spot (P)
- Lesson 4: Practice Getting Out of a Tight Spot (P)
- Lesson 5: Avoiding Fights and Resisting Gangs (P)
- Lesson 6: Weapons and Safety (P)
- Lesson 7: Personal Safety (S)

Phase III: Drugs Make the News—Bad News
- Lesson 6: Standing Up to Pressure to Use Drugs (P)
- Lesson 7: Getting Out of a Jam (P)

36. Peaceful Conflict Resolution—Young person seeks to resolve conflict nonviolently.

Phase I: Resolving Conflicts and Having Friends
- Lesson 4: Expressing Emotions in a Positive Way (P)
- Lesson 5: When You're Mad (P)
- Lesson 6: Gaining POWER in Positive Ways—Part I (P)
- Lesson 7: Gaining POWER in Positive Ways —Part II (P)
- Lesson 8: Using Positive POWER between Two People (P)

S — lessons that either support an asset or provide an opportunity for the asset to develop

P — lessons that actually teach a skill providing the asset

Relationship between the Developmental Assets, Resiliency,
and *Vermont's Framework of Standards and Learning Opportunities*

The Vermont Resiliency Network connected Search Institute's developmental assets to the state's Standards and Learning Opportunities, as well as to elements of resiliency. Highlighted here are excerpts of the Network's correlation of assets to the learning opportunities portion of the expectations.

Learning Opportunities	DEVELOPMENTAL ASSETS External and Internal Assets	RESILIENCY Environmental Resiliency Builders
A.5 A physically and emotionally safe, educationally supportive environment in which to learn. **B.1** Learning experiences that engage students in active learning, build on prior knowledge and experiences, and develop conceptual and procedural understanding, along with student independence. **B.3** Opportunities to learn through a variety of roles alone and with others. **B.4** Projects and assignments that require students to integrate and apply their learning in meaningful contexts, and to reflect on what they have learned. **C.4** Students use clear criteria and examples to evaluate their own work. **D.2** Learning experiences that have personal, community, and/or global relevance. **D.3** An educational climate that is collaborative, in which school staff, families, health and human services personnel, and community members work together to support all learners.	1. Family Support—Family life provides high levels of love and support. 3. Other Adult Relationships—Young person receives support from three or more nonparent adults. 4. Caring Neighborhood—Young person experiences caring neighbors. 5. Caring School Climate—School provides a caring, encouraging environment. 6. Parent Involvement in Schooling—Parent(s) are actively involved in helping young person succeed in school. 7. Community Values Youth—Young person perceives that adults in the community value youth. 8. Youth as Resources—Young people are given useful roles in the community. 9. Service to Others—Young person serves in the community one hour or more per week. 10. Safety—Young person feels safe at home, at school, and in the neighborhood. 12. School Boundaries—School provides clear rules and consequences. 14. Adult Role Models—Parent(s) and other adults model positive, responsible behavior. 21. Achievement Motivation—Young person is motivated to do well in school. 22. School Engagement—Young person is actively engaged in learning. 26. Caring—Young person places high value on helping other people. 30. Responsibility—Young person accepts and takes personal responsibility.	■ Promotes close bonds. ■ Values and encourages education. ■ Uses high warmth/low criticism style of interaction. ■ Sets and enforces clear boundaries (rules, norms, and laws). ■ Encourages supportive relationships with many caring others. ■ Promotes sharing of responsibilities, service to others, "required helpfulness." ■ Expresses high, and realistic, expectations for success. ■ Encourages prosocial development of values (such as altruism) and life skills (such as cooperation). ■ Provides leadership, decision-making, and other opportunities for meaningful participation. ■ Appreciates the unique talents of each individual.

tion (see Handout 9.7: How the 40 Developmental Assets Support the Maine *Learning Results* on page 260).

Each of these models illustrates the effort to align building developmental assets with the work of teachers and schools. District and state educational leaders promote taking the asset model one step further into the day-to-day work of teaching and learning in classrooms by connecting it with core curriculum and essential learnings applicable across many school districts.

Clearly, though, you as classroom teachers have a sound rationale for forging ahead with an asset mind-set within classrooms to influence students as much as district, regional and state specialists, and administrators. Take the initiative, facilitate positive change, and help teach young people in asset-rich ways that capitalize on sound instructional practices already at your fingertips.

Notes

1. Danielson, Charlotte. (1996). *Enhancing Professional Practice: A Framework for Teaching.* Alexandria, VA: Association for Supervision and Curriculum Development.
2. Ibid., 94.
3. Brainard, Muriel, and Peterson, Georgia. *Linking Assets to Action.* Lakewood, CO: Safe and Drug-Free Schools Prevention Program.
4. Lindenberger, Dee. (2000). *Asset-Building in Schools and Communities: Creating a Circle of Support.* Marquette, MI: Marquette-Alger Intermediate School District.
5. See Fullan, Michael. (1993). *Change Forces: Probing the Depths of Educational Reform.* London, New York: RoutledgeFalmer.
6. Jensen, Eric. (2000). *Brain-Based Learning: The New Science of Teaching and Training.* San Diego: Brain Store.
7. See Benard, Bonnie. (March 1993). Resiliency Requires Changing Hearts and Minds. *Western Center News,* 6(2). Pittman, Karen J., and Cahill, Michelle. (July 1992). Pushing the Boundaries of Education: The Implications of a Youth Development Approach to Education Policies, Structures, and Collaborations, as reprinted in Lindenberger, Dee. (2000). *Asset Building in Schools and Communities: Creating a Circle of Support.* Marquette, MI: Marquette-Alger Intermediate School District.
8. Association for Effective Schools, Inc., *Correlates of Effective Schools.* Web site accessed September 25, 2002: www.mes.org/correlates.html. This 501(c)(3) nonprofit is located in Styvesant, NY.
9. Senge, Peter M. (1994). *The Fifth Discipline: The Art and Practice of the Learning Organization.* New York: Currency/Doubleday.
10. Zajac, Sharon. (1997). *A Correlation of the Michigan Model for Comprehensive School Health Education with the Search Institute's Forty Developmental Assets.* Mt. Pleasant, MI: Educational Materials Center, Central Michigan University, i.
11. State of Maine Department of Education. (1997). *Learning Results.* Augusta, ME: Author.

How the 40 Developmental Assets Support the Maine *Learning Results*

Working together, the Portland Partnership, a vehicle for connecting schools to businesses in Portland, Maine, and the Safe and Drug Free Schools in the Portland School District, developed this chart showing how Search Institute's developmental assets support the "Learner Expectations" in the Learning Results,[1] *the state-approved standards for students.*

Learner Expectations	Developmental Assets	Percentage of Portland Youth Reporting the Asset[2]
Collaborative Worker	33. **Interpersonal Competence**—Young person has empathy, sensitivity, and friendship skills.	47%
	34. **Cultural Competence**—Young person has knowledge of and comfort with people of different cultural/racial/ethnic background.	50%
	36. **Peaceful Conflict Resolution**—Young person seeks to resolve conflict nonviolently.	48%
Knowledgeable Person	21. **Achievement motivation**—Young person is motivated to do well in school.	67%
	22. **School Engagement**—Young person is actively engaged in learning.	58%
	23. **Homework**—Young person reports doing at least one hour of homework every school day.	57%
	25. **Reading for Pleasure**—Young person reads for pleasure three or more hours per week.	27%
	17. **Creative Activities**—Young person spends three or more hours per week in lessons or practice in music, theater, or other arts.	20%
Quality Producer	16. **High Expectations**—Both parent(s) and teachers encourage the young person to do well.	49%
Versatile Thinker	32. **Planning and Decision Making**—Young person knows how to plan ahead and make choices.	31%
Involved Citizen	26. **Caring**—Young person places high value on helping other people.	53%
	27. **Equality and Social Justice**—Young person places high value on promoting equality and reducing hunger and poverty.	55%
	28. **Integrity**—Young person acts on convictions and stands up for her or his beliefs.	69%
	29. **Honesty**—Young person "tells the truth even when it is not easy."	67%
	30. **Responsibility**—Young person accepts and takes personal responsibility.	64%
Self-Directed Learner	37. **Personal Power**—Young person feels he or she has control over "things that happen to me."	47%
	39. **Sense of Purpose**—Young person reports that "my life has purpose."	61%

Notes
1. State of Maine Department of Education. (1997). *Learning Results.* Augusta, ME: Author.
2. Based on Search Institute's *Profiles of Student Life: Attitudes and Behaviors* survey.

Appendix A

Lists of the 40 Developmental Assets

Appendix A.1

40 Developmental Assets for Adolescents (Ages 12–18, English)

Search Institute has identified the following building blocks of healthy development that help young people grow up healthy, caring, and responsible.

EXTERNAL ASSETS

Support

1. **Family support**—Family life provides high levels of love and support.
2. **Positive family communication**—Young person and her or his parent(s) communicate positively, and young person is willing to seek advice and counsel from parents.
3. **Other adult relationships**—Young person receives support from three or more nonparent adults.
4. **Caring neighborhood**—Young person experiences caring neighbors.
5. **Caring school climate**—School provides a caring, encouraging environment.
6. **Parent involvement in schooling**—Parent(s) are actively involved in helping young person succeed in school.

Empowerment

7. **Community values youth**—Young person perceives that adults in the community value youth.
8. **Youth as resources**—Young people are given useful roles in the community.
9. **Service to others**—Young person serves in the community one hour or more per week.
10. **Safety**—Young person feels safe at home, at school, and in the neighborhood.

Boundaries and Expectations

11. **Family boundaries**—Family has clear rules and consequences and monitors the young person's whereabouts.
12. **School boundaries**—School provides clear rules and consequences.
13. **Neighborhood boundaries**—Neighbors take responsibility for monitoring young people's behavior.
14. **Adult role models**—Parent(s) and other adults model positive, responsible behavior.
15. **Positive peer influence**—Young person's best friends model responsible behavior.
16. **High expectations**—Both parent(s) and teachers encourage the young person to do well.

Constructive Use of Time

17. **Creative activities**—Young person spends three or more hours per week in lessons or practice in music, theater, or other arts.
18. **Youth programs**—Young person spends three or more hours per week in sports, clubs, or organizations at school and/or in the community.
19. **Religious community**—Young person spends one or more hours per week in activities in a religious institution.
20. **Time at home**—Young person is out with friends "with nothing special to do" two or fewer nights per week.

INTERNAL ASSETS

Commitment to Learning

21. **Achievement motivation**—Young person is motivated to do well in school.
22. **School engagement**—Young person is actively engaged in learning.
23. **Homework**—Young person reports doing at least one hour of homework every school day.
24. **Bonding to school**—Young person cares about her or his school.
25. **Reading for pleasure**—Young person reads for pleasure three or more hours per week.

Positive Values

26. **Caring**—Young person places high value on helping other people.
27. **Equality and social justice**—Young person places high value on promoting equality and reducing hunger and poverty.
28. **Integrity**—Young person acts on convictions and stands up for her or his beliefs.
29. **Honesty**—Young person "tells the truth even when it is not easy."
30. **Responsibility**—Young person accepts and takes personal responsibility.
31. **Restraint**—Young person believes it is important not to be sexually active or to use alcohol or other drugs.

Social Competencies

32. **Planning and decision making**—Young person knows how to plan ahead and make choices.
33. **Interpersonal competence**—Young person has empathy, sensitivity, and friendship skills.
34. **Cultural competence**—Young person has knowledge of and comfort with people of different cultural/racial/ethnic backgrounds.
35. **Resistance skills**—Young person can resist negative peer pressure and dangerous situations.
36. **Peaceful conflict resolution**—Young person seeks to resolve conflict nonviolently.

Positive Identity

37. **Personal power**—Young person feels he or she has control over "things that happen to me."
38. **Self-esteem**—Young person reports having a high self-esteem.
39. **Sense of purpose**—Young person reports that "my life has a purpose."
40. **Positive view of personal future**—Young person is optimistic about her or his personal future.

Appendix A.2

40 Developmental Assets for Elementary-Age Children (Ages 6–11, English)

Search Institute has identified a framework of 40 developmental assets for elementary-age children (ages 6 to 11) that blends Search Institute's research on developmental assets for 12- to 18-year-olds with research on healthy child development.

EXTERNAL ASSETS

Support

1. **Family support**—Family life provides high levels of love and support.
2. **Positive family communication**—Parents and children communicate positively. Children are willing to seek advice and counsel from their parents.
3. **Other adult relationships**—Children have support from adults other than their parents.
4. **Caring neighborhood**—Children experience caring neighbors.
5. **Caring out-of-home climate**—School and other activities provide caring, encouraging environments for children.
6. **Parent involvement in out-of-home situations**—Parents are actively involved in helping children succeed in school and in other situations outside the home.

Empowerment

7. **Community values children**—Children feel that the family and community value and appreciate children.
8. **Children are given useful roles**—Children are included in age-appropriate family tasks and decisions and are given useful roles at home and in the community.
9. **Service to others**—Children serve others in the community with their family or in other settings.
10. **Safety**—Children are safe at home, at school, and in the neighborhood.

Boundaries and Expectations

11. **Family boundaries**—The family has clear rules and consequences and monitors children's activities and where-abouts.
12. **Out-of-home boundaries**—Schools and other out-of-home environments provide clear rules and consequences.
13. **Neighborhood boundaries**—Neighbors take responsibility for monitoring children's behavior.
14. **Adult role models**—Parents and other adults model positive, responsible behavior.
15. **Positive peer interaction and influence**—Children interact with other children who model responsible behavior and have opportunities to play and interact in safe, well-supervised settings.
16. **Appropriate expectations for growth**—Adults have realistic expectations for children's development at this age. Parents, caregivers, and other adults encourage children to achieve and develop their unique talents.

Constructive Use of Time

17. **Creative activities**—Children participate in music, art, drama, or other creative activities for at least three hours a week at home and elsewhere.
18. **Out-of-home activities**—Children spend one hour or more each week in extracurricular school activities or structured community programs.
19. **Religious community**—The family attends religious programs or services for at least one hour per week.
20. **Positive, supervised time at home**—Children spend most evenings and weekends at home with their parents in predictable, enjoyable routines.

INTERNAL ASSETS

Commitment to Learning

21. **Achievement expectation and motivation**—Children are motivated to do well in school and other activities.
22. **Children are engaged in learning**—Children are responsive, attentive, and actively engaged in learning.
23. **Stimulating activity and homework**—Parents and teachers encourage children to explore and engage in stimulating activities. Children do homework when it's assigned.
24. **Enjoyment of learning and bonding to school**—Children enjoy learning and care about their school.
25. **Reading for pleasure**—Children and an adult read together for at least 30 minutes a day. Children also enjoy reading or looking at books or magazines on their own.

Positive Values

26. **Caring**—Children are encouraged to help other people.
27. **Equality and social justice**—Children begin to show interest in making the community a better place.
28. **Integrity**—Children begin to act on their convictions and stand up for their beliefs.
29. **Honesty**—Children begin to value honesty and act accordingly.
30. **Responsibility**—Children begin to accept and take personal responsibility for age-appropriate tasks.
31. **Healthy lifestyle and sexual attitudes**—Children begin to value good health habits and learn healthy sexual attitudes and beliefs as well as respect for others.

Social Competencies

32. **Planning and decision making**—Children begin to learn how to plan ahead and make choices at appropriate developmental levels.
33. **Interpersonal skills**—Children interact with adults and children and can make friends. Children express and articulate feelings in appropriate ways and empathize with others.
34. **Cultural competence**—Children know about and are comfortable with people of different cultural, racial, and/or ethnic backgrounds.
35. **Resistance skills**—Children start developing the ability to resist negative peer pressure and dangerous situations.
36. **Peaceful conflict resolution**—Children try to resolve conflicts nonviolently.

Positive Identity

37. **Personal power**—Children begin to feel they have control over things that happen to them. They begin to manage frustrations and challenges in ways that have positive results for themselves and others.
38. **Self-esteem**—Children report having high self-esteem.
39. **Sense of purpose**—Children report that their lives have purpose and actively engage their skills.
40. **Positive view of personal future**—Children are hopeful and positive about their personal future.

Appendix A.3

40 elementos fundamentales del desarrollo (de 12 a 18 años)

La investigación realizada por el Instituto Search ha identificado los siguientes elementos fundamentales del desarrollo como instrumentos para ayudar a los jóvenes a crecer sanos, interesados en el bienestar común y a ser responsables.

ELEMENTOS FUNDAMENTALES EXTERNOS

Apoyo

1. **Apoyo familiar**—La vida familiar brinda altos niveles de amor y apoyo.
2. **Comunicación familiar positiva**—El (La) joven y sus padres se comunican positivamente. Los jóvenes están dispuestos a buscar consejo y consuelo en sus padres.
3. **Otras relaciones con adultos**—Además de sus padres, los jóvenes reciben apoyo de tres o más personas adultas que no son sus parientes.
4. **Una comunidad comprometida**—El (La) joven experimenta el interés de sus vecinos por su bienestar.
5. **Un plantel educativo que se interesa por el (la) joven**—La escuela proporciona un ambiente que anima y se preocupa por la juventud.
6. **La participación de los padres en las actividades escolares**—Los padres participan activamente ayudando a los jóvenes a tener éxito en la escuela.

Fortalecimiento

7. **La comunidad valora a la juventud**—El (La) joven percibe que los adultos en la comunidad valoran a la juventud.
8. **La juventud como un recurso**—Se le brinda a los jóvenes la oportunidad de tomar un papel útil en la comunidad.
9. **Servicio a los demás**—La gente joven participa brindando servicios a su comunidad una hora o más a la semana.
10. **Seguridad**—Los jóvenes se sienten seguros en casa, en la escuela y en el vecindario.

Límites y expectativas

11. **Límites familiares**—La familia tiene reglas y consecuencias bien claras, además vigila las actividades de los jóvenes.
12. **Límites escolares**—En la escuela proporciona reglas y consecuencias bien claras.
13. **Límites vecinales**—Los vecinos asumen la responsabilidad de vigilar el comportamiento de los jóvenes.
14. **El comportamiento de los adultos como ejemplo**—Los padres y otros adultos tienen un comportamiento positivo y responsable.
15. **Compañeros como influencia positiva**—Los mejores amigos del (la) joven son un buen ejemplo de comportamiento responsable.
16. **Altas expectativas**—Ambos padres y maestros motivan a los jóvenes para que tengan éxito.

Uso constructivo del tiempo

17. **Actividades creativas**—Los jóvenes pasan tres horas o más a la semana en lecciones de música, teatro u otras artes.
18. **Programas juveniles**—Los jóvenes pasan tres horas o más a la semana practicando algún deporte, o en organizaciones en la escuela o de la comunidad.
19. **Comunidad religiosa**—Los jóvenes pasan una hora o más a la semana en actividades organizadas por alguna institución religiosa.

20. **Tiempo en casa**—Los jóvenes conviven con sus amigos "sin nada especial que hacer" dos o pocas noches por semana.

ELEMENTOS FUNDAMENTALES INTERNOS

Compromiso con el aprendizaje

21. **Motivación por sus logros**—El (La) joven es motivado(a) para que salga bien en la escuela.
22. **Compromiso con la escuela**—El (La) joven participa activamente con el aprendizaje.
23. **Tarea**—El (La) joven debe hacer su tarea escolar por lo menos durante una hora cada día de clases.
24. **Preocuparse por la escuela**—Al (A la) joven debe importarle su escuela.
25. **Leer por placer**—El (La) joven lee por placer tres horas o más por semana.

Valores positivos

26. **Preocuparse por los demás**—El (La) joven valora ayudar a los demás.
27. **Igualdad y justicia social**—Para el (la) joven tiene mucho valor el promover la igualdad y reducir el hambre y la pobreza.
28. **Integridad**—El (La) joven actúa con convicción y defiende sus creencias.
29. **Honestidad**—El (La) joven "dice la verdad aún cuando esto no sea fácil".
30. **Responsabilidad**—El (La) joven acepta y toma responsabilidad por su persona.
31. **Abstinencia**—El (La) joven cree que es importante no estar activo(a) sexualmente, ni usar alcohol u otras drogas.

Capacidad social

32. **Planeación y toma de decisiones**—El (La) joven sabe cómo planear y hacer elecciones.
33. **Capacidad interpersonal**—El (La) joven es sympático, sensible y hábil para hacer amistades.
34. **Capacidad cultural**—El (La) joven tiene conocimiento de y sabe convivir con gente de diferente marco cultural, racial o étnico.
35. **Habilidad de resistencia**—El (La) joven puede resistir la presión negativa de los compañeros así como las situaciones peligrosas.
36. **Solución pacífica de conflictos**—El (La) joven busca resolver los conflictos sin violencia.

Identidad positiva

37. **Poder personal**—El (La) joven siente que él o ella tiene el control de "las cosas que le suceden".
38. **Auto-estima**—El (La) joven afirma tener una alta auto-estima.
39. **Sentido de propósito**—El (La) joven afirma que "mi vida tiene un propósito".
40. **Visión positiva del futuro personal**—El (La) joven es optimista sobre su futuro mismo.

Appendix A.4

40 elementos fundamentales del desarrollo para niños de escuela primaria o básica (de 6 a 11 años)

El Instituto Search ha identificado un sistema de 40 elementos fundamentales de desarrollo para niños entre 6 a 11 años de edad que combina la Investigación del Instituto Search sobre los elementos fundamentales del desarrollo para chicos entre 12 y 18 años de edad con una extensa literatura sobre desarrollo infantil.

ELEMENTOS FUNDAMENTALES DEL DESARROLLO EXTERNOS

Apoyo

1. **Apoyo familiar**—La vida familiar brinda altos niveles de amor y apoyo.
2. **Comunicación familiar positiva**—Los padres y el niño se comunican positivamente. El niño está dispuesto a buscar consejo y consuelo en sus padres.
3. **Otras relaciones con adultos**—El niño recibe apoyo de adultos que no son su padre ni madre.
4. **Una comunidad comprometida**—El niño experimenta el interés de sus vecinos por su bienestar.
5. **Un plantel educativo que se interesa por el niño**—La escuela proporciona un ambiente que anima y se preocupa por los niños.
6. **La participación de los padres en las actividades escolares**—Los padres participan activamente ayudando al niño a tener éxito en la escuela.

Fortalecimiento

7. **La comunidad valora los niños**—El niño siente que los adultos en la comunidad valoran y aprecian a los niños.
8. **Los niños tienen papeles útiles**—El niño está incluido en las decisiones de la familia y le es dado papeles útiles en el hogar y en la comunidad.
9. **Servicio a los demás**—El niño y los padres brindan servicios a otros y a la comunidad.
10. **Seguridad**—El niño está seguro en el hogar, en la escuela y en el vecindario.

Límites y expectativas

11. **Límites familiares**—La familia tiene reglas y consecuencias bien claras, además vigila las actividades del niño.
12. **Límites escolares**—En la escuela proporcionan reglas y consecuencias bien claras.
13. **Límites vecinales**—Los vecinos asumen la responsabilidad de vigilar el comportamiento del niño.
14. **El comportamiento de los adultos como ejemplo**—Los padres y otros adultos tienen un comportamiento positivo y responsable como ejemplos.
15. **Interacciones positivas con compañeros**—El niño juega con otros niños que muestran comportamiento responsable como ejemplos.
16. **Expectativas para el crecimiento**—Los adultos son realistas en sus expectativas de desarrollo a esta edad. Los padres, un adulto responsable para los niños y otros adultos animan el niño para que logre y desarrolle sus propios talentos únicos.

Uso constructivo del tiempo

17. **Actividades creativas**—El niño participa en música, arte o teatro tres horas o más semanales a través de actividades en el hogar y fuera del hogar.
18. **Programas de niños**—El niño pasa una hora o más a la semana en actividades extracurriculares de la escuela o programas estructurados de la comunidad.
19. **Comunidad religiosa**—La familia asiste a programas o servicios religiosos por al menos una hora una vez por semana.
20. **Tiempo positivo y supervisado en casa**—El niño pasa la mayoría de las noches y los fines de semana en casa con los padres disfrutando de rutinas predecibles y divertidas.

ELEMENTOS FUNDAMENTALES DEL DESARROLLO INTERNOS

Compromiso conel aprendizaje

21. **Motivación por sus logros**—El niño es motivado para que salga bien en la escuela.
22. **Compromiso con la escuela**—El niño es atento y demuestra interés en el trabajo y participa activamente en el aprendizaje.
23. **Tarea**—Cuando el niño le es dada tarea, la hace.
24. **Preocuparse por la escuela**—Al niño debe importarle su escuela.
25. **Leer por placer**—El niño y un adulto que se preocupa por él leen juntos por al menos 30 minutos al día. El niño también disfruta leer sin que un adulto esté involucrado.

Valores positivos

26. **Preocuparse por los demás**—El niño es animado a ayudar a otras personas y compartir sus posesiones.
27. **Igualdad y justicia social**—El niño comienza a mostrar interés en mejorar la comunidad.
28. **Integridad**—El niño comienza a actuar con convicción y defiende sus creencias y valores.
29. **Honestidad**—El niño comienza a valorar la honestidad y actúa de acuerdo con este valor.
30. **Responsabilidad**—El niño comienza a aceptar y tomar responsabilidad por deberes apropiados de acuerdo con su edad.
31. **Un estilo de vida sano y actitudes sexuales saludables**—El niño comienza a valorar hábitos saludables. El niño aprende actitudes y valores sexuales sanos y respeto a los demás.

Capacidad social

32. **Planeación y toma de decisiones**—El niño aprende habilidades básicas de cómo planificar y hace elecciones en un nivel apropiado de acuerdo con su desarrollo.
33. **Capacidad interpersonal**—El niño interactúa con adultos y niños y puede hacer amigos. El niño expresa y articula sus sentimientos de una manera apropiada y tiene simpatía por los demás.
34. **Capacidad cultural**—El niño tiene conocimiento y sabe convivir con gente de diferente marco cultural, racial o étnico.
35. **Habilidad de resistencia**—El niño comienza a desarrollar la habilidad de resistir la presión negativa de los compañeros así como las situaciones peligrosas.
36. **Solución pacífica de conflictos**—El niño busca resolver los conflictos sin violencia.

Identidad positiva

37. **Poder personal**—El niño comienza a sentir que él tiene el control de "las cosas que me suceden". El niño comienza a manejar las frustraciones y desafíos de la vida a través de maneras que dan resultados positivos para el niño y para otros.
38. **Autoestima**—El niño afirma tener una alta autoestima.
39. **Sentido de propósito**—El niño afirma que "mi vida tiene propósito".
40. **La familia tiene una visión positiva del futuro**—El niño es optimista sobre su futuro mismo.

Appendix A.5

40 Acquis dont les jeunes ont besoin pour réussir (12 à 18 ans)

Le Search Institute a défini les pierres angulaires suivantes qui aident les jeunes à devenir des personnes saines, bienveillantes et responsables. Les pourcentages des jeunes détenant chaque acquis sont le fruit d'un sondage mené durant l'année scolaire 1999-2002 auprès de 220 100 jeunes Américains de la 6ᵉ à la 12ᵉ année.

ACQUIS EXTERNES

Soutien

1. **Soutien familial**—La vie familiale est caractérisée par un degré élevé d'amour et de soutien.
2. **Communication familiale positive**—Le jeune et ses parents communiquent positivement, et le jeune est disposé à leur demander conseil.
3. **Relations avec d'autres adultes**—Le jeune bénéficie de l'appui d'au moins trois adultes autres que ses parents.
4. **Voisinage bienveillant**—Le jeune a des voisins bienveillants.
5. **Milieu scolaire bienveillant**—L'école fournit au jeune un milieu bienveillant et encourageant.
6. **Engagement des parents dans les activités scolaires**—Les parents aident activement le jeune à réussir à l'école.

Prise en charge

7. **Valorisation des jeunes par la communauté**—Le jeune perçoit que les adultes dans la communauté accordent de l'importance aux jeunes.
8. **Rôle des jeunes en tant que ressources**—Le jeune se voit confier des rôles utiles dans la communauté.
9. **Service à son prochain**—Le jeune consacre à sa communauté au moins une heure par semaine.
10. **Sécurité**—Le jeune se sent en sécurité à la maison, à l'école et dans le quartier.

Limites et attentes

11. **Limites dans la famille**—La famille a des règlements clairs accompagnés de conséquences, et elle surveille les comportements du jeune.
12. **Limite à l'école**—L'école a des règlements clairs accompagnés de conséquences.
13. **Limites dans le quartier**—Les voisins assument la responsabilité de surveiller les comportements du jeune.
14. **Adultes servant de modèles**—Les parents et d'autres adultes dans l'entourage du jeune affichent un comportement positif et responsable.
15. **Influence positive des pairs**—Les meilleurs amis du jeune affichent un comportement responsable.
16. **Attentes élevées**—Les parents et les professeurs du jeune l'encouragent à réussir.

Utilisation constructive du temps

17. **Activités créatives**—Le jeune consacre au moins trois heures par semaine à suivre des cours de musique, de théâtre ou autres, et à mettre ses nouvelles connaissances en pratique.
18. **Programmes jeunesse**—Le jeune consacre au moins trois heures par semaine à des activités sportives, des clubs ou des associations à l'école et/ou dans la communauté.
19. **Communauté religieuse**—Le jeune consacre au moins trois heures par semaine à des activités dans une institution religieuse.

20. **Temps à la maison**—Le jeune sort avec des amis sans but particulier deux ou trois soirs par semaine.

ACQUIS INTERNES

Engagement envers l'apprentissage

21. **Encouragement à la réussite**—Le jeune est encouragé à réussir à l'école.
22. **Engagement à l'école**—Le jeune s'engage activement à apprendre.
23. **Devoirs**—Le jeune consacre au moins une heure par jour à ses devoirs.
24. **Appartenance à l'école**—Le jeune se préoccupe de son école.
25. **Plaisir de lire**—Le jeune lit pour son plaisir au moins trois heures par semaine.

Valeurs positives

26. **Bienveillance**—Le jeune estime qu'il est très important d'aider les autres.
27. **Égalité et justice sociale**—Le jeune accorde beaucoup d'attention à la promotion de l'égalité, et à la réduction de la faim et de la pauvreté.
28. **Intégrité**—Le jeune agit selon ses convictions et défend ses croyances.
29. **Honnêteté**—Le jeune « dit la vérité même si ce n'est pas facile ».
30. **Responsabilité**—Le jeune accepte et assume ses propres responsabilités.
31. **Abstinence**—Le jeune croit qu'il est important d'éviter d'être sexuellement actif et de consommer de l'alcool ou d'autres drogues.

Compétences sociales

32. **Planification et prise de décisions**—Le jeune sait comment planifier à l'avance et faire des choix.
33. **Aptitudes interpersonnelles**—Le jeune fait preuve d'empathie et de sensibilité, et noue des amitiés.
34. **Aptitudes culturelles**—Le jeune connaît des personnes d'autres cultures, races et ethnies, et se sent à l'aise avec elles.
35. **Résistance**—Le jeune est capable de résister à des pressions négatives exercées par ses pairs et à des situations dangereuses.
36. **Résolution pacifique de conflits**—Le jeune tente de résoudre les conflits sans recourir à la violence.

Identité positive

37. **Pouvoir personnel**—Le jeune sent qu'il a le contrôle sur les choses qui lui arrivent.
38. **Estime de soi**—Le jeune affirme avoir un degré élevé d'estime de soi.
39. **Sentiment d'utilité**—Le jeune croit que sa vie a un sens.
40. **Vision positive de l'avenir**—Le jeune est optimiste quant à son avenir personnel.

Appendix A.6

40 Acquis dont les enfants d'âge scolaire ont besoin pour réussir (6 à 11 ans)

Le Search Institute a dressé une liste de 40 acquis conduisant à l'épanouissement pour les enfants d'âge scolaire de 6 à 11 ans. Cette liste combine les résultats de l'étude menée par le Search Institute sur les acquis pour les jeunes de 12 à 18 ans et la documentation exhaustive existant sur le développement de l'enfant.

ACQUIS EXTERNES

Soutien

1. **Soutien familial**—La vie familiale est caractérisée par un degré élevé d'amour et de soutien.
2. **Communication familiale positive**—Les parents et l'enfant d'âge scolaire communiquent positivement. Celui-ci est disposé à leur demander conseil.
3. **Relations avec d'autres adultes**—L'enfant d'âge scolaire bénéficie de l'appui d'adultes autres que ses parents.
4. **Voisinage bienveillant**—L'enfant d'âge scolaire a des voisins bienveillants.
5. **Milieu à l'extérieur de la maison bienveillant**—L'école et d'autres activités fournissent à l'enfant d'âge scolaire un milieu bienveillant et encourageant.
6. **Engagement des parents dans les activités à l'extérieur de la maison**—Les parents aident activement l'enfant d'âge scolaire à réussir à l'école et dans d'autres situations à l'extérieur de la maison.

Prise en charge

7. **Valorisation des enfants par la communauté**—L'enfant d'âge scolaire croit que sa famille et sa communauté accordent de l'importance aux enfants et les apprécient.
8. **Rôles utiles des enfants**—L'enfant d'âge scolaire participe à des tâches et des décisions familiales appropriées à son âge, et se voit confier des rôles utiles à la maison et dans la communauté.
9. **Service à son prochain**—L'enfant d'âge scolaire sert les autres membres de la communauté au sein de sa famille ou dans d'autres milieux.
10. **Sécurité**—L'enfant d'âge scolaire est en sécurité à la maison, à l'école et dans le quartier.

Limites et attentes

11. **Limites dans la famille**—La famille a des règlements clairs accompagnés de conséquences, et elle surveille les activités et les allées et venues de l'enfant d'âge scolaire.
12. **Limites à l'extérieur de la maison**—L'école et les autres milieux à l'extérieur de la maison ont des règlements clairs accompagnés de conséquences.
13. **Limites dans le quartier**—Les voisins assument la responsabilité de surveiller les comportements de l'enfant d'âge scolaire.
14. **Adultes servant de modèles**—Les parents et d'autres adultes affichent un comportement positif et responsable.
15. **Interaction et influences positives de la part des pairs**—L'enfant d'âge scolaire interagit avec d'autres enfants affichant un comportement responsable, et il a l'occasion de jouer et d'interagir dans un milieu sûr et bien supervisé.
16. **Attentes appropriées par rapport au développement**—Les adultes ont des attentes réalistes par rapport au développement de l'enfant d'âge scolaire à cet âge. Les parents, les personnes qui en prennent soin et d'autres adultes encouragent celui-ci à réussir et à développer ses talents particuliers.

Utilisation constructive du temps

17. **Activités créatives**—L'enfant d'âge scolaire consacre au moins trois heures par semaine à des activités de musique, d'art, de théâtre, ou à d'autres activités créatives à la maison ou à un autre endroit.
18. **Activités à l'extérieur de la maison**—L'enfant d'âge scolaire consacre au moins une heure par semaine à des activités parascolaires ou des programmes communautaires structurés.
19. **Communauté religieuse**—La famille consacre au moins une heure par semaine à des activités ou programmes religieux.
20. **Temps de qualité supervisé à la maison**—L'enfant d'âge scolaire passe la majorité de ses soirées et ses fins de semaine à la maison avec ses parents, et s'adonne avec eux à des activités prévisibles et agréables.

ACQUIS INTERNES

Engagement envers l'apprentissage

21. **Attentes et encouragements relativement à la réussite**—L'enfant d'âge scolaire est encouragé à réussir à l'école et dans d'autres activités.
22. **Engagement à apprendre**—L'enfant d'âge scolaire est réceptif, attentif et activement engagé à apprendre.
23. **Activités stimulantes et devoirs**—Les parents et les professeurs encouragent l'enfant d'âge scolaire à explorer et à participer à des activités stimulantes. Celui-ci fait les devoirs qui lui sont assignés.
24. **Plaisir d'apprendre et appartenance à l'école**—L'enfant d'âge scolaire aime apprendre et se préoccupe de son école.
25. **Plaisir de lire**—L'enfant d'âge scolaire consacre au moins 30 minutes par jour à la lecture en compagnie d'un adulte. Il aime aussi lire ou feuilleter seul des livres ou des revues.

Valeurs positives

26. **Bienveillance**—L'enfant d'âge scolaire est encouragé à aider les autres.
27. **Égalité et justice sociale**—L'enfant d'âge scolaire commence à se montrer intéressé à améliorer la communauté.
28. **Intégrité**—L'enfant d'âge scolaire commence à agir selon ses convictions et à défendre ses croyances.
29. **Honnêteté**—L'enfant d'âge scolaire commence à accorder de l'importance à l'honnêteté et agit en conséquence.
30. **Responsabilité**—L'enfant d'âge scolaire commence à accepter et assumer ses propres responsabilités en accomplissant des tâches appropriées à son âge.
31. **Mode de vie sain et bonnes attitudes envers la sexualité**—L'enfant d'âge scolaire commence à accorder de l'importance à un mode de vie sain, et à développer des croyances et des attitudes saines envers la sexualité, ainsi que le respect envers les autres.

Compétences sociales

32. **Planification et prise de décisions**—L'enfant d'âge scolaire commence apprendre à planifier à l'avance et à faire des choix à des niveaux appropriés à son développement.
33. **Aptitudes interpersonnelles**—L'enfant d'âge scolaire interagit avec des adultes et d'autres enfants et peut nouer des amitiés. Il exprime et articule ses sentiments de façons appropriées et fait preuve d'empathie envers les autres.
34. **Aptitudes culturelles**—L'enfant d'âge scolaire connaît des personnes d'autres cultures, races et ethnies, et se sent à l'aise avec elles.
35. **Résistance**—L'enfant d'âge scolaire commence à développer la capacité de résister à des pressions négatives exercées par ses pairs et à des situations dangereuses.
36. **Résolution pacifique de conflits**—L'enfant d'âge scolaire tente de résoudre les conflits sans recourir à la violence.

Identité positive

37. **Pouvoir personnel**—L'enfant d'âge scolaire commence à sentir qu'il a le contrôle sur les choses qui lui arrivent. Il commence à gérer les frustrations et les défis de façons qui ont des résultats positifs pour lui et pour les autres.
38. **Estime de soi**—L'enfant d'âge scolaire affirme avoir un degré élevé d'estime de soi.
39. **Sentiment d'utilité**—L'enfant d'âge scolaire croit que sa vie a un sens et utilise activement ses compétences.
40. **Vision positive de l'avenir**—L'enfant d'âge scolaire est rempli d'espoir et positif quant à son avenir personnel.

Appendix B

Charts of What's in This Book

Appendix B.1

Assets Promoted by Contributors' Practices

Column groups: **Brain Research** — Lindenberger, p. 42 · **Instructional Strategies** — Paine, p. 53; Taccogna, p. 64; Taccogna, p. 68; Mitchell, p. 73 · **Language Arts** — Brown, p. 85; Johnson, p. 99; Mitchell, p. 101; Goddard, p. 114; Almendinger, p. 117; Karno, p. 126; Widmann, p. 131; Arnason & Schaney, p. 138 · **Social Studies** — Miller-Lane, p. 145; Guile, p. 157; Taccogna, p. 159; Duffey, p. 163; Perry, p. 171; Guile, p. 181 · **Math & Science** — Mahoney, p. 193 · **Health Education** — Lindenberger, p. 203; McComb, p. 206; Teppert, p. 210 · **Visual Arts** — Willett, p. 215; Shafer, p. 223 · **Beyond the Classroom** — Henderson, p. 235; Tulli, p. 247; Taccogna, p. 251

Asset	Lind.42	Paine53	Tacc.64	Tacc.68	Mitch.73	Brown85	John.99	Mitch.101	Godd.114	Almen.117	Karno126	Widm.131	Arn&Sch138	Mill-L145	Guile157	Tacc.159	Duffey163	Perry171	Guile181	Mah.193	Lind.203	McC.206	Tepp.210	Will.215	Shaf.223	Hend.235	Tulli247	Tacc.251
EXTERNAL ASSETS — Support																												
1. Family Support										■	■									■				■	■			
2. Positive Family Communication										■	■									■								
3. Other Adult Relationships	■	■	■			■					■	■									■	■				■	■	■
4. Caring Neighborhood						■				■																		
5. Caring School Climate	■	■	■	■	■	■	■			■	■	■	■	■		■		■	■	■	■	■	■	■	■	■	■	■
6. Parent Involvement in Schooling		■								■											■	■						
Empowerment																												
7. Community Values Youth		■				■			■											■	■			■			■	
8. Youth as Resources	■	■			■	■		■		■	■			■	■	■		■		■	■					■	■	■
9. Service to Others		■							■		■		■							■						■		■
10. Safety	■																					■						
Boundaries and Expectations																												
11. Family Boundaries																								■				
12. School Boundaries		■											■		■			■		■		■	■	■				
13. Neighborhood Boundaries																								■				
14. Adult Role Models	■					■				■	■			■				■	■	■	■					■	■	■
15. Positive Peer Influence		■	■	■	■	■		■		■		■					■			■	■	■	■	■		■		■
16. High Expectations		■	■	■		■	■					■							■	■								
Constructive Use of Time																												
17. Creative Activities		■							■				■			■								■		■		
18. Youth Programs																								■				
19. Religious Community																								■				
20. Time at Home																								■				
INTERNAL ASSETS — Commitment to Learning																												
21. Achievement Motivation	■		■	■	■	■	■		■		■	■	■					■	■	■				■		■	■	■
22. School Engagement	■		■	■	■	■	■	■		■	■	■	■	■		■	■	■	■	■	■					■		
23. Homework			■			■						■								■	■						■	
24. Bonding to School			■	■		■				■			■	■	■			■	■			■		■	■	■	■	
25. Reading for Pleasure		■																										
Positive Values																												
26. Caring	■			■	■		■	■	■					■		■			■	■	■		■	■	■			■
27. Equality and Social Justice				■				■						■	■	■												
28. Integrity					■	■																		■				
29. Honesty					■																							
30. Responsibility		■	■	■	■	■			■		■				■	■	■							■				
31. Restraint										■					■	■								■				
Social Competencies																												
32. Planning and Decision Making	■	■	■	■	■	■		■						■	■	■		■	■	■				■		■	■	■
33. Interpersonal Competence	■	■	■	■	■	■														■	■	■				■		■
34. Cultural Competence		■	■	■	■				■	■				■		■				■	■					■		
35. Resistance Skills		■												■						■	■					■		■
36. Peaceful Conflict Resolution	■	■	■	■	■	■			■		■			■	■					■	■	■				■		■
Positive Identity																												
37. Personal Power	■	■	■	■	■									■	■	■	■		■	■				■		■	■	■
38. Self-Esteem		■	■	■	■	■							■	■						■							■	
39. Sense of Purpose	■	■	■		■																					■	■	
40. Positive View of Personal Future	■	■		■		■							■								■			■		■	■	

Appendix B.2

Asset-Rich Strategies for Supporting Student Diversity

One way to think about approaching asset building in your classroom is to think about incorporating it through addressing student diversity. Valuing diversity is a thriving indicator in Search Institute's research, meaning that youth who value diversity tend also to report other behaviors and attitudes that indicate they are thriving as adolescents. It follows, then, that if we as teachers use strategies in our schools and classrooms that celebrate and incorporate the diversity of our students, we will be building the cultural competence asset in the process. Contributors to this resource use a number of asset-rich strategies that also meet diverse student needs. This chart shows where those are located in the text.

Asset-Rich Strategies That Support Diversity	Developmental Assets Supported	Author and Page Location in Book	How/Why This Strategy Addresses Student Diversity
Use the wide range of asset-building strategies shown below	16. High Expectations 21. Achievement Motivation 22. School Engagement 24. Bonding to School 30. Responsibility 33. Interpersonal Competence 34. Cultural Competence 38. Self-Esteem	Taccogna, 20–21 Taccogna, 32 Taccogna, 47–48	■ One significant finding from the data collected on Search Institute's *Profiles of Student Life: Attitudes and Behaviors* survey is that the number of assets present in the lives of students is stable across diverse racial and ethnic groups. ■ In addition, male and female students who report more assets in their lives also show greater strength in academic areas traditionally not strong for their gender. ■ Good instruction is both asset-supportive and meets the needs of diverse students.
Differentiate curriculum and instruction	16. High Expectations 21. Achievement Motivation 22. School Engagement 24. Bonding to School 30. Responsibility 32. Planning and Decision Making 38. Self-Esteem	Paine, 54–55 Taccogna, 64–67 Mitchell, 104–110	■ Differentiation addresses needs of students across ability levels, interests, and readiness. An underlying assumption is that all students can learn. ■ Differentiation strategies address many kinds of differences: ability, prior knowledge, cultural experience, and socioeconomic background. They allow the teacher to meet each learner where he/she is and to move forward from that point. ■ The work team activity illustrates differentiation.
Use cooperative learning	14. Adult Role Models 15. Positive Peer Influence 16. High Expectations 21. Achievement Motivation 22. School Engagement 24. Bonding to School 26. Caring 30. Responsibility 33. Interpersonal Competence 34. Cultural Competence	Paine, 56–57 Taccogna, 68–71 Mitchell, 73–75	■ Family heritage night is an example illustrating use of cooperative learning in building cross-cultural understanding. ■ Cooperative learning reduces prejudice, enhances intergroup understanding, and builds skills for cross-cultural communication. It also is of equal benefit to all socioeconomic groups. ■ The five-square activity is an example of a group exercise that contributes to building cultural competence.
Use heterogeneous grouping	14. Adult Role Models 15. Positive Peer Influence 30. Responsibility 33. Interpersonal Competence 34. Cultural Competence 36. Peaceful Conflict Resolution	Brown, 91–93 Widmann, 133–135	■ In the compass points activity, students understand the value of including those who are different from them in their work groups. ■ Heterogenous writing groups combine efforts to create a story.
Design lessons that incorporate multiple intelligences and learning styles; provide a variety of learning paths to accommodate different learning styles	5. Caring School Climate 16. High Expectations 21. Achievement Motivation 22. School Engagement 24. Bonding to School 37. Personal Power 38. Self-Esteem	Taccogna, 41 Widmann, 132–133 Arnason and Schaney, 138–141 Perry, 176 Willett, 215–221	■ Diversity may also be thought of as including the diversity in ways individuals learn. Several authors reinforce the fact that incorporating multiple intelligences and varying learning styles into lesson designs better meets the needs of a wider range of students. In turn, when students' needs are being met they are likely to be more engaged in school and want to do better—assets are built by attending to this form of diversity.

Asset-Rich Strategies That Support Diversity	Developmental Assets Supported	Author and Page Location in Book	How/Why This Strategy Addresses Student Diversity
		Shafer, 226–227	■ Diversity in school involves more than race, ethnic, or socioeconomics levels. It also includes the multiple ways in which students learn best.
		Widmann, 135–137	■ Presenting information and activities that address all of the learning styles helps assure diverse learners are engaged in learning: visual, auditory, tactile, and kinesthetic.
Use wait-time regularly	16. High Expectations 21. Achievement Motivation 22. School Engagement	Miller-Lane, 148	■ Teachers typically wait one second or less after asking a question and before moving on to the next student for a response. Waiting longer assists students learning English in processing information and participation.
		Perry, 177, 179	■ Strategies also include wait-time.
Structure learning opportunities to build interpersonal skills	21. Achievement Motivation 22. School Engagement 24. Bonding to School 33. Interpersonal Competence 34. Cultural Competence 36. Peaceful Conflict Resolution 37. Personal Power 38. Self-Esteem	Mitchell, 102–104 Mitchell, 105–113	■ The partnership project develops other-centered-ness and skills needed in long-term relationships. Both have applications to building cross-cultural relationships. ■ The legislative activity and community-based final project both build skills in taking the perspective of another person.
Incorporate into your instructional processes ways to get to know your students and to allow them to know each other: books at breakfast, cooperative learning activities, ice-breaker activities, class meetings	5. Caring School Climate 15. Positive Peer Influence 22. School Engagement 24. Bonding to School 33. Interpersonal Competence 34. Cultural Competence	Taccogna, 68–71 Brown, 89–93 Mitchell, 103–104 Mahoney, 194–195 Lindenberger, 203–205	■ Students who know each other personally but are from different racial, ethnic, or socioeconomic backgrounds are less likely to demonstrate prejudice, stereotyping, or other negative behaviors toward people in other groups.
Design opportunities for students to develop knowledge skills and attitudes necessary for good citizenship for life in a diverse, democratic republic	7. Community Values Youth 8. Youth as Resources 14. Adult Role Models 15. Positive Peer Influence 21. Achievement Motivation 22. School Engagement 26. Caring 27. Equality and Social Justice 30. Responsibility 33. Interpersonal Competence 34. Cultural Competence 36. Peaceful Conflict Resolution 37. Personal Power	Miller-Lane, 145–156 Guile, 181–190	■ All three social studies model lessons address civic responsibility and good citizenship. ■ Fifth graders help create a school in which learning and demonstrating civic responsibility are themes.
Design lessons and use strategies that help students explore the meaning of cultural competence explicitly	8. Youth as Resources 15. Positive Peer Influence 26. Caring 27. Equality and Social Justice 33. Interpersonal Competence 34. Cultural Competence 35. Resistance Skills	Miller-Lane, 149–152 Taccogna, 159–162 Willett, 220	■ The concept formation activity focuses explicitly on the meaning and development of cultural competence. ■ The headband activity from Comprehensive Health Education Foundation (CHEF) helps students get the feel of stereotyping and labeling, and encourages them to avoid both. ■ Fifth-grade activity in the Assets in Art Program using Katie Couric's book *The Brand New Kid* explores appreciating diversity and people who are different from us.

Asset-Rich Strategies That Support Diversity	Developmental Assets Supported	Author and Page Location in Book	How/Why This Strategy Addresses Student Diversity
Foster skills in consensus building	33. Interpersonal competence 34. Cultural competence	Taccogna, 70–71 Mitchell, 79–80	▪ Teaching students how to disagree constructively (as in academic controversy) helps bridge cultural differences. ▪ A class learns to build consensus through a construction activity.
Include a variety of content and materials representing differences in ethnicity, race, socioeconomic status, gender, and ability	5. Caring School Climate 14. Adult Role Models 21. Achievement Motivation 22. School Engagement 25. Reading for Pleasure 33. Interpersonal Competence 34. Cultural Competence	Brown, 85–87, 93–96 Almendinger, 117–124 Shafer, 223–229	▪ Books included in the "Grisham Novels" class address a wide range of social issues, engaging youth who can relate to various circumstances in the books and broadening their understanding of complex issues as well. ▪ The characters examined in *Romeo and Juliet* represent elements of diversity in ethnicity and world view. ▪ The study of the Hopi culture and one element of its artistic expression provides a model for learning about cultures.
Create lessons that provide opportunities for students to cross socioeconomic lines	3. Other Adult Relationships 5. Caring School Climate 6. Parent Involvement in Schooling 8. Youth as Resources 14. Adult Role Models 16. High Expectations 21. Achievement Motivation 22. School Engagement 26. Caring 30. Responsibility 32. Planning and Decision Making 33. Interpersonal Competence 37. Personal Power 38. Self-Esteem 39. Sense of Purpose	Karno, 126–130	▪ The thought of applying to colleges, much less applying for a scholarship, is often out of the realm of possibility in the mind of some students, particularly those in lower socioeconomic groups and those without college-attending role models. Having this experience as part of class opens to all the possibility of attending college regardless of a student's socioeconomic level.
Organize cross-generational activities to engage students in skill building and service learning	8. Youth as Resources 14. Adult Role Models 18. Youth Programs 21. Achievement Motivation 22. School Engagement 26. Caring 33. Interpersonal Competence 34. Cultural Competence 39. Sense of Purpose 40. Positive View of Personal Future	Goddard, 114 Karno, 127–128 Mahoney, 200	▪ The opportunities to learn to appreciate persons of other generations—older or younger—must often be structured; for many they do not occur naturally. Joint ventures contribute to diminishing stereotypical attitudes and behaviors. ▪ The integral involvement of parents in completing the VIP survey for the essay provides cross-generational understanding and appreciation. ▪ "Let's Talk It Over" activity involves parents and children.
Facilitate group decision making by setting up situations in which students must work collaboratively to make decisions and come to consensus	30. Responsibility 32. Planning and Decision Making 33. Interpersonal Competence 36. Peaceful Conflict Resolution	Mitchell, 78–80 Mitchell, 110–115	▪ The consensus-building activity requires students of different cultures, genders, and abilities working together to create a successful project. ▪ The whole class project puts all students in the class in the position of needing to respect others' needs and views with its emphasis on perceptual differences and its incorporation of diverse work styles (see Handout 4.6B).
Provide opportunities for students to write reflectively in order to monitor their learning and responses to projects	21. Achievement Motivation 22. School Engagement 33. Interpersonal Competence 34. Cultural Competence 37. Personal Power 38. Self-Esteem	Mitchell, 103–104 Brown, 94, 96 Arnason and Schaney, 141 Miller-Lane, 148–156	▪ Written reflections enable you to look in on how individual students are responding to projects and gaining understanding. The reflective writing assignment elicits revealing responses from students of different cultures. ▪ Several other authors use reflection as well.

Asset-Rich Strategies That Support Diversity	Developmental Assets Supported	Author and Page Location in Book	How/Why This Strategy Addresses Student Diversity
Create structures that support students over time	16. High Expectations 21. Achievement Motivation 22. School Engagement 23. Homework 24. Bonding to School 32. Planning and Decision Making 33. Interpersonal Competence 34. Cultural Competence 36. Peaceful Conflict Resolution 37. Personal Power 38. Self-Esteem	Henderson, 235–246	■ Transition from one level of schooling to the next (particularly from middle to high school) is difficult for many students, especially those already challenged by deficits in skills or cross-cultural learning issues. ■ Structured approaches to helping students make major transitions in their schooling not only help them bond to school and be engaged in learning, but also increase student achievement and build and maintain assets. Students from diverse backgrounds may be in particular need of such support.
Establish peer tutoring opportunities	15. Positive Peer Influence 21. Achievement Motivation 22. School Engagement 25. Reading for pleasure 33. Interpersonal skills	Johnson, 99–100 Henderson, 245	■ Cross-age tutoring arrangements build confidence as well as skills in students on both ends of the age range. Such arrangements help bridge diverse learning abilities and promote skills of valuing people of different ages as individuals. ■ Same-age tutoring arrangements also provide for underachieving students.
Use technology to provide challenge, engagement, and learning-enhancement opportunities	5. Caring School Climate 15. Positive Peer Influence 17. Creative Activities 21. Achievement Motivation 22. School Engagement 30. Responsibility 32. Planning and Decision Making 33. Interpersonal Competence 36. Peace Conflict Resolution 38. Self-Esteem 39. Sense of Purpose	Arnason and Shaney, 138–141	■ Special education students respond well to active learning situations that allow them to participate as equals in learning opportunities and produce products that have appeal to their peers.

Appendix B.3

Connecting Asset Building to Instructional Strategies

Contributors to this resource use a number of effective instructional strategies that are particularly asset rich. This chart summarizes the major strategies they use, the assets they support, and where in the book to find examples of their use.

Instructional Strategy	Developmental Assets Supported	Author and Page Location in Book	References or Applications
Academic or Constructive Controversy	21. Achievement Motivation 22. School Engagement 33. Interpersonal Competence 34. Cultural Competence 36. Peaceful Conflict Resolution 37. Personal Power	Taccogna, 70–71 Mitchell, 105–107	■ Description of formal process of teaching academic controversy ■ R.A.Y. Congress activity using elements of academic controversy
Active Learning (active participation)	16. High Expectations 21. Achievement Motivation 22. School Engagement 30. Responsibility 33. Interpersonal Competence 34. Cultural Competence 37. Personal Power 38. Self-Esteem	Lindenberger, 43 Brown, 85–97 Johnson, 99–100 Mitchell, 73–80, 102–104, 110–115 Goddard, 114 Widmann, 132, 136–137 Arnason and Schaney, 138–141 Taccogna, 159–162 Perry, 171–173, 180 Guile, 183–190 Mahoney, 193–201 Willett, 215–221 Shafer, 223–229 Tulli, 247–249	■ Effects in brain of activities that actively involve students ■ Breakfast and books; joint planning; group activities ■ Prepare for reading to others ■ Cooperative learning; partner project; consensus building activities ■ Interviewing; writing ■ Multiple learning modes ■ iMovie technology to engage youth; skits ■ Addressing issues of labeling and stereotypes through headband activity developed by CHEF ■ CMP Amusement Park Design Company activities ■ Schoolwide naturescape project ■ Recommendation that actual learning and opportunities for real-life application foster greater engagement and incorporation of knowledge into practice; youth mapping project; writing creative advertising spots; youth advocacy activities ■ Visual arts activities interpreting each asset category ■ Kachina sculpture art project ■ A multiyear graduation project
Brain-based Teaching	3. Other Adult Relationships 8. Youth as Resources 14. Adult Role Models 21. Achievement Motivation 22. School Engagement 26. Caring 33. Interpersonal Competence 36. Peaceful Conflict Resolution 37. Personal Power 39. Sense of Purpose 40. Positive View of Personal Future	Lindenberger, 42–43 Almendinger, 119 Widmann, 132–133	■ Alignment with developmental assets framework ■ Structure of unit addresses brain research ■ Using imagination as a source of content
Concept Formation	8. Youth as Resources 21. Achievement Motivation 22. School Engagement 23. Homework	Miller-Lane, 149–152 Willett, 218	■ Cultural competence unit models how to unpack the meaning of any of the 40 assets ■ Students learn what a value is

Instructional Strategy	Developmental Assets Supported	Author and Page Location in Book	References or Applications
Cooperative Learning	8. Youth as Resources 16. High Expectations 21. Achievement Motivation 33. Interpersonal Competence 36. Peaceful Conflict Resolution	Paine, 57 Taccogna, 68–71 Mitchell, 73–80 Brown, 91–93 Mitchell, 105–106 Miller-Lane, 151 Perry, 172–173, 175	■ Family heritage night building cultural competence ■ Overview as an asset-rich strategy ■ Five-square puzzle, candy distribution challenge, and consensus construction activities ■ Compass points activity honoring student differences ■ Health-o-meter activity to process group dynamics ■ Think-pair-share in cultural competence lesson ■ Simulation activity; problem-solving groups; interval table investigations activity
Critical Friends ■ Coaching ■ Student as worker, teacher as coach	8. Youth as Resources 30. Responsibility 32. Planning and Decision Making 33. Interpersonal Competence 37. Personal Power	Brown, 91–93	■ Compass points; students arrange speakers
Differentiation of Curriculum and Instruction ■ Classroom adaptations of content, process, or product to meet individual needs ■ Programmatic options	8. Youth as Resources 22. School Engagement	Paine, 54 Taccogna, 64–67 Brown, 87 Mitchell, 101–104 Widmann, 132	■ Overview of differentiated programs ■ Alignment of asset building with differentiation strategies ■ Involving youth in decision making about content ■ Reflective writing to assess projects ■ Addressing various learning styles and using differentiation
Integration of Curriculum and Interdisciplinary Instruction	16. High Expectations 21. Achievement Motivation 22. School Engagement 32. Planning and Decision Making	Paine, 55–56 Almendinger, 118–124 Duffey, 163–167 Shafer, 227–228	■ Overview; cross-grade interdisciplinary salmon project ■ Integration of literature and guidance curricula to heighten student engagement and increase connections between course contents and real-life issues for teens ■ Integration of language arts, social studies, science, and mathematics in a unit ■ Integration of visual arts with European history and literature, French, and family/consumer sciences classes
Literature: Analysis	15. Positive Peer Influence 30. Responsibility 31. Restraint 32. Planning and Decision Making 33. Interpersonal Competence 40. Positive View of Personal Future	Brown, 93–94 Almendinger, 121–123 Widmann, 135	■ Analyses of characters in John Grisham novels ■ Analysis of characters in *Romeo and Juliet,* the influences around them, and the asset implications of their beliefs and actions. ■ Analysis of fiction to prepare for writing a story
Multiple Intelligences	16. High Expectations 21. Achievement Motivation 22. School Engagement 37. Personal Power	Taccogna, 41 Widmann, 132–133, 136–137 Willett, 215–221 Shafer, 223, 226, 227	■ Overview, connections to asset building ■ Brainstorming in multiple learning modes; incorporating multiple intelligences into the lesson ■ Teaching about the assets by relating asset categories to elements of visual arts ■ Artistic expression as an alternative way for some students to succeed

Instructional Strategy	Developmental Assets Supported	Author and Page Location in Book	References or Applications
Organizers ■ Advance organizers ■ Graphic organizers	21. Academic Achievement 22. School Engagement	Paine, 59 Mitchell, 110–112 Almendinger, 122–123 Perry, 177	■ Use of advance organizers in preteaching material; K-W-L closure technique ■ Use of graphic organizer (Handout 4.6B) ■ Use of graphic organizer (Handout 4.7) ■ Math investigation sheet and K-W-H-L organizer and process
Peer Tutoring	5. Caring School Climate 8. Youth as Resources 9. Service to Others 21. Achievement Motivation 22. School Engagement 26. Caring 38. Self-Esteem	Paine, 59–60 Johnson, 99–100 Teppert, 210–211 Henderson, 245	■ Strategies to practice, remediate, motivate ■ Middle school special education students reading for kindergarteners ■ High school students teaching younger students about health concepts and issues through club activities ■ Student mentors in an intervention transition program to address underachieving students
Questioning: Higher-Level	16. High Expectations 21. Achievement Motivation 22. School Engagement	Paine, 57–58 Miller-Lane, 146–149 Perry, 176	■ Rationale for use of higher-level questioning strategies and programs that support differentiation ■ Use of questioning in a Socratic seminar discussion ■ Modeling questions to solve math problems
Reflection ■ Reflective or responsive writing ■ Self-reflection ■ Mental mapping	16. High Expectations 21. Achievement Motivation 22. School Engagement 23. Homework 30. Responsibility 37. Personal Power 38. Self-Esteem 39. Sense of Purpose	Brown, 94, 96 Mitchell, 101–103, 107–109, 113–115 Arnason and Shaney, 141 Miller-Lane, 148–149 Miller-Lane, 150–156	■ Various responsive writing activities ■ Reflective writing to assess projects ■ Oral reflection on video about developmental assets ■ Writing reflections after a Socratic seminar ■ Mental map activity studying perceptions of school priorities
Service Learning	8. Youth as Resources 9. Service to Others 38. Self-Esteem	Paine, 55–56 Brown, 93–96 Mitchell, 110–115 Johnson, 99–100 Karno, 129 Arnason and Schaney, 138–141 Guile, 181–190 Mahoney, 197–198 Teppert, 210–211	■ Connections between asset building and service learning ■ Youth decision making in service-learning opportunities ■ Community-based project ■ Middle school special education students help kindergarteners read ■ Seniors share essay-writing lessons with juniors ■ Special education students teach other students with iMovie technology ■ Environmental naturescape project ■ Marketing projects ■ High school students provide health presentations to younger children
Shared Inquiry	8. Youth as Resources 16. High Expectations 21. Achievement Motivation 22. School Engagement 30. Responsibility 33. Interpersonal Competence 37. Personal Power 38. Self-Esteem	Paine, 57 Widmann, 135	■ Using Junior Great Books ■ One aspect of her approach to creative writing
Skill-Building Instruction	5. Caring School Climate 8. Youth as Resources 14. Adult Role Models 15. Positive Peer Influence 22. School Engagement 27. Equality and Social Justice	Paine, 58 Mitchell, 73–80 Taccogna, 70–71	■ Skills instruction as asset building ■ Candy distribution challenge (negotiation, conflict resolution skills), five-square puzzle (interpersonal and cultural competence), and consensus construction (consensus-building) activities ■ Academic controversy

Instructional Strategy	Developmental Assets Supported	Author and Page Location in Book	References or Applications
Skill-Building Instruction (cont.)	28. Integrity 30. Responsibility 32. Planning and Decision Making 33. Interpersonal Competence 34. Cultural Competence 37. Personal Power 39. Sense of Purpose	Taccogna, 159–162 Mahoney, 197 Lindenberger, 204 McComb, 208 Henderson, 237, 238	■ Headband activity developed by Comprehensive Health Education Foundation (CHEF) to recognize and avoid stereotyping and labeling ■ Recommendation that similar skills be taught as applicable to many risk areas ■ General communication skills and coping skills ■ Becoming a positive peer role model ■ Academic skills common to many high school content areas
Socratic Seminar/ Socratic Dialogue	8. Youth as Resources 21. Achievement Motivation 22. School Engagement 27. Equality and Social Justice 31. Restraint 33. Interpersonal Competence 37. Personal Power	Paine, 57 Miller-Lane, 146–149	■ Tool for engaging and empowering students ■ Pledge of allegiance lesson
Team Teaching	3. Other Adult Relationships 5. Caring School Climate 14. Adult Role Models 21. Achievement Motivation 22. School Engagement	Almendinger, 117–123 Perry, 176 Arnason and Schaney, 138–141 Henderson, 235–246	■ Counselor and classroom teacher collaboration to bring content expertise and adult modeling to sensitive topics ■ Team teaching by special education and regular middle school teachers ■ Two special education teachers collaborate to enable youth to produce iMovie about the developmental assets ■ Team teaching an end-of-summer institute for underachieving students becoming high school freshmen
Technology/Media Integration	16. High Expectations 21. Achievement Motivation 22. School Engagement	Arnason and Schaney, 138–141 Mahoney, 198	■ Creating asset messages through video technology ■ Creating media spots to advocate for positive health practices
Transitions ■ Looping ■ Transitions from level to level of schooling	3. Other Adult Relationships 5. Caring School Climate 6. Parent Involvement in School 10. Safety 12. School Boundaries 15. Positive Peer Influence 22. School Engagement 24. Bonding to School	Paine, 60–61 Henderson, 235–236 Tulli, 247–249	■ Looping to enhance relationships and maintain learning levels through grade-level transitions ■ Transition program to address underachieving students moving from middle to high school ■ A multiyear graduation project with assessment features
Understanding by Design	8. Youth as Resources 14. Adult Role Model 32. Planning and Decision Making	Guile, 181–188	■ Systematically planning backward from objective of infusing assets throughout the curriculum
Writing: creating essays, stories, scripts, and articles	4. Caring Neighborhood 5. Caring School Climate 7. Community Values Youth 8. Youth as Resources 9. Service to Others 12. School Boundaries 16. High Expectations 21. Achievement Motivation 22. School Engagement 23. Homework 26. Caring 32. Planning and Decision Making	Goddard, 114 Karno, 126–130 Widmann, 131–137 Arnason and Shaney, 138–141	■ Magazine to reflect the history of the people of a rural area ■ Writing college and scholarship essays ■ Writing an asset-based story ■ Students who have learning disabilities developing and editing scripts for a video

Contributors

AMY ALMENDINGER, M.ED.

Almendinger teaches high school English and has also served as the K–12 language arts department head for the New Richmond (Wisconsin) School District. For seniors, she has developed and teaches an interdisciplinary course called "Great Ideas." With a B.A. in English and secondary education and an M.Ed. in teaching and learning, she now also works as an educational facilitator for St. Mary's University's M.Ed. program. She received the Sallie Mae First Year Teacher Award in her early teaching career, and has since received the Herb Kohl Fellowship.

CONTACT INFORMATION: Amy Scott Almendinger, New Richmond High School, 701 East 11th Street, New Richmond, WI 54017; telephone 715-243-7451; amya@newrichmond.k12.wi.us.

JOYCE ARNASON, M.A.

With a B.A. in English and an M.A. in special education, both from the University of Denver, Arnason has for 23 years taught middle and high school students with emotional or behavioral disabilities and learning disabilities. Her interest in technology not only inspired the unit she shares in this resource but also spurred her participation on the Smoky Hill High School (Aurora, Colorado) Technology Committee. She has also served as a coordinator in the Pupil Services Department at another Cherry Creek high school.

CONTACT INFORMATION: Joyce Arnason, Smoky Hill High School, 16100 East Smoky Hill Road, Aurora, CO 80015; telephone 720-886-5601; jarnason@mail.ccsd.k12.co.us.

ANDREA GODFREY BROWN, M.A.T.

During her teaching career, Brown has worked with students at all levels, grades 1–12, as a classroom teacher, a teacher of gifted and talented students, and as a counselor. Most recently, she is a high school language arts teacher in Manchester, Missouri, where she also serves as a coach and coordinator of Parkway's Critical Friends Groups. A graduate of Principia College in Elsah, Illinois, with a B.A. in English and education, and of Webster University, St. Louis, Missouri, with an M.A.T. in communications, she was honored in 1998 by the University of Missouri as an "Excellent Teacher."

CONTACT INFORMATION: Andrea Godfrey Brown, Parkway South High School, 801 Hanna Road, Manchester, MO 63021; telephone 314-415-7700; Abrown@pkwy.K12.mo.us.

BRENDA DUFFEY, M.S.W.

Duffey teaches at a juvenile correctional facility in Oregon, focusing on developing assets and life skills while helping students there obtain either GEDs (graduation equivalency degrees) or high school diplomas. Her example here reflects integrated curriculum developed when she taught humanities and served as department head at John Adams Middle School in Albuquerque, New Mexico, a school with a majority population of Hispanic students and a large group of American Indian students. Prior to that she worked in high schools in Indiana, Kentucky, and North Carolina. With an M.S.W. in social justice from Kent School of Social Work and a B.A. in history (both at the University of Louisville), she also worked for two years in the Middle School Initiative Project funded by the city of Albuquerque to deter gang activity through tutoring and after-school activities. She is a regional representative and has presented twice to the Oregon Alternative Educators Association Conference, once about infusing assets into curriculum.

CONTACT INFORMATION: Brenda Duffey, 4823 Gloria Gayle Way, Florence, OR 97439; telephone 541-902-9694; tworaisn@presys.com.

H. WALLACE GODDARD, PH.D.

Goddard's role as an extension specialist at the University of Arkansas culminates a career in public schools that included teaching gifted and talented students, photography, filmmaking, yearbook, and, as he puts it, "every variety of science and math." He is the author of a youth identity program called the Great Self Mystery and has provided training to support it. In addition, he coauthored *The National Extension Parent Education Model*. He is currently chair of the education and enrichment section of the National Council on Family Relations. He holds a Ph.D. in family and human development from Utah State University in Logan, an M.Ed. in educational administration, and a B.S. in physics education, both from Brigham Young University in Provo, Utah.

CONTACT INFORMATION: H. Wallace Goddard, 4407 Kenyon, Little Rock, AR 72205; telephone 501-666-4407; wgoddard@uaex.edu.

DAVE GUILE, M.S.

With a B.S. in elementary education and an M.S. in counseling, both from Oregon College of Education and postgraduate work at the University of Oregon, Guile's background served him well as a principal opening a new elementary school based on the developmental assets model. He has also worked as principal in four other K–6 schools and has been the director of instructional services for the Salem-Keizer School District in Oregon. He received the Oregon Pioneer Award from the Oregon Elementary Principals Association in 1994 as well as the Distinguished Principal Award from the Western Oregon Region of Oregon Elementary School Principals Association in 1988, and was named Educator of the Year in 1985 by the

Keizer Chamber of Commerce. He participates in his community as a youth basket-ball coach, as a Little League coach, and on the Kids Vote Organizing Committee.

CONTACT INFORMATION: Dave Guile, Forest Ridge Elementary, 7905 June Reid Place North, Keizer, OR 97303; telephone 503-399-5548; guile_dave @salkeiz.k12.or.us.

STEVE HENDERSON, M.A.

With an M.A. in athletic administration from St. Mary's College of California in Moraga, and a B.A. in psychology from San José State University, San José, Cali-fornia, Henderson is a history teacher and coach at Aragon High School in San Mateo, California, teaching U.S. and world history. He has continued to pursue his social studies area by participating as a traveling teacher on the "Sojourn to the Past" Civil Rights Educational Journey in 2000 and as a traveling scholar in the Fulbright-Hays Seminars Abroad program in 2002. He received a Who's Who Among America's Teachers Award as well as the Distinguished Teacher Award at Aragon High School for several different years. He serves as a presenter and trainer for the Positive Coaching Alliance at Stanford University, Stanford, California, pro-moting innovative techniques in coaching to youth sports organizations.

CONTACT INFORMATION: Steve Henderson, Aragon High School, 900 Alameda de las Pulgas, San Mateo, CA 94402; telephone 650-762-0129; shenderson@smuhsd.k12.ca.us.

KAREN KUPFER JOHNSON, M.ED.

Johnson works as a reading specialist in the Minneapolis, Minnesota, public school system, in an urban center for middle and high school students who have special learning needs. In addition, she serves as a private tutor and volunteers to train other tutors as well as to coordinate read-aloud opportunities for homeless children in this urban area. With a B.S. in English and language arts, and an M.Ed. in curric-ulum and instruction with a reading focus, both from the University of Minnesota, she has taught 6th- through 12th-grade students and has served as a family daycare provider for children 11 years old and younger. She is working on a second master's degree in special education. She has received recognition for her work with the Harrison Service Learning Program at her current school and a certificate of excel-lence in 1997 for her volunteer tutoring of homeless youth.

CONTACT INFORMATION: Karen Kupfer Johnson, Harrison Education Center, 501 Irving Avenue North, Minneapolis, MN 55405; telephone 612-668-2680; karenkupferjohnson@msn.com.

STEPHANIE KARNO. M.S.

In addition to her role as a high school English teacher in western Wisconsin, Stephanie has served as the Associate Director of the Master of Teaching and Learning Program at Saint Mary's University in Minnesota, where she has facili-tated three learning communities of teachers getting their master's degrees. She has also been a staff developer in areas such as the Dimensions of Learning and in inquiry and research. She has a B.A. in English from Luther College in Decorah, Iowa, an M.S. from Winona State University, Winona, Minnesota, and is working on her Ed.D. in educational leadership. A member of the editorial board for *Alliance*, an educational journal of southeast Minnesota, she has had various articles published in educational and outdoor journals. In addition to her school roles, she has been the Summer Ventures camp director at Luther College and family camp director in the Boundary Waters Canoe Area in far northern Minnesota.

CONTACT INFORMATION: Stephanie Karno, New Richmond High School, 701 East 11th Street, New Richmond, WI 54017; telephone 715-243-1235; skarno@smumn.edu.

DEE LINDENBERGER, M.A.

While her early career involved elementary school teaching, Lindenberger has had experience teaching at all grade levels (K–12 and university level) in her current role as consultant-trainer for Marquette-Alger Regional Education Service Agency and the Strategic Alternatives in Prevention Education Association, both in Michigan. She provides training and technical assistance to school districts throughout Michigan in prevention programming, youth leadership, and brain-based learning. Her B.A. in English from St. Lawrence University in Canton, New York, and her M.A. in health education from Northern Michigan University in Marquette, provide good background for that role, in which she has co-developed and coordinated the Upper Peninsula Teen Leadership Program. This program has been recognized on both the state and national levels. A middle school risk-reduction curriculum that she co-developed also has been recognized on the national level by the Centers for Disease Control and Prevention in the U.S. Department of Health and Human Services. She has authored five training manuals in the areas of student assistance, risk reduction, violence prevention, asset building, systems change, and bullying prevention.

CONTACT INFORMATION: Dee Lindenberger, 211 East Kaye Avenue, Marquette, MI 49855; telephone 906-225-1568; lindenberger@optimal-learning.org.

COLLEEN MAHONEY, PH.D.

Mahoney's background includes serving as a college faculty member who for the past 10 years trained school and community health educators at State University of New York College at Brockport, the University of Maryland, and Kent State University in Ohio. Her education includes a Ph.D. in health education from the University of Maryland, an M.Ed. in counseling and a B.A. in child and adolescent psychology, both from Stetson University in DeLand, Florida. She now is an Ohio-based consultant providing training and technical assistance to schools and communities working on asset-based initiatives. Currently, she is working with Columbiana County's Building Assets Together and Wadsworth's Assets in Motion initiative. She has had more than 15 articles published in professional journals and was editor of two college-level texts on human sexuality.

CONTACT INFORMATION: Colleen Mahoney, Mahoney Consulting Group, 301 Windfall Lane, Wadsworth, OH 44281; telephone 330-335-4800; cmahoney@wadsnet.com.

KARLA MCCOMB, M.S.

McComb was a director in the Curriculum and Professional Development Division of Clark County School District (Las Vegas) in Nevada, where she supervised social studies, health, physical education, Indian education, multicultural education, and the Safe and Drug-Free Schools program. With a B.A. from California State University, Sacramento, and an M.S. from Nova Southeastern University, Ft. Lauderdale, Florida, her prior experience was as a social studies and English teacher in middle schools, where she also served as department chair. She currently serves as the chair of several councils and commissions, including the Nevada Commission on Substance Abuse Education, Prevention, Enforcement and Treatment, and she works with Raising Nevada, the statewide asset-building initiative in Nevada. She has written and/or edited many publications and curriculum materials and has served as adjunct professor in multicultural education.

CONTACT INFORMATION: Karla McComb, Community Relations Coordinator, Easter Seals Southern Nevada, 6200 West Oakey Boulevard, Las Vegas, NV 89416; telephone 702-870-7050; kmccomb@eastersealssn.org.

JONATHAN MILLER-LANE, M.ED.

With an M.Ed. in education and a B.A. in African and Middle Eastern history, Miller-Lane brings to his contributions here background in teaching social studies at the high school and college levels as well as in international living (in the Middle East, Africa, Australia, and New Zealand). He now is a doctoral candidate in curriculum and instruction at the University of Washington, Seattle. At Bainbridge High School outside of Seattle, Washington, he taught a senior honors humanities seminar as well as a variety of history, world affairs, and civilization courses. He was also faculty adviser to the class of 1999 and coordinated production of two summer institutes for teachers in leading better discussions. He was named Teacher of the Year at Bainbridge High School in 1998, 1999, and 2001. He has presented papers to the American Educational Research Association as well as to the Washington State Council for the Social Studies and the Council of Public Legal Education. He also served as moderator and organizer of "Rethinking Citizenship: A Series of Five Youth/Adult Forums," sponsored by the Bainbridge Island Humanities Council.

CONTACT INFORMATION: Jonathan Miller-Lane, 1210 North 43rd Street, Seattle, WA 98103; telephone 206-547-4815; millerlane@wans.net.

JAN MITCHELL, M.A.

Retiring in 2002 as a high school communications teacher, Mitchell now is an adjunct instructor for Buena Vista University in Marshalltown, Iowa, where she teaches communications courses for professionals. With a B.A. in English and speech from Westmar College in LeMars, Iowa, and an M.A. in English from the University of Northern Colorado, Greeley, she also works as a consultant and a writer. She was named Iowa Teacher of the Year in 1997 and one of four finalists for National Teacher of the Year. She also received a U.S./Russia/Ukraine Award for Excellence in Teaching, resulting in travel to eastern Russia to train teachers in 1997. She earned certification from the National Board for Professional Teaching Standards in 1999.

CONTACT INFORMATION: Jan Mitchell, 1500 Lincoln Towers Circle, Marshalltown, IA 50158; telephone 641-752-7666; lincotower@thewebunwired.net.

STAN PAINE, PH.D.

With experience in both public and private school systems and with learners from preschool through graduate school, Paine continues to serve as an elementary school principal. He also shares his expertise in that role with future school principals by teaching and mentoring in the administrative licensure program at the University of Oregon in Eugene. His education includes a Ph.D. in special education and administration from the University of Oregon, an M.S. in applied behavior analysis from Southern Illinois University, and a B.A. in psychology from St. Cloud State University in Minnesota. In 1997, he was recognized by the National Association of Elementary School Principals as the National Distinguished Principal for the state of Oregon, and received the Human Rights Leadership Award in 2002 from a community organization. He has authored two books and several chapters and articles on various educational topics. He has also served on advisory boards for a high school, a public library, a church, and a community-based educational enrichment academy.

CONTACT INFORMATION: Stan Paine, Springfield School District, 525 Mill Street, Springfield, OR 97477; telephone 541-744-6308; spaine@sps.lane.edu.

HELENE LOUISE PERRY

With an early childhood education degree from the University of Wisconsin-Milwaukee, Perry teaches middle school mathematics and communication skills in the Minneapolis Public Schools. In addition to having taught all elementary grade levels in a variety of public and private settings, she has provided mathematics inservice to teachers and has presented at the Minnesota and National Council of Teachers of Mathematics conference. Her work has earned her the Presidential Award for Excellence in Mathematics Teaching in 1993, 1994, and 1996, and she was a Fulbright Memorial Teacher Fund award recipient in 2001. Beyond her school day, she has initiated and coordinated a program that encourages African American girls to achieve and began a mentoring program for African American students.

CONTACT INFORMATION: Helene Louise Perry, Clara Barton Open School, 4237 Colfax Avenue South, Minneapolis, MN 55409; telephone 612-822-8193; helenelouisep4616@msn.com.

CHERI SCHANEY, M.A.

Currently teaching high school special education students at Smoky Hill High School in Aurora, Colorado, Schaney has also had teaching experience with middle school students. Her B.A. is in elementary education from the University of Northern Colorado in Greeley, and her M.A. is in educationally handicapped instruction from Colorado University at Denver. Her role on the Colorado State Assistive Technology Committee supports her interest in using technology in the classroom, illustrated in her contribution to this resource.

CONTACT INFORMATION: Cheri Schaney, Smoky Hill High School, 16100 East Smoky Hill Road, Aurora, CO 80015; telephone 720-886-5601; cschaney@mail.ccsd.k12.co.us.

JAIME L. SHAFER

As a high school art teacher in Latrobe, Pennsylvania, Shafer has also participated in the Pennsylvania Service Learning Alliance and was a minigrant recipient in 2001. She cosponsored the "art-to-wear" program at the school and assisted in managing the Greater Latrobe Art Collection as well as the Visiting Artist Career Orientation Program. She was also named in the 2002 edition of *Who's Who Among America's Teachers*. She earned her B.F.A. from Edinboro University of Pennsylvania.

CONTACT INFORMATION: Jaime L. Shafer, Greater Latrobe Senior High School, 131 Arnold Palmer Drive, Latrobe, PA 15650; telephone 724-539-4225; shafer@s10345.netschools.com

JUDY TACCOGNA, ED.D.

Through 2002, Taccogna was the education director at Search Institute in Minneapolis, coming to that role from Beaverton School District, a 30,000-student suburban district outside of Portland, Oregon. Her contributions to this resource are drawn from years she served there as the executive administrator for K–12 curriculum and instruction, an elementary principal at two schools, a middle school teacher, and a middle and high school counselor, as well as earlier years teaching all but 3rd grade at the elementary level. Her education includes an Ed.D. in educational administration and supervision from Portland State University, Portland, Oregon, an M.Ed. in counseling from Oregon State University, Corvallis, and a B.A. in elementary education and literature from Westmont College in Santa Barbara, California. Her publications include an asset-related article cowritten with Peter C. Scales in the *NASSP* (National Association of Secondary School Principals) *Bulletin* and a supplementary social studies text about the Oregon economy, coauthored with Oregon teachers. At Search Institute, she has led the organization in applying the asset research to educational settings; helped districts and educational organizations understand the asset model through consultation, training, and presentations; and worked to develop resources, including training for educators. She is currently under contract to work with the institute on resources to support its new school climate survey.

CONTACT INFORMATION: Judy Taccogna, 8460 Rosewood Drive, Chanhassen, MN 55317; telephone 952-974-5082; jtaccogna@visi.com.

GEORGIA TEPPERT, M.ED.

As assistant principal at Greater Latrobe Senior High School as well as in her former role as Mrs. Pennsylvania, Teppert has encouraged the application of the asset model in her school as well as the community. Her education includes an M.Ed. in education and secondary administration from the California University of Pennsylvania in California, Pennsylvania, and a B.S. in health and physical education from Slippery Rock University of Pennsylvania. Her roles have included those of principal of a junior/high school and high school assistant principal, high school health and physical education teacher, and elementary/middle school sports teacher. She also has worked with students as a coach of competitive cheerleading, field hockey, and lacrosse and as the adviser of the Leaders of Tomorrow Club featured in her contribution here. She coordinates the student assistance program at the high school, is a member of the Greater Latrobe Asset Developers (GLAD), and volunteers for several community organizations such as Latrobe Parks and Recreation and the Candlelighters Children Career Network.

CONTACT INFORMATION: Georgia Teppert, RR15 Box 390, Greensburg, PA 15601; telephone 724-834-1158; tepperg@hotmail.com.

DENNIS J. TULLI, ED.D.

Tulli recently retired from his role as superintendent of Lebanon School District in Lebanon, Pennsylvania. His experience also included serving as an assistant superintendent as well as a high school principal, vice-principal, counselor, and social studies teacher. With an Ed.D. in educational administration from Temple University in Philadelphia, as well as an M.Ed. in counseling and a B.A. in psychology, he is particularly attuned to the support elements provided in the district graduation project about which he writes. He is also active in his community, serving as chair of the Lebanon County Community Health Council (a county organization promoting quality of life in the community) and on the state and local YMCA boards of directors. He has received the Paul Harris Fellow honor and was a Jefferson Award nominee, both for community service.

CONTACT INFORMATION: Dennis J. Tulli, 19 Locust Lane RD9, Lebanon, PA 17042; telephone 717-274-1318; tulli@comcast.net.

PAMELA N. WIDMANN

When Widmann wrote for this resource, she was the Gifted and Talented Program Assistant in the Cherry Creek School District in Aurora, Colorado, working in the areas of drama, creative writing, geography, and history. She currently serves as a language arts teacher at Liberty Middle School in that district, where she has also been on the staff of the English as a Second Language program and in the Communications Department. With a B.A. in communications (theater) from Metropolitan State College in Denver, Colorado, she is now working toward a master's in communications (writing) at Regis University, Denver. She is a published songwriter and author of *Sneeze in Threes*, a children's book that supports the bully-proofing program in the district.

CONTACT INFORMATION: Pamela N. Widmann, pwidmann@mail.ccsd.k12.co.us.

KRISTINE WILLETT, M.A.

With an M.A. in information and learning technology from the University of Colorado and a B.A. in art and elementary education from Fort Lewis College in Durango, Colorado, Willett fits perfectly into her position teaching art and technology at Canyon Creek Elementary in Colorado's Cherry Creek School District. Her prior experience infusing assets into art curriculum at nearby Independence Elementary, as well as teaching at two other elementary schools adds insights to her work with young children.

CONTACT INFORMATION: Kristine Willett, Canyon Creek Elementary, 6070 South Versailles Parkway, Aurora, CO 80015; telephone 720-886-3600; kwillett@mail.ccsd.k12.co.us.

Other Education Resources from Search Institute

Great Places to Learn: How Asset-Building Schools Help Students Succeed (1999).

NEAL STARKMAN, PETER C. SCALES, AND CLAY ROBERTS

This foundational book offers a practical, proactive approach to helping students succeed both academically and developmentally. It shares interesting and encouraging real-life stories and strategies for building asset-rich school communities. Handouts, charts, and action lists give you the tools needed to actively and intentionally build developmental assets for and with all students.

Handouts and Overheads from **Great Places to Learn** *(2000).*

Use this ready-to-copy set of tools to help you build an asset-rich school climate and asset-rich students. Taken directly from Search Institute's best-seller *Great Places to Learn* (see above), these charts, lists, and worksheets are packaged in a format that will let you easily copy and distribute or make overheads. This set also includes 13 never-before-published, bonus handouts for a total of 45 photocopiable handouts and 10 ready-to-use overheads.

Ideas That Cook: Activities for Asset Builders in School Communities (2001).

This resource offers next steps for people who have read *Great Places to Learn* (above) and who have seen the *"You Have to Live It"* video (below) and are ready to take action. Written and organized like a cookbook, *Ideas That Cook* offers recipes that help you build strong relationships, a caring school environment, and effective and innovative programs through stories and examples. Each activity includes ideas focused on learning, unique mentoring and service-learning opportunities, and activities for fun and recognition.

"You Have to Live It": Building Developmental Assets in School Communities (1999).

Winner of the Association of Education Publisher's 2000 Distinguished Achievement Award, this 27-minute VHS video lets you see and hear for yourself how schools around the country are building assets for and with students from elementary to the high school level. Its message is both inspiring and instructive as teachers, principals, coordinators, and students provide firsthand accounts of how, intentionally and informally, they have built assets in school communities and how anyone can do it.

These resources, as well as posters, workbooks, trainings, and survey services, are available from Search Institute. For more information and a free catalog, call toll-free 800-888-7828 or visit the Web site: www.search-institute.org.